Khayelitsha

KHAYELITSHA

uMlungu in a Township

Steven Otter

PENGUIN BOOKS

PENGUIN BOOKS

Published by the Penguin Group
Penguin Books (South Africa) (Pty) Ltd, 24 Sturdee Avenue, Rosebank,
Johannesburg 2196, South Africa
Penguin Group (USA) Inc, 375 Hudson Street, New York, New York 10014,
USA
Penguin Group (Canada), 90 Eglinton Avenue East, Suite 700, Toronto,
Ontario, Canada M4P 2Y3 (a division of Pearson Penguin Canada Inc)
Penguin Books Ltd, 80 Strand, London WC2R 0RL, England
Penguin Ireland, 25 St Stephen's Green, Dublin 2, Ireland (a division of
Penguin Books Ltd)
Penguin Group (Australia), 250 Camberwell Road, Camberwell, Victoria
3124, Australia (a division of Pearson Australia Group Pty Ltd)
Penguin Books India Pvt Ltd, 11 Community Centre, Panchsheel Park,
New Delhi – 110 017, India
Penguin Group (NZ), 67 Apollo Drive, Mairangi Bay, Auckland 1310,
New Zealand (a division of Pearson New Zealand Ltd)

Penguin Books (South Africa) (Pty) Ltd, Registered Offices:
24 Sturdee Avenue, Rosebank, Johannesburg 2196, South Africa

www.penguinbooks.co.za

First published by Penguin Books (South Africa) (Pty) Ltd 2007
Reprinted 2008 (twice), 2010 (twice)

Copyright © Steven Otter 2007
Photographs © Steven Otter except where otherwise credited
Cover photograph © Denzil Maregele

ISBN 978-0-143-02547-4

Typeset by CJH Design in 10/14 pt Charter
Cover design: Flame Design, Cape Town
Printed and bound by Interpak Book Printers, Pietermaritzburg

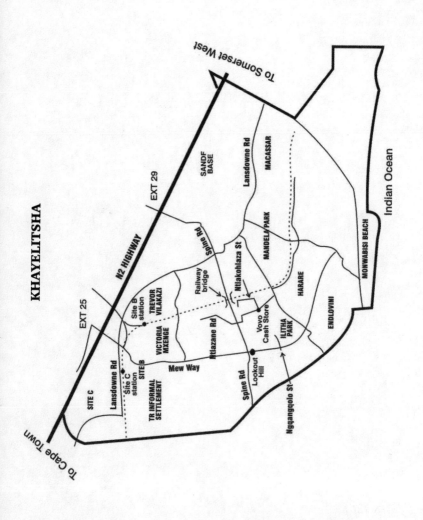

KHAYELITSHA

To Cape Town
To Somerset West

N2 HIGHWAY
EXT 25
EXT 29

SANDF BASE
Lansdowne Rd
MACASSAR

MANDELA PARK

Spine Rd
Railway bridge
Ntlakohlaza St
Lansdowne Rd

Site B station
TREVOR VILAKAZI
VICTORIA MXENGE
SITE B

Vovo Cash Store
ILITHA PARK
HARARE

MONWABISI BEACH

Indian Ocean

Site C station
SITE C
TR INFORMAL SETTLEMENT
Mew Way
Ntlazane Rd
Lansdowne Rd

Spine Rd
Lookout Hill
Ngqangqolo St
ENDLOVINI

New Home

'You've taken the wrong train,' the plump woman finally said.

She'd been staring at Aletta and me for some time with the look of someone building up the courage to speak, carefully piecing the words together so as not to offend. One of four passengers sitting opposite us on the bright yellow third-class bench, she'd also looked concerned, I'd thought earlier, before looking back down the tracks to admire the slowly receding form of Table Mountain in the late morning air.

'Isn't this the train to Khayelitsha?' I asked her, troubled; her statement had been delivered with disturbing certainty.

She looked surprised.

'Is that where you're going?' she asked, drawing her neatly plucked eyebrows even closer to the bridge of her wide nose.

It was late January 2002 and my girlfriend Aletta was returning home to the Netherlands at the end of the month. Once she was gone I knew that our one-bedroom apartment on the slopes of Table Mountain, in the upmarket suburb of Tamboerskloof, would be rather too extravagant a home for me alone. I'd asked a number of my newspaper colleagues to keep an eye out for a single room.

'Are you prepared to live in a black area?' asked Mzondi, a fellow journalist.

South Africa doesn't officially still have 'black areas', I'd thought to myself, although on the few occasions I'd been to Khayelitsha I hadn't noticed any whites or coloureds about, not even just driving through the township in their motor cars. And 'Khaya' did not fall into the category of a 'no-go area', in light of the rather glaring fact that well over a million people lived there. But Mzondi's frank question stripped all political correctness from the issue. His home, he was reminding me, was a 'no-go area' for the vast majority of whites and coloureds.

'Actually, I *am* prepared to live in a black area,' I'd replied, for the first time expressing openly the desire to break down my inner prejudices and feel truly South African.

The next day he handed me a torn-off piece of newspaper with a telephone number scribbled on it in black ink.

'Tshidi has an outside room for you,' he said. 'Her place is five minutes away from mine. Call her.'

Tshidi had arranged to meet Aletta and me, so we took the train to iLitha Park, Khayelitsha. As we travelled, the houses grew smaller and the litter more pronounced: it looked like an era generally thought to have passed.

The last stop, iLitha Park, seemed to be one of Khayelitsha's more affluent suburbs, I thought as we were led to Ntlakohlaza Street by Wanda, our new and concerned friend from the train. The houses, although small, were neat and new, in light, cheerful yellows, pinks, blues and whites, lining the dusty, tarred roads of the neighbourhood. It was January, the middle of summer, and as we walked from the station we saw a suburb almost entirely devoid of greenery, although a cow stood grazing contentedly on a solitary clump of grass nearby. But then a cool breeze blew in from the sea, just out of sight to the south, and I caught a whiff of braai meat, as some of those heading for the station stopped to study us unabashedly.

'If you need someone to transport your furniture from town, you can call my father,' offered Wanda, handing me a piece of paper with a number written on it. I saw that she was offering the services of Mr Ncuba and his bakkie.

'How much does he charge?' I asked.

'This is not my father's job,' she replied, 'so pay him some money for petrol if you can afford to.' She pointed towards her home, a few hundred metres away. 'Even if you don't need his help be sure to visit me some time anyway,' she said.

We found Tshidi with a duster in her hand at Number 8 Ntlakohlaza Street. Although the word *ntlakohlaza* means 'autumn', it was difficult to imagine these summery houses in the hot lanes shrouded in cold and rain. The cow had finished its lunch: there was now officially no greenery left in sight.

Mzondi had said Tshidi and her husband Molefe were Sotho so my rudimentary Xhosa would be useless.

'Hello sisi,' I called to her from the other side of her crumbling garden wall.

Tshidi, a voluptuous woman in her late twenties, was giving her stately dining room table – squeezed into a room barely large enough to hold it – one final, proud wipe. She was wearing a floral blue and white blouse over a long skirt, and she wiped her hands on a yellow apron strung about her broad waist. It was easy to see the Sotho influence in her sharp features, with her petite nose and thin lips. She waved to us to come in. Our shoes crunched over the gravel as we passed through the empty space where the gate in the wall should have been, and then Tshidi unlocked the padlocked security gate at the front door and invited us in.

At the table sat her brother-in-law Foamy, a young man who radiated intelligence from a smiling, warm face. He stood to greet us, and after an elaborate round of handshakes between the four of us, we were offered seats at the massive table. Aletta briefly studied her reflection in the wood.

'Molefe is still at work,' Tshidi said, explaining that his shift at the insurance company where he worked ended at 5pm. A homely aroma of gravy and mieliepap wafted in from the kitchen, suggesting that his dinner was already under way.

Foamy, it turned out, had arrived at his brother's house a week earlier to begin a search for work. He'd completed a course in agriculture in his home province of the Free State and, although he'd had plans to become a farmer, he'd been instructed by his father to travel to South Africa's second city. A rolled-up sleeping mat lay beside one wall, revealing the dual purpose of the room. One of the two bedrooms in the main house, Tshidi explained, had been occupied the week before by a Burundian refugee named Frederick.

'But he's out looking for a job right now,' she said. 'Would you like to see your room?'

We headed around the side of the peach-painted house to a pair of freestanding rooms at its rear. The available one had a glossy red vinyl floor and, at around nine square metres, barely managed to house a tiny table and wardrobe. Although the half-empty cement bags lying to one side of the doorway suggested the rooms had been erected recently, the walls of the one in which we stood were already in a state of considerable disrepair: a dusty pile of plaster and cement pebbles lay below each of the many yawning cracks. The signs of a recent and thorough sweep of the floor suggested that while those walls were apparently still sturdy, they were disintegrating at a rapid rate. But, I thought, weighing up my options and looking over the back garden wall, the train station was just a couple of minutes away. We knocked fifty rand off the monthly rental of three hundred and fifty, and said our farewells.

'You can move in on Friday, the first day of the month,' Tshidi waved after us.

I hadn't seen the necessity of making an official announcement in the newsroom about my move to Khayelitsha, so Lukhanyo did it for me. It was all rather awkward; without speaking to a soul he'd typed an in-house email and right-clicked 'All'.

'Notice,' it read. 'Steven is white on the outside, but black on the inside'; it seemed that I was an inside out coconut, in effect.

It was easily the most interesting prose Lukhanyo had

written in months. Participants in the daily news conferences at the paper had been finding it increasingly difficult to suppress their laughter as the circle of ideas bore down on him.

'What's your story idea for today?' the news editor would ask him, and once again it would emerge that Lukhanyo was still in the research stages of his package on tourism. The email introduced a new era for him, though, as one by one the reporters stopped at my desk to question me about its contents. There is perhaps no place in the world where news travels faster than in a newspaper office with a large staff. Like the ripples of a pool, in less than sixty minutes everyone was in the know.

'I don't want you coming to work without a decent bath in the mornings,' quipped the news editor, whose coloured status permitted such jokes.

Bulelaaaneee!

At first I was glad they had left: her euphoric moaning, and the creaking of his bed, had left me feeling not only embarrassed but lonely. Aletta and I had shared a sad farewell at the airport the day before. There had been tears, and a feeling that this would be a permanent parting. She was going back to Holland, where I'd never been. She, and my memories of her, would no longer be part of my frame of reference. I couldn't imagine her country, although she'd described it to me. Perhaps she's riding a bicycle to the cheese shop, I thought, trying to make light of the pain that had consumed me since she'd left.

'Bulelani,' the girl had whispered throatily an hour before. The 'Bule' (pronounced Boo-le) had come out quickly, the 'la' had lasted far longer, 'laaaaaaaaaa', with the 'neeee ...' gradually fading into blissful silence: 'Bulelaaaaaaneeee'.

That's great, I thought as I focused on the positive side of sharing their intimacy against my will: now I know my neighbour's name.

My shyness, however, had ensured that I hadn't made a sound since they'd arrived – they'd begun their lovemaking almost instantly – even though I'd needed to empty my bladder. Not that they would have stopped, of course. At one point I crept across my room, eyes fixed on the gap above the wall that separated us, and carefully opened the door. A blast of southeaster knocked a plastic cup off the table and on to the floor, where it bounced around deafeningly loudly between the vinyl and my clumsy hand. But the creaking bed didn't abate: my companions seemed deaf to the happenings beyond their love nest.

By the time I climbed back under the covers their affection had entered a new phase, with Bulelani, as I now knew him, joining in with a variety of grunts and moans. Of the three of us I must have been the only one who was fretful about their bed: I lay there speculating about its make and guarantee.

Then, as suddenly as it had begun, it was over, its ending signalled by a two-strong final sigh. After a brief period of silence, she began to talk in that singsong tone so characteristic of the Xhosa language. She'd obviously been energised a great deal, but I couldn't help wondering whether Bulelani had taken a turn for the worse. If he was responding to her pillow talk at all it must have been by means of a simple nodding of the head. Reassured that the worst (for me, at least) was over, I began to get drowsy.

Would sleep be at all possible, I wondered, as my neighbours now hopped out of bed and began to dress? But then they were gone, out into the warm Khayelitsha night. I would introduce myself to Bulelani tomorrow, I thought, as I looked at my watch: it was an hour to midnight.

◆

As I tried to fall asleep on my first night in Khayelitsha, my mind drifted back to my first venture into a black township. This was in the 1990s in my home town of Uitenhage, a few months after I'd completed my one-year military conscription.

I was employed at Volkswagen at the time, and it was there that I got to know a young, stoutly built Sotho named Rakwena.

One Friday Rakwena invited me to a shebeen in Kwa-Nobuhle, Uitenhage's largest black township. Nelson Mandela had been released from prison a few years earlier and Chris Hani's murder was only a few weeks old, so it was with a sense of trepidation that I accepted the invitation.

In my memory the night remains a sequence of largely unconnected events involving a hand in my back pocket; Rakwena holding a youngster by the neck, his legs kicking frantically above the floor; a dangerously obese girl, and a missing shoe.

At the second shebeen that we visited, a square room packed bumper to bumper with bodies, I became the victim of a pickpocket. Rakwena and I were pushing through the pulsing mass of dancing patrons towards the shebeen counter when I felt the hand against the right side of my bum. Those were the days – in Uitenhage at least – of skin-tight jeans so I felt the hand immediately. I was stunned by the sheer speed with which it moved. Not only had it entered the correct pocket, but it bunched into a fist and scooped out my last ten rand note – all at the speed of lightning. I spun around just in time to see a black arm disappearing into the mass of people.

'What's wrong, Steve?' Rakwena shouted above the music. He'd obviously seen my swift about-turn.

'Someone stole my ten rand note,' I cried.

'Who?'

'I'm not completely sure,' I shouted, 'but I think it might have been him.' I pointed to a youth who couldn't have been more than sixteen years old.

Although the youngster was moving fast, Rakwena caught up to him in a flash and hoisted him up against the nearest wall. Before I could remonstrate or suggest a more circumspect approach, the boy, whose body was hanging limply under the grip of my friend's fist around his throat, began digging frantically in one of his pockets. Out came the ten rand note and Rakwena carried the boy to the door of the shebeen and tossed him roughly into the night outside.

'Don't worry, my brother, he won't do that again,' he smiled at me upon his return.

What had bewildered me most about this episode had not been Rakwena's quick reaction, but rather the support I was given by the other black patrons. I had always seen South Africa's race relations as a simple matter of black versus white, yet not one of the black people there that night had stuck up for the thief, despite their shared race. Although in any 'normal' society this would have been a simple matter of right versus wrong, in the South African context I had genuinely expected at least some of the patrons to turn on me because I had accused one of their black brothers of theft.

Although Rakwena was the best escort I could have wished for, the evening had deteriorated rapidly after that.

To be frank, I'd never pondered the possibility that I'd ever be forced into sex, but the lady who deposited herself on my lap made me think it was a very real prospect. She must have weighed close on two hundred kilograms, judging from the very small quantity of air that I was managing to suck desperately into my lungs.

'I luuuuuuuv you,' she announced, looking into my eyes with aggression rather than any other emotion on her gigantic round face.

She had beautiful wide eyes, but her forceful approach had fallen well short of anything even close to a turn-on.

'Rakwena,' I'd gasped desperately from under her.

'She really luuuuuuuvs you, Steve,' he replied, nodding his head approvingly. 'You are really a man.'

'Rakwena,' I repeated with a mighty effort, 'I want to go home.'

Not only had my admirer refused to budge, but she actually told my friend that I had no choice in the matter. Just when I'd started to come to terms with the fact that her decision was final, Rakwena managed to persuade her to let me go to the toilet. When I finally plucked up the courage to come out of that room, my friend was waiting nervously at the door.

'If you want to get away from that girl, we must go to your car at once!' he shouted above the music, taking my arm and leading me quickly to the door.

Unable to hide my relief as we pulled away in the car seconds later, I'd turned to Rakwena and smiled.

'That woman was fucking dangerous, man.'

'Eish, Steve, we were too much lucky to escape,' he sighed in agreement.

Just then something ricocheted off the roof of the car.

'What was that?' I shouted, before another bang from above.

'Drive, Steve, drive!' Rakwena screamed in a high-pitched voice. 'She is throwing rocks at us!'

I raced through the gears roughly, my head bent low over the steering wheel. As we rounded the first corner to safety Rakwena lifted both feet on to the dashboard.

'Look, Steve, one of my shoes is missing,' he groaned.

'I'm not going back,' I said.

'You have to!'

'I'll buy you a new pair, Rakwena!'

My thoughts returned sleepily to the present. It had been a good day. Everything had gone smoothly.

Mr Ncuba, Wanda's father, had recognised me instantly outside the Cape Town library, where we'd agreed to meet. I'd told him to look out for 'a very white guy with very short hair wearing blue jeans'. The four-by-four we drove to the Tamboerskloof apartment looked brand new and Mr Ncuba, in his smart brown pants and collared, checked shirt, was a cultured man. Greying around the ears, he had the eyes of someone who'd achieved much for his age. As we drove up Long Street, I asked him where he worked.

'I'm on pension,' he said, 'but my wife Christina still runs a crèche.' He said it with a great deal of pride, smiling contentedly through the windscreen. Her mother Christina, Wanda had told us on the train, had been Cape Town's Woman of the Year in 2001. 'Are you married?' Mr Ncuba asked, with a smile soaked in experience.

'I have a girlfriend,' I replied, not really wanting to talk about her.

Mr Ncuba elaborated on what to look out for in a good wife.

'She should be a hard worker and love you very much. Then she will do anything for you and will never find another man. It is easy to find a beautiful woman, but these two qualities are far more important.'

Twenty minutes later, with my belongings dwarfed by my king-sized mattress on the back, we were on the N2 highway heading out of Cape Town proper.

From Langa, the closest black township to central Cape Town, much of the highway is lined with shacks. Many look as though they've been put up in the dead of night, perhaps after a long journey from a home far away in the old Ciskei or Transkei homelands; rocks squat on the corrugated iron roofs, there to defy the violent southeaster.

Drive fast along the national highway and the shacks seem to be laid out in rough grids; but it is a deceptive order. The lanes between the rows of shacks represent nothing less than a nightmare to the City's fire authorities, the most common cause of blazes being a haphazardly placed paraffin stove knocked over in the night, sometimes leaving several dead. I'd seen the effects of boiling water in a confined space, another cause of burns, on a visit to the Red Cross Children's Hospital, where numerous toddlers lay bandaged from head to toe. I winced as I remembered the mother I'd interviewed who, in her hurry to relieve herself, had left a pot of boiling water on the floor of her shack. The innocence of her two-year-old boy, lying sweetly on their bed, was stolen for ever when he rolled to one side and into the pot. It was a page two lead that gave me no pride; just another story in a typical township sequence of chaos and pain.

Between the township's border fence and the frantic N2 highway more youngsters were aiming for the headlines, this time with a soccer ball. Whether they would make the paper as a sports feature, or a page three short on how one of them had tried to retrieve the ball from the fender of a passing car was anyone's guess.

The Mew Way exit is the gateway to another world. Flat and featureless, the Cape Flats have been populated almost as quickly as they have been robbed of their marshes and sand dunes. Site C and Site B, whose lean-tos are a testament to innovation, lay before us. Here and there a double-storey shack, housing a family and its business, leaned jaggedly against the sky.

Locals lined the streets in the hope of flagging down a minibus taxi, while braaivleis stalls were already smoking away, their matrons busily placing liver, lamb fat, boerewors and chops on the grids, sizzling and spitting, tantalising passers-by. That delicious aroma of meat I'd noticed the week before was back in the air and I hoped to sample it, but Mr Ncuba had other plans.

'I want you to meet my wife,' he said, and we turned down a side street.

As we entered iLitha Park the disorderly shacks were abruptly replaced by a regimented grid of neat government homes, one of the nesting grounds for President Thabo Mbeki's newly created black middle class.

Ours wasn't the only car parked outside the crèche; mothers were coming and going. In the back garden the little children and two helpers were listening intently to Christina Ncuba's instructions. Although she was a huge woman, with a tent-sized dress and thick limbs, she moved with natural agility and grace. Her eyes overflowed with friendliness and affection as she greeted me, my soft suburbs paw warmly wrapped in one of her bear-like, calloused hands. I felt instantly mothered, and deeply sad that I was past crèche-going age.

After a complicated, three-phase handshake, Christina slipped easily into the role of public relations officer; she'd been told I was a journalist. Following a tour to every corner of the tiny crèche, she boomed, 'There's a German girl staying across the road from our house – my husband will introduce you!'

I told Mr Ncuba that wouldn't be necessary right now, as Christina waved us goodbye. Although I didn't tell him this, I hadn't moved to Khayelitsha to meet other white people and, besides, we probably wouldn't have felt the necessity to get to know each other if we'd been neighbours in the suburbs. He had a back-up plan, however: a visit to their impressive house. The biggest in the street, it had a satellite dish perched on the roof.

'You can come and watch rugby any time you like.'

'I don't like rugby that much,' I replied.

He looked surprised. I'd always wanted to play football, I explained, but because my school, like most white boys' schools in South Africa, had an almost religious infatuation with rugby and cricket, there had been nothing for it but to play them, and watch football on television.

Inside the house Mr Ncuba pointed out an empty room. 'Why don't you move in here?' he asked. 'Christina would really like that, and she's a good cook.'

I didn't doubt that as I remembered Mrs Ncuba, looking at the same time at her husband's hefty belly.

'No thanks, Tata,' I said, not without genuine regret. 'I've already paid the rent for the other place.'

'That doesn't matter; we can go there tonight and tell them

you've changed your mind. I'm sure they'll understand.'

I wanted to live close to my colleague Mzondi, I explained, so there was nothing to do but to stick with the original plan.

'Alriiight,' he finally sighed, with the drawn-out 'i' so characteristic of black South Africans. 'But you're welcome to watch rugby here any time you want,' he said, ignoring my earlier remark.

Vovo Cash Store

'Is the room fine?' Foamy asked as we watched Mr Ncuba drive off after depositing my belongings in my new home. It was. I asked him where I could get some food. 'There's a fish and chips shop near the station,' he said.

Foamy led the way – a walk of a few seconds – and ordered two portions of the oily grub through the gap in the powerful metal bars that stretched from the floor to the roof in the area in front of the cash register. A minute later we sat down on two warped plastic chairs and chatted with our mouths full of food.

I was happy to leave the staring customers behind. I'd never before been so conscious of my colour – I had felt as though I was eating and talking in slow motion. Foamy, in contrast, had handled the attention with ease, constantly greeting and smiling at newcomers. As we walked slowly homewards I realised by the position of the sun that it was already late afternoon.

'Want to go for a beer?' I asked Foamy.

We entered a little garage shebeen, Vovo Cash Store, which was three houses away from ours – dangerously close, I thought happily. It was a Friday afternoon, and there were already three one rand coins in the queue on the pool table.

'*Molweni*,' each of the five other customers greeted us.

'*Ewe*,' we replied.

I bought two quarts of ice-cold Black Label from the shebeen mama and, after putting a coin on the table, we sat down on two beer crates close enough to the pool table to watch the game. The level of play was impressive, with one of the two middle-aged contestants sinking four balls in a row. As the effects of the cold alcohol were steadied by the hot air pushing lazily in through the garage doorway, I decided I'd become quite comfortable where I was and removed the coin. Besides, my brain had been put into neutral by the beer, and taking on labyrinthine pool strategy seemed too big to ask.

'Are you frightened, my brother?' asked the man who'd just won.

I sat back on my crate. 'Frightened of what?'

'Well, your coin has vanished from the table,' he laughed. 'This *umlungu* is scared of me,' he announced to the patrons around us.

'I'm not scared,' I retorted. 'I just don't want to ruin your reputation.'

We had both sounded tough, but I was starting to get nervous. For those who take the game seriously, there is much more to pool than scratched green cloth and six holes. Every little sound, like the collision of two balls, or one hitting the side of the table before plunging into a pocket, reveals the true battle: a clash of egos. And this guy's ego – judging by his performance, eye contact and posture – was seeping like liquid iron into the street outside.

The lively conversation had abated, I noticed as I looked around. Even the shebeen mama had picked up the tension in the air; she was nervously watching us through the hole in the wire mesh where I'd got the beers. I placed my coin back on the table.

'First I'll beat this guy, an easy job,' he said, gesturing to his challenger, 'then I'll deal with you.'

He pushed a coin into the slot and packed the balls on the table. The challenger broke the pack, sinking three 'solids'. Not in the least bit fazed, the macho man downed six balls, with the confidence of a champion.

'Where are you from?' he asked.

I told him.

'I have only known you for five minutes and already you are lying,' he scorned.

Foamy backed me up.

'It's true; he lives in one of the rooms behind my house.'

'Then you are my neighbour,' he said confidently. 'Drink with us!' He pointed to a cluster of beers standing on the concrete floor next to his friends.

The game between us was close, with Vusi – for that was his name – getting one chance on the black. But he never stood a chance: as always, my patented 'mind-power and body action' technique worked. I stood a little way back from the pocket he was targeting and leaned slightly to the left. Then, fixing my eyes well to the left of the pocket, just before he hit the ball I lost my balance slightly and fell slowly, also to the left. It was a pathetic trick to fall for, especially for someone as good as he was.

'It's your game,' his previous victim grinned at me.

I didn't want the round of applause to lose its impact in a later defeat, so I gave the table to Vusi, downed the last of my beer, and left with Foamy.

◆

The gunshots told me I'd been dreaming.

They came in rapid succession. There were three of them, bang, bang, bang, followed by screeching tyres and a screaming engine. Sleep, the only true hiding place, where we are able to die without being forced to watch. Hands around the throat, the sound of a rusty gun being cocked; in sleep the details are meaningless.

Now I was awake, however, and in a matter of seconds I recalled the conversation I'd had with Mary, a colleague at the paper. She'd been right after all.

'You'll be fine for a few days,' she'd said, 'but after that they'll turn on you. Our cultures are too different and they're going to wonder what you're doing there. You won't live through it, not just because of the cultural differences, but because of the common crime. My advice to you is that you find a home here in the suburbs where you belong. I know it sounds terrible, but it's true. These are the facts.' She'd spoken with conviction.

The apartheid laws had been scrapped in a day's work, but the basic rules remained in place. Break them if you wish, but not without considerable risk. I'd put her words down to white paranoia, her childhood on the farm with blacks who'd been denied a proper education and the option to leave their slavery behind. The master's obvious superiority echoed in his servant's pathetic reply to his every instruction, 'Ja, baas.'

The bag of mielie meal, the sack of samp, the bag of beans and the tray of eggs that had forced them to remain in their filthy huts, fearfully thankful for their master's hand.

Of course they'll turn on you: I'd brushed her comments aside. Who wouldn't? But Mary was fluent in Xhosa – I'd heard her talking to the office cleaners in their own tongue.

'I know how they think,' she'd said, looking me in the eye, 'because I know how they talk. Death means less in their culture.'

She'd probably spent her first years playing with *their* kids (learned their language, like Verwoerd, before her own), until the words of her parents around the dinner table, spoken in front of the black cook as if she was a ghost, took their toll. Words that convinced her they were inferior. Not only words: there were also the facts. Her private schooling in the town far away, their pathetic education on the farm; her smart uniform, their tattered pants and skirts, hand-me-downs from the family of the white master: these were the facts that made her parents right. So that, driving past the shacks on the way from picking up their daughter from boarding school for the weekend, they could point at them and say, with all the authority of those fully civilised, 'Who would want to share a government with people who live like that, who actually choose to live like that?'

'I appreciate your concern, Mary, but I think you're wrong,' was all I could muster.

I know it sounds strange, but I didn't want to offend her because I actually liked her. I would have been desperately lonely if I hadn't been decent to the Marys that had surrounded me in my youth. I had parents from completely different cultures: my father a fairly strict Austrian, my mother a liberal English South African. In some sense that contributed to the adventurous natures evident in me and my siblings, and made us more open-minded. My parents had tried their best to instil values in us that were hard to instil in one's children in South Africa at that time, especially in a conservative place like Uitenhage.

I'd managed to keep my thoughts away from the gunshots seconds after they'd happened, but almost as quickly decided it was time to act. I thumped the palm of my hand against the wall that separated us. They'd left just before I'd fallen asleep and I hadn't heard him come back.

No reply.

'Bulelani,' I whispered, mimicking his girlfriend's voice from hours earlier, loud enough to travel the distance and no further.

He was gone, had abandoned me to my fate. He'd probably help them before me anyway, if Mary was right, I thought cynically.

Wearing only my sleeping shorts, I crept outside without making a sound. The wind had died down and all was ominously silent. I peered around the front wall in the direction of the infamous Town 2 informal settlement, yet another of Khayelitsha's communities. I'd heard a lot about it, this place where car hijackers and other criminals lived in outwardly ugly shacks that contained treasures lifted during some of the countless burglaries that strike the suburbs at night. The gangsters' cars were often bigger than their homes, I'd heard.

That was where the shots had come from, it seemed to me, as I peered over the railway line at the silhouettes cast by the roofs of the lean-tos. The full moon had given the now empty fields between Town 2 and iLitha Park the look of a battlefield lit up by lamp post flares of bright orange, with the train tracks cutting the scene in two. The lamp posts were more widely spaced and far higher than in the suburbs, taking on the appearance of the ominous watchtowers of old, when some black areas were fenced in and kept under tight surveillance by the military and the police. The houses of Ntlakohlaza Street were in total darkness.

The three gunshots had been my first, I thought as I crept stealthily back to my room, but perhaps for those who'd lived in these streets for years they were just three, only three gunshots among countless others. Who knows? Perhaps three a week, maybe even three a night?

Either way, I'd have to get used to them – or leave.

Zane

Zane and I, walking down the street, a quart of beer in each hand. It's just after 10pm on a Sunday evening and the only reason we're holding the beers is because I'm white, or at least that's what Zane says. He says it in his halting English, with a look of pure disgust on his face.

'That fucking bastard never sells me beer after 10 o'clock – it's only because an *umlungu* asked him that he sold it to us.'

I wonder at how this smooth opportunist has all of a sudden forgotten our constant thirst for alcohol and replaced it with self-righteous scorn. A man who – I'd been told – spent five years in Cape Town's infamous Pollsmoor Prison for armed robbery at a Bellville bank, a respected (read: feared) veteran, although ex-tsotsi, promoting black consciousness. In typical gangster fashion, Zane is a lovable mix of good and evil – if you're his friend you're fine, and that's why almost everyone greets him.

Zane must have had his fair share of enemies, proof of which erupted a few minutes later, as we neared Tata Hobe's home with Tata Hobe's beers.

An interesting man, Tata Hobe. Permanently inebriated, the old Xhosa medicine man spent his time between the sofa in his cosy lounge and the double bed in his bedroom. I never found out much about his healing powers, but the white beaded necklace and bracelet were evidence of his trade. I also learned very quickly that whistling was not tolerated in his presence. The first time I launched into a lovely rendition of one of Tchaikovsky's 'Swan Lake' pieces, the old man began to wail loudly, holding both hands to his ears in agony. At first I thought it was a pathetic attempt to sing along to a tune he didn't know, but Zane, with a finger held to my lips, quickly explained that whistling was not allowed in the company of sangomas. Although he wasn't exactly sure why this was, I discovered from others that it had something to do with dreams. Apparently the ancestors communicate with sangomas while they are asleep, a conversation that can be stunted by the sound of whistling. The shrill noise, if it echoes through the medicine man's sleeping hours, can very well lead to a breakdown in communication.

A few days before, a neatly framed photograph of Tata Hobe had appeared on his lounge wall. Clothed in a suave suit, seated at a desk with his face turned to the camera, his left hand resting on an impressive pile of papers, the younger, more vibrant Hobe peered through shiny spectacles that reflected his sober days, the very beginning of his sad journey into the bottle.

'I used to be an accountant,' he told Zane and me through

swollen lips. 'And I was very successful,' he added, his head wobbling.

Zane matched Tata Hobe's solemn look with one of his own.

'Anyone can make a picture like that. All you have to do is borrow a suit and glasses from your neighbour and pack your children's school books on the desk.'

But, truth be told, Hobe had achieved quite a bit for a blubbering drunk. He seemed to be one of that rare breed: the addict whose prophesies of personal wealth are actually fulfilled.

His middle-class station wagon stood outside his iLitha Park house, alongside his yellow container where a hired helper, who happened to be one of Zane's girlfriends, ran a roadside café. The income generated from his shop, which traded in the basics – cigarettes, sweets and oily *igwinya* (vetkoek) – was enough to keep Hobe on his uneasy flight from reality. It was also sufficient to keep Zane drunk, for whenever he ran out of capital he would politely offer his services to Tata Hobe, assuming almost instant control of all activities in the region of the heavy cash register. A little while later he'd be shooting pool at Vovo Cash Store, ordering beer after beer without a care in the world.

As Zane and I passed through the narrow gap created by the car and container and neared Hobe's closed front door, a white saloon screeched to a halt on the street behind us. There was a shout and a car door flew open. As Zane bolted around the back of the house, I flew through the air and, opening the door on the way, landed in the lounge where I took up position on one side of the door and out of quickly imagined firing range, with both quart bottles raised and ready to crash on to the heads of any unwelcome visitors.

After a weekend of heavy drinking and fragile conversation, one is often prone to edgy paranoia, me perhaps for white reasons, but Zane definitely for dark ones.

I was immediately comforted by the close presence of Hobe, who seemed ready to scold me for finding an unacceptable use for two of his precious Castle quarts. He tried to grab one of them out of my raised right hand, but missed, and just managed, by going into the Pollsmoor position – hands on table, raised buttocks – to avoid falling over the coffee table placed in the centre of his lounge.

The knock on the door was one heard a hundred times a day all over Khayelitsha – a persistent rumbling that increases in volume swiftly and does not give one much time to answer.

'Who is it?' I asked.

'Hey, Steve, it's me, Johnson,' came the nervous reply; it was a journalist from *City Vision*, a good friend of mine.

Zane knew how to travel light – we found two quarts lying side by side in the grass, barely a metre from the back wall which he must have cleared so athletically.

He returned, cautiously, half an hour later.

I had met Zane on my third day in Khayelitsha, at Vovo Cash Store. Also known as Steve's Place, the corner café and shebeen is on the corner of Ntlakohlaza Street and Ntlazane Road. Its owner and namesake Steve was a policeman who worked in the Strand and upped his income with the unlicensed garage shebeen.

A cunning businessman, Steve refused all friendships that were initiated by a second party because of his status in the iLitha Park community. A drunken patron once told me that he belonged to the same clan as Steve's wife, which made the two men brothers. This was said in front of Steve, who replied that the man was a cunning opportunist trying to create a familiarity that would pressurise the shebeen owner into some act of kindness, like the provision of a case of beers on the house. The discussion that followed, which attracted noisy opinion from almost all those at the shebeen that day, plunged deep into the unwritten roots of Xhosa culture. Steve finally gave in.

'All right, we are brothers,' he said.

The concession was forced by a verbal dissertation delivered by a young friend of mine, an intelligent man indeed. His grandmother had taught him in the rural old Transkei homeland that all the men whose blood flowed within the same clan were brothers. Steve was not merely a relative by marriage, for is not blood stirred into an equal mix through a bond as strong as this? Afterwards Steve sombrely told me that times were changing and some aspects of Xhosa culture were being destroyed by the Western values of business and profit.

'It's difficult to practise ubuntu when you're trying to make a profit,' he said ruefully.

A valuable source of advice, Steve was one of those rare types who can drink vast quantities of liquor and stay sensible. The fact that beer at Vovo Cash Store, as in other township shebeens, was half the price of that purchased in Cape Town proper, only added to its attraction. Rather than helping me save money, however, the low price of beer often just led to me downing double the volume of the foamy golden liquid.

No music was played at Vovo Cash Store: its physical attractions were minimal. The shebeen was about the size of two garages joined lengthways; a long, narrow room. At around 7am on weekday mornings Steve rolled up his garage door, reversed his car out of the shebeen into Ntlakohlaza Street and drove his kids to school. Vovo Cash Store was then open for business. Later, once the patrons had rolled in and there was no longer any space left on the long wooden bench that stretched halfway down one wall, or on the dilapidated white plastic chairs that surrounded the equally decrepit matching table, regulars had the option of sitting on an empty beer crate. Steve's wife and mother ran the business in his absence, often passing the time watching the closely contested pool games unfold.

A beautifully plump woman, with a perfectly round face and shiny brown eyes, Steve's wife Thandi had provided him with a steady supply of naturally tanned, angelic daughters. Yoliswa, who at twelve years was the oldest of the three, sometimes ran the shebeen, and did so with an efficiency that offered the patron regular distraction from the meagre entertainment on offer between those drunken walls. Steve once told of how a customer had tried to trick Yoli into giving him more change than was due to him by paying with a hundred rand note.

'He complained that Yoli gave him the exact amount,' Steve boasted.

The moment I first saw Yoliswa I could not take my eyes off her beautiful face. It shone with intelligence. Top of her class at school, she spent her spare time working in the shebeen, studying and playing soft music on a little plastic keyboard with keys barely large enough to press. Her two little sisters looked almost identical and moved about in tandem, often colliding with the knees of pool players as they went to ask their father for a sachet of the flavoured cool drink that he stored in the fridge just behind the beer.

Liquor was served through a little gap in a thick wire partition that separated the family from the patrons. A side door into the main house was within easy reach, should a group of tsotsis ever demand a share of the profits, although, to my knowledge, this had never happened.

Each Saturday Steve returned from who knows where in a bakkie loaded with crates of beer. As he unloaded the vehicle customers assisted in carrying the heavy crates through the shebeen to the wire partition.

It was here that I first met Zane. He seemed a quiet, thoughtful man, with the uncanny ability to convey a variety of warnings and messages by a glance or a wink. Of average height and build, he looked surprisingly healthy for someone who drank on a nearly daily basis, although an ominous-looking scar ran down the length of one cheek. I noticed him before he noticed me. He probably thought I was a visitor from the suburbs, and it was only after he found out that I lived in iLitha Park that Zane began to acknowledge me.

I suppose it would be fair to say that we developed an understanding. Zane would watch from a beer crate in the corner as I took on yet another opponent at pool, glancing from me to the table, smiling at my strategy. In the days that followed he began to nod towards the beers and mumble, 'Drink' – which I eventually learned to recognise as an offer of friendship in the Xhosa culture. It was through Zane that I began to develop an understanding of sharing, something I realised I had not had much experience of in the past.

True, the word ubuntu had been bandied about in certain pretentious white circles when I was a youngster, but this was first-hand experience of an act that I had always thought to be some kind of mystical, white-imagined, African quality.

When Zane invited me to join his group at Steve's Place,

I would also offer to buy a few beers, or inform him of my intention to get replacements at a later stage of the day. I needed to do business fairly, after all, in the European tradition: whatever you give me, I give you.

'Drink,' he would say again simply, shaking his head at my ignorance. I would look sheepish, sit down, and wait for him to pour me a glass of beer.

A still clearer understanding of sharing came towards the end of my first month in Khayelitsha, by which time I had spent every last cent of my salary. I lay in bed thinking mournfully that I would have to avoid Steve's Place until payday. The next morning I awoke with the same certainty and, still feeling sorry for myself, at around 10pm I decided to visit my fellow journalist Mzondi, who lived a few streets away.

Of course, part of the trouble with Steve's Place was that I always had to pass by it, whether on my way to the station to catch a train into town, or to visit a friend. This time was no different and, as I was about to move swiftly out of sight of those already there drinking, I heard Zane's voice calling to me.

'Steven, *yizapha bhuti.*'

I walked inside and solemnly declared I would be enjoying a sober weekend. He asked me why, to which I replied that it just wasn't healthy to drink on so regular a basis.

'Suka wena,' Zane laughed, rubbishing what I'd said.

Leaning forward I explained softly that I was out of cash, but quickly assured him I'd be back on the liquid beat on payday. A look of utter disgust passed over his face.

'Drink,' he said, nodding towards the team of Hansas standing on the plastic table.

Throughout my life I had been taught that wisdom usually emerged out of complex constructions, whether poetic parables or elegant innuendos. True, I had read Hermann Hess's *Siddartha*, which taught the wisdom of simplicity, but apart from those blurred, fantasy-laden pages, I had never before been taught such a humbling lesson. I had gone through life with a set of ledgers, attempting to balance brotherhood and the business of friendship, or if not balance, at the very least break even. But with the repeated use of only one word, Zane had forced me into an acceptance of a different set of principles altogether.

This kindness might have seemed uncharacteristic. Zane, after all, had once murdered a man in cold blood. Or at least, that's what people said.

Ultimately, I was to spend many months trying to find the catch: perhaps he wanted something from me – what criminal game was he playing?

But there was no catch.

Zane showed almost no emotion when he eventually spoke to me of that day, all those years ago, at a Bellville bank, although I felt him watching me closely, searching for a sign that his story was hurting, perhaps even killing, our friendship.

It was a simple, brutal tale. He and two of his friends had been drunk out of their wits when they arrived at the bank, their hearts and minds overrun by the lust for money and blood. I asked Zane the typically South African question.

'Was the man you shot black, coloured or white?'

Zane smiled.

'He was an Afrikaner.'

I had to ask whether or not he felt guilty about killing this Afrikaner. Zane answered without any visible emotion.

'I have never felt guilty for what I did.'

'Why not?'

'Because I hate the Boer.'

Mzondi

My friend Mzondi was a man of his word. He had fulfilled his promise to teach me Xhosa etiquette and to introduce me to the 'right people'. On our very first Friday evening appointment at Vovo Cash Store, however, it became clear that Mzondi's lessons on Xhosa etiquette would be drastically slowed by his obedience to African Time: on this occasion he had arrived four hours late for our 6pm appointment. After a few weeks I began to come to terms with the fact that insisting on meeting times with Mzondi was pointless. Nevertheless, he did teach me the ropes, guiding me from shebeen to house and back to shebeen, and introducing me to his seemingly endless family members.

'This is my brother Zwai,' he would say. 'This is my sister Lisa, and this is my other brother Zola.' And so it would go, until I became increasingly incredulous about the sheer size of Mzondi's family. Of course, in a week or two I would realise that they were in fact friends: biological brothers and sisters were soon distinguished from the thousands of other siblings by being introduced as 'my blood brother', or 'my father's second born', or it was revealed that 'we have the same mother'. But the echoes of family were everywhere: all married women and mothers were known as 'mama', while I addressed men old enough to be my father as 'tata.' Men two generations ahead were called 'tatamkhulu', or grandfather, and women of their age were 'makhulu'.

These titles were not casually dished out, to help get conversations started or allow for flippant greetings, but instead carried tremendous weight and respect. The meaningless formality and superficiality of so many of my encounters with whites was totally foreign here. In the suburbs, cliques reigned and appointments were everything. In Khaya, it was not uncommon for me to be visited in my room by someone I'd met only the day before, who had dropped by without an invitation. Forgetting his or her name would be met with a look of deep hurt; although an apology would completely clear the air. In the suburbs, in my previous experience, older people were secretly pitied or belittled, or ignored, but here they were shown the respect they deserved, the younger generation listening intently and often declining to make eye contact with the speaker out of deference.

With the air so full of genuine affection and respect, it did not take long for me to feel I had a gigantic family, one that boasted hundreds of siblings, parents and grandparents. Before, my family had referred merely to my three siblings and my parents; in Khaya, family can include people you have known only for a few days. My personal safety, which had so preoccupied me in my first days in Khaya, soon became the least of my worries, because wherever I went I bumped into dozens of friends.

In many ways, being white meant I was safer than anyone else, mainly because the colour of my skin brought me a strange kind of celebrity. For instance, I might walk into a shebeen in Site C, over five kilometres from where I lived, and be approached by a patron who'd tell me he'd heard I played a good game of pool. Soon I would be drinking in a group of five or six, all of them rooting for me at the pool table, with countless challengers lining up coins to take me on at the game. I began to notice that I seemed to be good for business: word of my whereabouts would spread, and shebeens that had been empty would fill to capacity half an hour after I arrived. And the victory dances that went on after I'd been beaten at the pool table suggested that whipping a white man at the game was something to be celebrated.

Very soon I felt that I had known this place and its people my whole life. I felt that I had returned home, home to a place I'd always pined for, but had never managed to find until now. I had always been mindful of the fact that as long as I felt like a white, English South African, I would be guilty of ignoring the truth of my identity. Although I couldn't speak a word of German and couldn't remember anything from the short time when my family lived in Austria, I had always identified more closely with a European identity than an African identity. My move to Khaya forced me to realise that I had far more in common with Africa than with any imagined European roots.

There were friends everywhere, even if I'd only met them five minutes earlier. On almost every train journey into work in the early afternoons I would meet acquaintances, old and new. The women were the most caring, many of them domestic workers on their way to scrub a white home in the suburbs. They would interrogate me warmly on my feelings about Khayelitsha, my opinion of the Xhosa people, and they would listen intently to my response. Their concern for my well-being was genuine and strong: I was often escorted on foot to my township destination by a motherly matron.

But it was more than humanity and a sense of camaraderie: there was a naturalness about relationships and public gatherings that was unlike anything I had experienced in the white world, and this was never more evident than on a pumping dance floor in a packed tavern, like Lulu's Tavern in Site B.

On one particular evening, Mzondi had taken advantage of my fame to try to organise a lift home from Lulu's for the two of us. He was getting restless, and although it was late – well after 10pm – and we'd been drinking all night, I wondered whether his eagerness to leave perhaps had something to do with an appointment with a girlfriend that he hadn't told me about. For my part, leaving was the last thing on my mind – jiving was what I wanted. I'd chosen Mapaputsi's 'Intro Umgan'wama Cala' as one of my two songs on the jukebox, an impossible track to waste, and just as Mzondi started yawning, it began, booming through the tavern: 'This is the police!' rang out in the guttural English of a uniformed *boertjie*. 'You are surrounded!' it blared. 'Come out with your hands on top of your head!' It was my battle cry, and before Mzondi could say a word I sprang up and headed for an empty spot on the dance floor.

Being a white boy on the skinny side of thin, I had soon found myself very under-endowed in the backside area in the township. Indeed, my complete lack of any kind of rear end had made me the butt, so to speak, of endless jokes from my friends. But tonight I wasn't letting my genetic handicap slow me down: the irresistible kwaito beat gave my bum a life of its own.

I had always been a self-conscious dancer, but a month in Khayelitsha had changed that. White men couldn't jump, I'd been told on countless occasions; did that mean they also couldn't dance? It was a friendly jibe, but it had a serious undertone. Dancing is central to Xhosa culture, from Nelson Mandela doing his famous shuffle in front of the global media, to disgruntled workers toyi-toying, sticks in hand, to the director's office. For men it is an instinctive expression of rhythm and strength, while for women it is a chance to flaunt their beauty, with sensual gyrations and clever hands. In Khaya, it is common to see toddlers, only walking for a week or two, being coaxed by their elders to dance. Many of their moves, enhanced by pronounced nappy bums, were enough to make me lose any confidence I might have had left. However, as the weeks and months passed, I had stopped worrying about how I looked to others. Here, the forms of beauty dictated by glossy magazines were not important.

The dance floor was overflowing with all shapes and sizes; men with massive beer bellies joined their more muscular fellows in dancing with the ladies, some of them enormously fat, others rake-thin. Everyone smiling at everyone, something I'd only ever seen years before among dancers stuffed to the gills with LSD at Cape Town's outdoor trance parties – but the difference here was that the smiles would still be just as wide in the morning.

The song over, I returned to our table sweating from head to toe. Mzondi waited for me to sit down.

'Hey, Steve, I know it's a Saturday night,' he said carefully, 'but I'm feeling very tired. I've asked my brother over

37

there if he can drive us home.'

Sipho, who worked as a foreman for a construction firm, drove a wreck – at about 20 kilometres an hour and in third gear, with both hands placed lovingly on the steering wheel. Despite the car's ruined state, he took a lot of pride in being a good chauffeur, and during the drive he asked me time and time again whether I was comfortable. I was. A large pile of papers and school books had been cleared off the front seat to make room for me, and it was a pleasure not to be walking.

When we pulled up outside a house on the outskirts of iLitha Park, miles from my own, I wasn't surprised, accustomed as I had become to being spirited around to meet people. Sipho seemed peculiarly excited, and honked his horn several times before bounding out of the car. This, it turned out, was Sipho's own house – an old, unsightly green government house with a crumbling front wall.

Before I knew what was happening, Sipho's wife was introduced and immediately sent away. 'She's gone to wake our baby,' he announced proudly.

The infant was duly produced, as the kettle boiled cheerfully and tea was poured. I put my cup down as the little bundle was carefully placed in my arms. He was three months old, but still had the squint of the newborn, while his nose was about the size of a button, and about as flat. As I got my clumsy hands into the right position on the baby, I was aware that Sipho was retreating to the doorway, and when he called my name and I looked up I saw that he was grinning at his child and me through a camera lens. By the third snap I was smiling cheerfully.

'Thank you, Steve,' said Sipho, snapping one more picture.

Later, as Mzondi and I staggered up towards my house, I tried to understand the last half hour.

'Why did he take that photograph of me with the baby, Mzondi?'

My friend grinned. 'Sipho told me in the shebeen he was going to go past his house first.'

'But why?'

'Because he's never had a white man there before,' said Mzondi, 'and because when the baby is older he can show him the picture of the two of you together. It will make the boy happy. Look at it this way, Steve …' He began walking unsteadily away. 'It's not every day we have a white person in the township.'

He waved, and swayed off into the night.

Vuyo

'Steve, are you a man or a moffie?' Zane asked again. Our two companions, sitting with us on my double bed, guffawed; our game of checkers, played with beer bottle caps, was well under way.

I'd known James and Mzo for many months, but still often wondered why Mzo was part of our tiny circle of close friends. He reminded me of a buddy I'd had in Uitenhage years before, whose only contribution to conversation had been a series of rhyming clichés, delivered with smug drunkenness. An enquiry as to how he was doing was greeted with 'Going like a Boeing', while the misfortunes of his enemies got a knowing, 'What goes around comes around'. Mzo had the same love for hard liquor and an equally swift about-turn in personality came upon him as the brandy filled his belly.

He spent weekdays slumped in his sister's little home

watching daytime television, but I had no doubt that if Mzo had had a car and a job like my cliché-spewing Uitenhage buddy, he too would have driven around with a bottle of gin in his cubbyhole and a beer mug by his side. However, Mzo had long ago lost his compass on his journey to find work, and now lived for Fridays, when his hard-working sister got paid. (I must confess, however, that Zane, James and I were also not totally innocent in this regard, having drunk a fair share of his sister's wages – perhaps this went some way towards explaining why we still tolerated Mzo.)

This particular afternoon Mzo was at his most tolerable as he sat on my bed: he had all of his sister's charity in his pocket, putting him in a splendid mood as he anticipated the drinking to come. Because the drinking had not yet begun, the aggression and drunkenness that made him so unlikeable were still hours away.

'Steve,' said James through dreadlocks so long that they brushed the checkers board, 'you must tell this girl you love her.' He underlined his statement by banging down his Castle cap over two of my Black Label caps.

For the umpteenth time, I protested that I had a girlfriend.

'And where is she now when you need her?' asked Zane.

'She's in Holland.'

'Holland!' cried Zane, rolling himself a cigarette of my peach tobacco. 'And how far is Holland from here, my brother?'

'Zane,' I said impatiently, changing the subject, 'let me explain something to you. I buy one packet of peach tobacco at the beginning of every month. Now,' I continued slowly and patronisingly, 'that bag has to last me the whole month, so if we smoke it all today, I will be without cigarettes for three weeks. Have you ever had to go without tobacco?' I looked up from the game – it was lost, in any case.

'No, I haven't,' said Zane, 'because when I don't have anything to smoke, my friends do, and what they have they share with me.' He shot me a pointed look, lit the cigarette, and passed it to James: a smoke covers a lot of mileage in the township.

'How far is Holland?' he began again. He just would not let it go. 'A few thousand kilometres north of Khayelitsha?'

'You are taking too long to learn checkers, Steve,' complained James.

'If you start walking now,' Zane continued, taking my place at the board, 'you will get some *pathla pathla* in about five years.' He touched the fly of his pants with his pinkie. 'By which time that thing will have shrivelled up and died.' He pronounced it *'shreeevalled'*.

I shrugged, and tried to sound sure of myself. 'In my culture men and women are expected to stay faithful to each other.'

'Yes, but many of them don't,' Mzo chipped in, surprising us all with a vaguely intelligent contribution. 'And anyway, now you are living with us.'

'When in Rome ...' said James, in his Model C accent, slamming down a cap on Zane's side of the board.

'Why I am asking you if you are a moffie,' said Zane, 'is because we have never met this lady from Holland. And you are always trying to hug us when you're drunk, so how can we be sure she's real? Why isn't she here?'

'She's completing her studies.'

'If this lady really loved you,' James said, 'she'd be here with you.'

It was a familiar routine for all of us but, although we all knew our lines, my resolve had weakened over the months and I think we all sensed that this time it was different. Perhaps it was the tone of my voice when I'd told them I'd seen Vuyo on the train earlier that afternoon, and the look in my eyes as I'd described her.

Even years after she first came into my life, I am moved by the memory of her smile. Just the thought of it, so many months after our last contact, leaves me longing to see her smile one more time. For I know for sure that there was not a single occasion after the first time we met, passing each other in a bland Technikon corridor, on which I did not blush, thrown completely by a beauty that flowed from her deep coffee eyes and sparkled from her smile. Her little freckles, uncommon on the nose of a Xhosa girl, only added to the power she held over me. And to top it all, to make her completely irresistible, she seemed delightfully oblivious to the spell she'd cast on me.

I'd thought about Vuyo often, in that space that exists despite being in a relationship with someone else, a space reserved for those fleeting contacts with might-have-been love. In my case, this space was big; the daytime blushes and night-time fantasies (more the goddess-worshipping type than anything more lurid) had gone on for eighteen months. Perhaps because I was in a relationship, and perhaps because she was clearly too perfect to touch, the most I'd ever said to her in that time was, 'Are you on your way to fashion class?'

My infatuation had quickly reached a masochistic point, where I would arrive half an hour early for class in the hope that I could somehow embarrass myself in the corridor and catch her eye. It couldn't have been subtle. I've seen many black faces blush, but on my pale one, I might as well have announced my feelings with a display of fireworks.

43

Given how I felt, and how she flitted in and out my thoughts for so many months, it was extraordinary that I hadn't recognised her sitting across from me on the train to Khayelitsha one particular day, months after I'd last seen her, before the start of my internship at a Cape Town newspaper. She and another girl, somewhat younger than her, stepped lightly aboard the train at Site C station, one stop from iLitha Park, and soon after the train got rolling again, she had begun to whisper into her companion's ear and to giggle. I am no stranger to giggling girls, but there was a loveliness in her smile that started pulling me out of the reverie one slips into on trains, where you hardly notice the people around you. Her smile brightened, and suddenly my self-consciousness slipped away: I smiled back. It was then that she leaned forward.

'How are you, Steven?'

How on earth did she know my name?

I managed to stutter a reply, something about being well. Only then did I recognise her.

'Vuyo?' I cried.

'I'm fine,' she said with grin.

She was wearing an orange full-length *umbhaco* traditional dress, with a majestic *iqhiya* turban in the same colour. The orange went with the creamy brown shade of her skin so flawlessly that I was hardly surprised to see a hint of blue in her eyes. The old smile lit up, her lovely features worked their magic, and once again I had the happy, disturbing feeling that I'd lost control of my eyes.

'You look so beautiful!' I blurted out. 'Where have you been?'

A few fellow passengers had pricked up their ears, and were grinning. This time Vuyo blushed.

'Thanks,' she said shyly. 'My sister and I belong to a traditional choir in Site C. We've just come from practice.' Her sister – for it was she, sitting with Vuyo – gave me a polite smile, as the train jerked and began to slow down, its brakes screeching as we pulled in to the platform.

'I never knew you lived in iLitha Park.'

'I live in Harare,' answered Vuyo, referring to another area in Khayelitsha, not the Zimbabwean capital, as we climbed off the train into the tremendous press of commuters. 'Over there,' she added, pointing to the far end of Ntlazane Road.

Harare, a huge undulating stretch of scrub covered with shacks and a few isolated houses, was one of the places I'd been warned to steer clear of, although Foamy had taken me to a shebeen on its outskirts that sold the cheapest *umqomboti* (traditional beer) for miles.

'Do you live with your parents?'

'With my mother,' she said. We began to climb the stairs to the dull grey pedestrian skywalk. 'And you?'

I told her I lived in Ntlakohlaza Street, and pointed towards my home.

We rounded the corner at the top of the stairs, and joined the masses of people making their way through the revolving gates where Metrorail employees checked their tickets. A man next to us said something to Vuyo, but it was lost in the noise of shoes and conversation, and she and I had been shunted apart by the tide of people. She smiled across at me.

'He's joking about us,' she laughed, raising her voice across the din. Even though she was almost shouting, her voice still held its delightful softness. 'He says I will become famous because an *umlungu* is in love with me!'

At that point some people might have been swept away by emotion, but just then I was swept away far more physically.

The crowd, being forced through a narrower section, had become a flood, and I realised I was no longer choosing my direction. I relaxed my body, and let myself shuffle wherever the press took me. Brown heads surrounded me, and whenever I caught someone's eye, they smiled inquisitively at me.

Beyond the crush I found Vuyo and her sister waiting for me, and we walked in shy silence down the cement ramp towards the little market at the bottom, where hawkers sold everything from cigarettes to live chickens. But the shyness quickly melted away in the warm breeze that swirled dust around our feet and we began to chat easily, as if we were old friends – about how long we'd both lived here; how amazing it was that we hadn't run into each other before; and all the other insignificant details that go on in flirtation when neither of you wants the conversation to end. In fact, we became so lost in our conversation that Vuyo's sister, Zodwa, began shifting from one foot to the other and looking uncomfortable in the way that people do when they feel they are intruding on someone else's intimacy. At last she politely insisted that she had to hurry home to meet a friend, and left us alone. Vuyo and I talked on and, as I watched her shade her face from the sun with a slender, elegant hand, I wondered about how to time my first advance. In the end I settled for a compromise: a lie, and a fast-forward.

'I need to go now,' I said, entirely untruthfully, 'but, Vuyo, could I have your phone number?' I stumbled on. 'Then maybe I can visit you some time?'

I had (perhaps unforgivably) skipped the first rule of township courtship, riding roughshod over the 'I'll call you' and moving straight to talk of visits, and I felt myself blushing – yet again. Vuyo studied my blazing face a little longer than was fair, even my eyeballs seemed to be inflamed.

'Okay,' she said at last. 'That would be nice.'

For a moment I wondered if I should ask whether she had a boyfriend, but then I remembered Zane's advice – if you love a woman, you love her regardless. With a parting smile, she began to walk away.

'What do you do in the afternoons?' I called after her.

She grinned shyly.

'I watch the Teletubbies.'

Bin Laden of iLitha Park

I'd walked home over sea sand and scrub, and had it not been for a small dose of guilt, I would also have been walking on air. It was the kind of guilt you feel when you know you've taken a small step towards unfaithfulness, and in order to justify the move I had just made, I began to analyse what had just happened. I may have a girlfriend, I thought, but she is very far away.

After all, it had been an incredible coincidence meeting Vuyo on the train – surely this was fate taking a hand? And if fate was involved, what could I possibly do to change the course of my destiny, other than let it bring her closer to me?

Of course, had I been honest, I would have seen that loneliness was also taking its toll. In an environment where I did not have one friend who was single – most of the guys

I knew claimed to have upwards of three girlfriends – I had become desperate for intimate female company. It didn't help that now and then my male friends would politely ask me to leave so that they could be alone with their lovers. Deep down I knew that I was looking for justification.

Zane would have agreed with whatever rationalisations I came up with. It was his view that my romantic and sexual drought was due to my inexperience with Xhosa girls, but then again none of his lectures on township courtship contained any useful information about what to do with girls who spent their afternoons watching the Teletubbies.

But there was one far more serious issue that I couldn't wish away or leave in the hands of fate. HIV and Aids are rampant in the townships, with infection rates far higher than in other areas, and I decided I would at least be responsible in one respect, and bring it up with my friends later that evening.

And so it was that once Zane, James and Mzo had finished mocking my lack of courtship prowess and poor game of checkers, we relocated to Vovo Cash Store; Mzo bought an armful of quarts and I broached the subject of condoms. Did any of them have one for me? They shook their heads.

'So where's the closest place to buy some?'

'I don't know Holland that well,' said Zane. James thought there might be some at the all-night garage café in Site B. Mzo had downed three glasses and was already a basket case, and not answering any questions.

'So do you guys wear condoms?' I asked my more conscious companions.

'Every time,' said James.

'Never,' said Zane. Although I'd discussed the issue of Aids with Zane before, I'd always got the feeling that his views were shaped according to what he knew would irritate me most. 'When you buy meat at a shop, do you eat it with the plastic still on?' he asked.

I got angry. 'But if I take the plastic off the meat, I won't die a horrible death.'

My temper was short, because I'd been here before – literally. The last time we'd had the condom debate, we'd been at the same shebeen, early on a Saturday morning. We'd just settled down with our beers when a terrible commotion broke out across the road in Zane's house. He was gone in a flash, and we followed more slowly. There was no wall in front of the house, and so we had a clear view.

A bundle of clothes flew through the front door, followed by a dishevelled woman wearing pyjamas. Soon another woman appeared in the doorway, this one smartly dressed, and the two proceeded to scream at each other. Zane finally appeared and casually came wandering back towards us.

'What's going on?' I asked as he took his place with us again.

'Those are my girlfriends,' he said.

'And?'

'They are fighting.'

'I can see that,' I said impatiently.

'The one in the garden slept with me last night,' sighed Zane. 'The other one has just arrived.'

'But which one is your real girlfriend?'

He shrugged. 'I love them both.' He watched them go at each other disinterestedly, and I noticed that no one else seemed particularly interested in the fight either. The few pedestrians passing by hardly noticed the hullabaloo, and Zane's neighbour, who was wearing the characteristic apron and headscarf of a married Xhosa woman, continued hanging out washing on the line between the two houses as if nothing was out of the ordinary.

'It looks like you're in trouble, my brother,' I said. 'What are you going to do?'

'Nothing,' he said, blankly. 'They will sort it out.'

I was more than a little taken aback by his detached attitude. I asked him which of the women he'd been with the longest.

'That is not the question,' he replied. 'This never would have happened if that one' – he motioned to the well-dressed woman in the doorway – 'hadn't come. I didn't phone her to come here, so she was not invited. What she has done is wrong.' He shrugged and turned to the pool table to watch the latest game.

But the shrieking continued from across the road, and finally he swigged down the last of his beer with an irritated jerk and stood up to leave.

'I'll be back soon,' he said curtly. 'Put a coin on the table for me.' With that, he walked over the road, motioned the two women into the house with him, and shut the door.

About ten minutes later he opened the door and guided one of the women outside. Following her, he lifted a bundle from the ground and hailed a taxi. She climbed in, the taxi pulled away in a cloud of exhaust fumes, and Zane crossed the road and returned to my side.

'I made a choice,' he said in response to my raised eye-brows.

'Which one did you choose?'

'The one who came this morning.'

'Why?'

'Because,' said Zane, 'I had the other lady last night, and this one I have not had for a long time.'

I knew that arguing against Zane's behaviour from a moral standpoint was useless, as he always simply claimed that our cultures were different, and that I did not understand. Besides, I would always have to admit that countless white men and women cheated on their partners. But while sexual lapses happened, for me there was no negotiation about condoms. And although Zane's protests about safe sex that morning had been presented with a smile, with his two girlfriends fighting over him, I could tell that tonight he was completely serious about his convictions. If it hadn't been for James backing me up, I would have become extremely angry.

Instead I took a different angle, and told Zane about my visit to a Catholic home for Aids orphans in town during the first year of my studies; how I'd read a children's story to them, as they were racked by hacking coughs that spoke of deadly lung infections, and how I'd tried not to touch their faces which were covered in excruciating blisters.

'Your babies might end up there, Zane,' I said.

'Steve,' he said, 'a condom is not foolproof. It often breaks.' James tried to talk probability and statistics, but Zane pulled him up, irritated by the lecture. 'Ag, man,' he snapped, 'if I get sick I will throw myself in front of a train.'

It was then that Osama bin Laden spoke up from where he was leaning over the pool table.

He had been named for his looks. Although his lips were thicker and his skin darker, his long beard and light brown eyes gave him an uncanny resemblance to the Al-Qaeda leader, and for a few months after the New York attacks it was widely acknowledged, with much laughter, that Bin Laden was hiding out in iLitha Park. The name had stuck, and now everyone called him Osama.

'You are mad if you don't wear a condom,' Osama said.

Zane laughed. 'How can you guys listen to someone who lives in a cave with thirty-five wives and fifty camels?'

Osama wasn't laughing. 'My father is a chief in the old Ciskei. He has four wives and many more girlfriends, and he doesn't have HIV or Aids.' I understood now where Osama, who spent his whole life between home and Vovo Cash Store, got his money. He also apparently had similar sexual tastes to his father – I had never seen him with the same girl twice.

James sighed. 'Another one who doesn't believe the disease exists.'

'I do believe it exists,' said Osama, 'but it is a bigger problem in the cities than in the rural areas. That's why I use condoms when I'm here.'

I'd had enough, and thought about other things while they talked: of Vuyo, neatly preparing for bed somewhere deep in the Harare squatter camp. I hoped she was safe. Much later, lying in my own bed, I turned off my phone and switched off the light. I'd resisted the urge to call her for one night; but there would be hundreds more. I wasn't sure how long I could hold out.

Beans

According to township wisdom, the only way to recover from a *bhabhalaza* is to drink a quart or two of beer in the morning. However, the lore insists, the best option is to prevent a *bhabhalaza* altogether, by drinking non-stop so that the pain of the next morning is indefinitely delayed.

And so it was that on those bright March mornings I was usually to be found working on my headache, with plenty of similarly hard-working sufferers who had been at the same shebeen the night before. Drinkers in the townships have a massive advantage over their counterparts in the suburbs. In a place where the close-knit sense of community and the culture of sharing exist, drinking buddies and beer money are always on hand.

Conversation with my new friends was always slow and meandering, but after some weeks I discovered that there was a widespread belief that I was an undercover policeman. It later emerged that my companions at Steve's Place deliberately kept their conversation vague and innocent, in case I was carrying tales to my uniformed superiors. But as the weeks passed, and no police raids were forthcoming on the unlicensed drinking holes I frequented, a new rumour began to take hold. It seemed I wasn't working for the law at all, but rather that the confidence that had brought me to live as a white man in Khayelitsha was a sure sign that I was a hardened, fearless drug dealer. The image began to rub off on me, and I quickly began to feel more confident about walking out on my own; much of my white paranoia was evaporating.

But of course it was inevitable that this version of my persona would fade too. The truth would out, and after I showed some of the patrons at Vovo a selection of my stories in the paper, word spread that I peddled news rather than drugs, and I began to be taken at face value.

It had been that face – a white one – that had earned me much of the interest and respect I'd experienced in my first months in the townships, and as much as I had wanted to be treated as an ordinary resident, I had to admit to myself that, as people got used to my presence and paid less attention to me, I began to feel a little neglected. I realised I had started to feel like a rock star, waving to my fans in the street: I had even begun to harbour delusions of grandeur, fantasies in which I ran for the position of street committee head, or even local councillor. And when I was brought back down to earth – by a dog, in this case – it was with a big bang.

One Saturday afternoon I had gone to my Ghanaian hairdresser John, who operated out of a large ship container five minutes away from my home. As always, it was a pleasant visit, a chance to relax and be pampered in relative peace. Even though the little rectangular space was one of a plethora of containers lining Ntlazane Road, it was always an oasis for me as I listened to the buzzing of razors and the banter of the mostly female customers and staff, and looked at the Black Like Me products on the shelves.

The guys at Vovo Cash Store always said I looked like a woman when my hair grew to anything close to a centimetre in length, and so John had become essential in keeping me looking manly. But his main custom came from the women who streamed in to be transformed by his clever hands, his nimble and slim fingers belying his squat, short frame and thick neck.

I've always enjoyed having my head shaved. The pleasant combination of the whirring of the shaver, hair falling softly past my face and the firm touch of fingertips on my scalp has never failed to send me into a state of dreamy reflection. By the time John was done, and I had paid him the three rand for the cut (he returned a further rand I tried to give him, saying that three rand was all he'd take), those dreamy reflections had spiralled into full-blown megalomania. I was winning international awards, making important speeches, and being inaugurated as a mayor, premier and president. I left John's container on a cloud.

Taking the route back to Vovo Cash Store, I passed the shoe repair, cellphone and Telkom containers on my left. Everything was so much cheaper here and, because the service was so personal, my love of bargaining was tolerated and guarantees for work done often continued indefinitely. On my right was the station, where a train had drawn to a stop a few minutes earlier, judging by the mass of bodies coming down the stairs. My life had reached a peak, I thought as I crossed the road to the station side and moved slowly along the pavement. I had finally lost the feeling that I stood out like a sore thumb.

It was at this point that I noticed a few people looking in my direction. This was still fairly normal, but this time there was a little girl – children are always less inclined to be tactful – saying something to her mother, all the time motioning in my direction. Her giggling continued, even though her mother seemed to be scolding her, and some of the adults walking in twos and threes from the station seemed to be making a point of not noticing me. I checked my fly: it was up. Perhaps it was someone behind me. I glanced over my shoulder ...

The dog was white, an unusual shade for a township mutt. They are usually light brown, and difficult to spot as they flit around after dark looking for scraps with an air of shadiness about them. This one appeared to have a touch of Jack Russell in it, because it had a smudge of brown down one side, and held its head at a cocky angle. Its eyes were fixed intently on me. Then, as the dog came closer, I realised what had appealed to the little girl's humour. The creature, which had its backside planted firmly on the ground, was using its front legs to pull itself forward. It was giving its backside an almighty scrape on the road. Apparently my stalker had a particularly bad case of worms.

'Get away,' I shouted at it, trying not to think about how we must have looked to those around us.

He had obviously seen a kindred spirit in me, though, because each time I shouted he would retreat, still in that unpleasant position, before moving after me again once I'd resumed my journey. This frustrating situation continued for some time, until a passing woman had the decency to hurl a large stone at the dog. This did the trick, even getting the little creature to lift its bum off the ground and run. After saying a quick thank you, I slunk away bashfully.

But there were other times when my whiteness gave me credit I did not deserve, and if I must be entirely truthful, I have to concede that at these times I happily hid behind my neighbours' misperceptions. But I still feel guilty about the episode of the beans.

After moving to Khaya, my diet had changed to one consisting mainly of meat, beans and beer. The rice and pap I ate served to dissipate at least some of the more negative effects of the animal fats and legumes, but there was one rather violent reaction with which I grappled desperately on an almost hourly basis: wind. The legumes and beer in particular produced a certain windiness, whose main goal seemed to be escaping from my rear at the most inopportune moments. Frequently, and without warning, I farted like a racehorse.

My dayshift at the paper was punctuated by quick darts around the large, open-plan office to avoid being identified as the source of the noxious fumes. Knowing from the escalating rumble deep inside my belly, and the simultaneous build-up of pain that accompanied it, that trouble was on the way, I'd spring up from my desk and head for the bathroom. Now and then, halfway there, I'd be shaken into accepting that my ambition had been too great and I'd do a quick left turn towards the fax machine. After not picking up a fax, I'd head for the smoking room, the only room in the building where most of the occupants were unable to smell. After work, relieved that I'd made it through the day without anyone noticing my avoidance of all forms of communication delivered from a stationary position, I headed for the taxi rank.

There were days I took a train and there were days I took a taxi. The choice depended on a number of factors. For one, during rush hour I found the trains were the best option since car fumes were avoided. Away from the inevitable traffic jams, trains were also faster. Then there was the issue of privacy; whenever I did not want to bump into someone I knew, or feel out of place as the only white face, I caught a taxi. However, the speed at which some taxi drivers drove and the fact that they regularly shot down highways inside the yellow line sometimes saw me with my head crunched between my legs, screaming in the most horrible, silent way.

Today's choice was the result of a simple calculation of casualties. In the case of the train, the casualties would have numbered well over sixty, I estimated, while a taxi holds only sixteen at a stretch.

And so it was that I found myself squashed between three big mamas on the back seat of a taxi, rushing down that nightmarish curve in the N2 highway past Groote Schuur. However, crossing the excruciating boundary between stomach cramps and relief with a dreadful shriek on my face, the speed of the vehicle was the furthest thing from my mind. Instead, the smell that consumed every inch of air in the taxi dominated my every thought, adding a new element to my make-up as a male; that feeling of silent hysterics at so horrible a habit. The smell had spread extremely quickly and ended with an ominous silence taking hold of driver and passengers alike. There was no doubt in my mind – as even the sound of the engine faded away – that we had hit an air pocket at ground level. It was then that the big lady in front of me turned around, her lips curled in disgust.

'I'm really sorry about this,' she said apologetically. 'Some of our people don't have any manners.'

Baas John

As the black people who lived in my area began to realise that I was there to stay and attitudes towards me normalised, I began to be treated like everybody else, soon getting flak for some of my more strange opinions and especially for my rare bouts of arrogant behaviour, which usually unfolded around the pool table. There, a common strategy of mine was to list the years in which I claimed to have won the Pool Championships of Khayelitsha.

'Khayelitsha Champion 2000, 2001 and 2002,' I would announce, with my hands held above my head like a boxer.

Opponents who took this type of thing badly were few, most of them coming up with a far-fetched claim of their own.

But even though attitudes normalised, my pale complexion still followed me everywhere, especially when I ventured into areas where people didn't know me. My whiteness stalked me into the shebeens and on to the trains, into neighbours' houses and to traditional functions. I think much of this can be put down to my own mind, constantly reminded as it was by my eyes, which looked forever past the milky white shade of my spotted nose. For weeks on end I donned sunglasses whenever I ventured away from my area, which, although effective in combating at least some of my paranoia, inevitably buttered up my gangster image. But there was no way of getting around it: I was white.

This should not be misunderstood. I've never had a problem with my race. It was just that my colour saw me having to deal with some irritating situations. I was regularly asked if my father could organise someone a job. It was usually older men who did this, dressed in tattered clothes and sometimes a little drunk. The idea that most white people in South Africa have always been far wealthier than most blacks is certainly not a misperception, but rather an unfortunate result of an unequal political state, and it was precisely this truth that embarrassed me. But as my number of friends increased and some of them began to notice my feelings of awkwardness, so they began to explain in Xhosa that I was a local student and not the son of a wealthy businessman.

Probably the thing I hated most about those first weeks was the 'thank you speech', which happened almost every day for two months. This also usually involved an older man, drunk or sober. Walking up to me, he'd have his hand outstretched. A look of absolute adoration in his eyes, he would cup one of my hands in both of his, saying simply, 'Thank you.'

Then the speech would start; each was the same as the one before. Its message might have been genuine and based on a sad reality, but it soon got under my skin; perhaps it was some kind of guilt that made me feel so intensely embarrassed. I'd expected to find anger over the injustices that had been meted out to black South Africans over the centuries by people my colour. When I found no anger at all, my guilt somehow always intensified.

'Thank you for coming to see how we live,' the speech would go. 'Thank you for showing white people that we can live together in peace. Most white people don't bother to see how we live, but you are different.' One particular speechmaker shared with me his philosophy on race; one I heard a thousand times over. 'My skin is black,' he said, 'and yours is white. But if you cut us on the hand, then you will see that my blood is red like yours.'

But there were also times when we all saw the funny side of our misperceptions and shared warm laughter, one of the most effective ways to deal with ignorance. Many of the younger men took to calling me 'Baas John', a hangover from the apartheid days, when many whites used 'John' as a name for black men in general. To their credit, however, those who *did* call me 'Baas John' would never fail to crumple in fits of laughter when I replied appropriately to the apartheid banter, with a sharp, 'Voetsak!'

My whiteness was never more amusingly highlighted to me than on one particular train ride to Cape Town, as we rattled and roared between the iLitha Park and Site C stations.

I was watching a beggar work his way down the third-class carriage, with its two bright yellow benches running down either side of the rectangular compartment. Stopping in front of each commuter, leaning slightly forward with a severe expression on his face, the middle-aged man was saying, in a fairly demanding tone, 'Twenty cents ...'

It was barely light outside and the autumn air was howling through the gaping holes where the windows should have been and down the back of my neck.

'Twenty cents ...' I heard the strangely intense man say to someone about five seats down from mine.

Now that he was nearer to me I was able to study him a little more closely. His hair was extremely dishevelled, at the stage when the onset of dreadlocks can only be beaten with soap, a razor and a bucket of warm water. Tattered clothes and an unwashed body are by no means signs of mental illness, but there was something about the fanatical expression in his eyes that made one think twice.

'Twenty cents?' he asked my neighbour, who handed him a coin.

Shuffling a little to the left, until he was standing in front of me, the bedraggled man barely seemed to register my existence, but the voice was louder and the words slightly different:

'Twenty rand!' he demanded of me.

Perhaps I had hoped to become colour blind, but I realised that in the South African context colour blindness is probably more difficult to achieve than land redistribution. In my case, though, my habit of always noticing the race of the person I was talking to or looking at had begun to fade away. Only when someone brought up the subject of colour in a conversation would I remember I was white. I also found it interesting that so many of my black friends said that to them all whites looked the same, since this is what I had regularly heard white people say about black people when I was a child. In a strange way it made sense, though, because we had all been living in our separate areas and hadn't come to recognise differences in individuals we only had offhand contact with at work.

Now, because I was living as a close neighbour of black people on a day-to-day basis, a whole new world of facial expressions and interesting patterns of speech opened up before me, just as a kaleidoscope of personalities revealed itself. Previously, my sensitivities to race had seen me being uniformly polite to, and without exception interested in, each black person I'd met, but I could now choose friends based on their personality and sense of humour, as one would in any normal society. For instance, while my neighbour Bulelani was a very pleasant person, I was not interested in going beyond a merely formal relationship with him. I found him a little too strait-laced and decent, and I got the feeling he frowned on my habit of drinking beer on Christian church days, although it could have been my guilty conscience that made me look away when he passed by my local in his Sunday best shortly before noon.

On the other hand, I sometimes met gardeners and refuse collectors – people I would probably not usually have interacted with – who had more of a grasp on politics than some of the journalists I knew, arguing this way and that on the issues of the day. It is precisely because of the high level of contact and communication in Khaya that the calibre of debate is so impressive. While those in the suburbs are undoubtedly more educated, there is not the same abundance of ideas as in the township, where there is less technology to distract one. Making do with so little made me realise just how much time we waste on time-saving devices, that keep us so preoccupied, limiting our interactions with those around us. Children, too, are everyone's responsibility, so if the little boys play soccer, or the little girls play their popular skipping game, *ugqaphu*, on a busy section of a road, it is any adult's prerogative to instruct them to move somewhere safer.

Which is not to say that my discoveries in this new world were automatic, or easy. On the contrary, I found contact with gardeners and domestic workers particularly difficult at first, thanks to my white upbringing that demanded a list of qualifications and achievements, besides a particular skin colour, before I would consider speaking to someone as an equal. Immensely impressed by the person's grasp on politics and other topics, I would ask his or her profession. I never quite knew why I winced when the answer had something to do with gardening or domestic work, but the more I thought about it the more I became convinced it had something to do with guilt.

Of course, this was not a new experience for me. Most whites in South Africa have had their prejudice shown to them at some point, and I was no different. Some years before I moved to Khayelitsha, I had lived in a commune in Woodstock, Cape Town. The gay coloured man I'd discussed the tenancy with when I'd first visited the house told me that his only other housemate was a lesbian, but he failed to inform me she was black. Not that it would have mattered (so the white liberal in me would have claimed). But of course it always mattered.

Not being much of a morning person, I have always taken some time to wake up properly. This morning – my first in the commune – was no different, and, as I stumbled into the bathroom to take a shower, my characteristic charm and tact were not yet in top gear. Standing at the basin (which was filled with a huge pile of soaking clothes) was a short, muscular black girl with dreadlocks down to her shoulders.

'*Molo* sisi,' I said to her, even in my dazed state feeling some pride at my obvious talent for pronouncing the words.

'*Molo bhuti*,' she'd replied, squeezing the water from a particularly bright pair of lady's pants.

'I'll bring my washing in a minute, sisi,' I told her. 'Do I have to pay privately, or is laundry included in the ...?'

'Go fuck yourself,' snapped the stocky girl, knocking me straight back into the land of the living.

'Oh, I see,' I stuttered, 'so you're our lesb ... er, you're the other housemate.'

But in Khayelitsha I was quickly forgetting my colour. Even shaving in the morning would start with a double-take in the mirror when I saw a pale face staring back at me. I'd study him for a moment, just as the blacks on the train did, with the result that it soon became an image of something from the past, a person I'd left behind. The more at home I began to feel, the more this feeling of having a new identity consumed me.

And as this sense of belonging sank in, so I began to feel safer. At one time, back in my hometown in the Eastern Cape, I would tense up as I walked past a black man. Now I greeted most as individual friends and acquaintances. Countless black people had become friends, adopted family, neighbours and allies in day-to-day life. In fact, I had more black friends now than I'd ever had white friends. And for their part, they regarded that friendship as sacred: it meant we could give each other money or food whenever required, and visit whenever we felt the urge. I was beginning to trust black people at least as much as I had white people before them, individual by individual.

'The day will come when *they* will turn on you,' Mary had said. Even now, when I walked past her desk in the office, she would turn a cynical eye on me and snort, 'So, still alive, are you?' I began to pray that I wouldn't die some accidental death that would prove Mary's prejudices correct.

But a small part of me still remembered that there had been those gunshots on the first night. The townships were and still are ravaged by crime. Was I romanticising a dangerous place, and blinding myself to potentially lethal possibilities? Mary's version certainly wasn't anywhere near the truth, I told myself, but wasn't South Africa the murder capital of the world?

It was Nonceba, my recently divorced neighbour, who opened my eyes one day. Our friendship had begun over the vibrocrete wall between our respective houses, and I liked her feisty attitude. She had taken the government's liberal gender policies to heart, she said, and had lasted only a couple of weeks of cooking and sweeping as a good wife before she'd packed her bags and left her husband in his doorway. One afternoon, I mentioned the gunshots to her.

'Those weren't gunshots,' she said firmly.

'But seriously, on my first night here I clearly heard three gunshots.'

'Steve,' she said, with strained patience, 'what you heard was the popping of a car's ... *eish*, what do you call that thing at the back?'

'Exhaust?'

'That's him,' she cried. 'That's why you heard an engine at the same time. It was just an old car struggling to drive!'

Shame

One of my earliest memories of a black person is of an old Xhosa man who knocked on the door of our family home in Uitenhage one day. We did not have a fence then: it was only later that we began to wall ourselves in.

I opened the door and stared up at that wrinkled, ancient face and those watery eyes and wondered if the old *madala* was a hundred yet. His clothes were ragged and filthy, an effect only heightened by his withered frame.

'*Kleinbaas*,' he'd called me. 'Can *kleinbaas* call the Madam, please?'

I knew instantly how to act, because I was a white child in Uitenhage and had learned well from my fellow whites. I knew that understanding blacks was very simple, because blacks fell into four categories: the troublemakers; those who caused one to say 'shame'; good blacks; and clever blacks.

The 'troublemakers', usually males anywhere between the ages of twelve and thirty-five, the vanguard of *'die swart gevaar'*, were mostly brought to us through radio and television to keep us voting for the National Party. They were regarded as highly dangerous communists who were entirely unpredictable. Winnie Mandela was perhaps the one exception to this all-male club.

My only experience of the 'troublemakers' was during the days on either side of the Langa Massacre, on 21 March 1985. Although I am now able to reason that the actions of the police and soldiers on that day were nothing short of criminal, for many years I did not even know what had happened, remembering the period excitedly only in relation to a massive military helicopter. I would have been eleven years old at the time, in the 'I-want-to-be-a-pilot' stage of development, so the sight of such an imposing aircraft was a real treat. Actually there were two flying over our garden at an extraordinarily low altitude in the early evening in the direction of Langa; my heart absolutely leaped with delight. Thinking back, the two monstrosities must have produced a rather different reaction in the hearts of the black children, many of them my age, caught up in the struggle for freedom on that same dark night.

The blacks who fell into the 'shame' category were mostly those one met on a daily basis. They were generally dressed in rags and, despite their pathetic physical appearance, were usually docile and highly respectful. For anyone who actually thought about this for a second, trying to figure out whose 'shame' we were speaking of would have presented quite a dilemma. 'Shame', or 'Ag shame', could be dished out to describe almost any meeting with one of the 'poor blacks', whether made in reference to their impoverished appearance, or as a closing statement in a conversation we never had a clue how to continue, even if we wanted to.

'Good blacks' usually came singly, possibly because the 'troublemakers' functioned in gangs or groups that were associated with senseless violence, usually seen as a product of their 'group mentality'. An example of a 'good black' would have been one who did his work and said, 'Ja baas', with a suitably respectful smile on his slightly lowered face and downcast eyes. Also known as the 'honest black', the 'good black' had the ability to provide good company and work for the white person without ever crossing the line into insolence, or 'acting white'. The white person who had come into contact with him would often express a high level of surprise at his very existence, because he had somehow managed to break the rule that all blacks were troublemakers or stupid, or both.

The 'clever black' suffered the same risk of entering a catch-22 situation as the 'good black'. He was respected for knowing a lot, but hated just as quickly if that knowledge represented any kind of threat to the white person he was speaking to. He would be witty and have the ability to laugh at himself, all the while treading a tightrope between intelligence and impertinence.

The existence of these categories in those years could be proved by the general response of blacks to whites. Most blacks I came across as a child agreed with everything I said, or, if pushed to issue a reply, said whatever they thought I wanted to hear. This, in turn, backed up the perception among many white people that blacks were liars, or too stupid to think for themselves.

The old man in front of me asking for my mother could be effortlessly filed into the 'shame' category, although in my thinking he was also a 'good black' because of his traditional understanding of respect for the white boy.

A year or so later a black man selling potatoes rang the doorbell. This was during our dog Rosy's time. She was a mixed breed with the attitude and strength of a dog that is convinced it's a lion. Hearing the bell, she'd sneakily followed my mother through the house, territory she wasn't normally allowed to venture into. Because the dog was in the habit of doing this, my mother opened the door just wide enough to tell the salesman she did not want potatoes. But Rosy managed to squeeze through and chased the young man who, in his haste, left his wares behind and had hopped over the balcony and into the rose bushes, tearing up the road at lightning speed. In her rush to close the door, my mother unwittingly slammed it closed on Rosy's tail, a large piece of which lay, still wagging with the memory of aggression, on the lounge carpet. We'd packed the discarded sack of potatoes into our old Peugeot and searched the streets for its owner, but to no avail.

'Shame,' I had thought, as I sat on the back seat of my father's car.

My two brothers and I would sometimes pelt the 'garden boy' from next door, Jeffrey's Bay, with stones and mud balls. Named after a world famous surfing town nearby, Jeffrey's Bay had the presence of mind to approach my mother about our behaviour. We were ordered to stop at once, as some in Uitenhage say, 'throwing Jeffrey's Bay with stones'. I thought Jeffrey's Bay a rather 'clever black' for having had the courage to approach one of my parents in the first place.

Although the use of the word *kaffir* was forbidden in our home, in private my two older brothers and I would sometimes use it to describe each other, or someone else's behaviour. When someone lost his or her temper, 'he went *kaffir*'. Similarly, a white person who was over friendly towards blacks was disdainfully termed a *kaffir boetie*. Missing a bath one evening would result in my being told by one of my brothers the next day that I smelt 'like a *kaffir*'.

In my earliest years, when the 'trouble' was a concept too far away for me to fathom, venturing away from our home represented an exciting journey into the white world outside, a world that unfolded on pristine beaches and at timeless braaivleis stands, its white citizens never turning from the lamb chop or the boerewors roll to look beyond where they were congregated. The mere willingness to do so, no matter how short-lived, would have flown in the face of what most of us, deep down, were certain of; that our kind had not only made the land in which we had settled a better place for all, but was responsible for introducing a touch of civilisation and development to the lives of the savages around us. Not only had we discovered South Africa, but we had also civilised the *kaffirs* that roamed it in so disorderly a fashion. This mindset was backed up in our history books, where the Zulu King Shaka was the only black man treated with some degree of reverence, brilliant as he was at introducing discipline and order to the ranks of his tens of thousands of previously disorganised warriors.

Perfectly suited to the master and servant relationship between us and the blacks was the rudimentary Xhosa I learned at the junior English white boys' school I attended. I have never forgotten the phrases, like '*Ndifuna ipetroli,*' or 'I want petrol', that our white Xhosa teacher got us to learn in an effort to make us efficient masters in the South Africa of the time.

Other interactions between the different races during my

childhood occurred at church. Like most other denominations, the Baptist Church we attended was strictly segregated. Our all-white church was on rare occasions visited by small groups of singers from our sister black and coloured churches (when we invited them, of course). The black Baptist Church, however, was regarded with a great deal of suspicion, since much of the congregation still combined ancestral worship with the religion we had brought them. I remember one Sunday – I couldn't have been much older than ten – when a troupe of coloured men came to sing for us. Despite the guitarist's makeshift instrument, on which he had substituted a white shoelace for one of the strings, the performance was one of the most moving I have ever heard. The toothless trio, clothed in their Sunday best, crooned and swayed, their passion something entirely new in my limited experience.

The next Sunday, when the all-white congregation stood up to sing, I couldn't help but wonder which sound God preferred: ours, more like a choir of felines, or the lively song over in Rosedale, where the coloureds humbled themselves before Him as second-class citizens.

Despite all the odds being against me, I somehow liked black people. The ones I met seemed so passive, relaxed and obedient that I naturally felt the urge to help them, easily taking on liberal attitudes because they were a part of my parents' outlook on things. My father once told me that when he arrived in Johannesburg from Austria a white policeman had told him: 'Welcome to South Africa. If you see a *kaffir* walking on the pavement you can just push him off. The pavements are for white people.' My father spoke about the incident as though it didn't make much sense to him. My mother, on the other hand, told me that her father used to invite his black workers from Coca-Cola to his home in Port

Elizabeth for parties. Only years later had she realised why there had always been a police van or two parked across the road through the night.

The fact that at the age of about nine years I befriended a black boy named Shaun helped a great deal. Shaun was the son of one of our domestic workers (referred to in those days as 'girls') named Virginia, who regularly visited our home even after she stopped working for us. She was a charming person, with a warm temperament and motherly nature. I was proud of our friendship with Virginia and Shaun, not least because they drank out of our own teacups, instead of those usually reserved for the 'girl'. And they actually sat on the couch.

Although Shaun's English was rudimentary at best and we therefore struggled to communicate, we had a great deal of fun outside in the garden. We made mud balls and played hide and seek, things I also did with my white friends, but if we'd come up with the idea of going to the beach, that would have been problematic.

I always sensed that life for Shaun was very different from my life; I was always the one who came out with the toys. Shaun, unable at that age to hide his admiration for one more privileged than he, spent much of each visit looking from me to my possessions with wide, envious eyes. I was a kind-natured child, so I gained much enjoyment from teaching Shaun to ride a bicycle. Of course, in the national spirit of things, the bicycle was mine. In fact, when my neighbourhood friends and I saw a black person riding a bicycle, one of us would inevitably quip, 'I wonder where he stole it', to howls of laughter from the rest of us.

Shaun's reaction to my bicycle was one of absolute delight, which made me pity him immensely. So, when BMXes came in and I received one, I gave the old bike to him.

Although I still believe our friendship changed my perceptions of black people at least to some extent, our relationship was a replica of the national bond between white and black, as it always involved me as the one who had, and Shaun as the one who didn't.

Racism did not only reveal itself in all forms of human contact and interaction; even the dogs were guilty of it. White people walking down the road outside our home were greeted with a bored look by our dogs, while the arrival of a black beggar saw them, fangs bared and mouths frothing, barking madly from behind the gate.

To be sure, as the eighties arrived and sanctions kicked in, even in Uitenhage the lamb chops became fewer and the beer flowed a little more slowly, with the result that white people were forced to move away from free hospitality to the concept of the 'bring and braai'.

Things continued for me in this way up until the age of eighteen, when the first ten or so black children were graciously allowed into my school. However, I soon realised that mixing with black students would be harder than I'd thought. A black boy who'd gone to the bush to be cir- cumcised and arrived back at school with a shaven head was soon called Kojak, after the bald New York policeman from the series of the same name, something to which he took offence. It quickly became a racial issue, even though if he had been white he still would have been the target of jokes. Meanwhile, a squash game with a black friend saw him accusing me of cheating, a situation that rapidly took on a racial edge.

Indeed, in the twenty-first century, much has changed, with a slowly growing number of black people living in the suburbs, driving smart cars, as individualistic and fearful for their safety as the next man.

For each individual, the 'New South Africa' is defined quite differently. Visiting Uitenhage, the place where I'd grown up, I pondered what it meant to me and how my search for it had led me to Khayelitsha. I moved to Khaya determined to face my prejudices, the product of an ingrained racism, due mostly to the unnatural relations between people of different races during my youth. In effect, it was this abnormal development that brought me to a stage where I knew I had some kind of illness. Besides the typically South African generalisations I made about specific race groups over the years, I also had very mixed feelings towards freedom when it finally came. On the one hand, I had felt extremely emotional at the time of Nelson Mandela's release from prison, while on the other, I had an immense fear that the black hordes would rise up and kill us, not only because of our terrible treatment of them, but also as a confirmation of our theory that they were savages. In short, I never quite knew whether the racist or the non-racist within me was right.

By moving to Khayelitsha, I embarked on a search for the truth of the matter. I knew deep down that racism didn't make any kind of logical sense, but I very often thought racist things. What unfolded in Khayelitsha, therefore, was a journey to the heart of my racism, the only journey powerful enough to drown out the racist voices of the majority within the white society of my youth.

In Khayelitsha, the new South Africa did not bring about much change for hundreds of thousands of people. I moved into a community where many of the tribal customs remained intact, sharing and poverty lived side by side, and friendship and brotherhood were sacred. And I found that there was one thought that was foremost in my mind as I gazed out at Uitenhage: I was looking forward to going home to Khayelitsha.

Nightmare on Foamy Street

With its heavy winter rainfall and vicious winds, Cape Town stands out among South African cities as an exception to the rule of pleasant weather for much of the year. In winter icy gales batter the city from all directions, while rain cuts down from the sides, making escape from the wet an all but futile exercise. But there is perhaps no corner of the Mother City that is as exposed to the elements as Khayelitsha. The narrow lanes between the tiny houses and hotchpotch shacks may be faithful to the general evenness of the ground, but they serve as lethal channels for the gusts of wind which dump busloads of water on the long-suffering residents.

Scuttling here and there in their polished shoes, residents try unsuccessfully to sidestep the muddy pools that have made minefields of the streets and sidewalks, wearing makeshift raincoats – for the most part black or grey rubbish bags hastily modified to create slits for heads and arms. Umbrellas are often rendered useless as their owners venture out into the streets, battered by rain-laden gales with the velocity of a stream of rubber bullets.

My lesson in integration was beginning to make a tough local of me as I vainly attempted to keep the elements from fighting their way through the roof and under the door of my tiny room. Three months before I hadn't noticed the inch of space under the door, or the minute holes in the roof – there had been no reason to – but now they conspired against me on two fronts, creating the deadly combination of constantly dripping water and an ice-cube cold draught. The newspaper office became a warm, dry sanctuary for me, although it wasn't long before I was assigned to cover the floods.

A trip into Site C with a Salvation Army disaster relief team one rainy evening saw me feeling more involved than I'd ever been before. I wasn't exactly living in a shack, but at least I knew what it was like to sleep on a damp bed with the sound of dripping water driving you mad.

During a pause in the rain I informed my landlord, Molefe – who I couldn't help but notice looked particularly warm and dry in the more sturdily built main house – of the problem. His solution was to dispatch Foamy and me to the Shoprite in the Site B shopping centre to purchase a variety of buckets for catching the water.

This large shopping centre provides further evidence of the existence of a considerable bundle of township contradictions. Set smack bang in the centre of the thousands of shacks of Site B, it houses a fine selection of clothing shops and takeaway joints. With our purchases of three light pink water catchers and an electric kettle beside us, we'd taken advantage of the break in the rain and sat on the steps out at the front of the shopping centre and watched in wonder as a cash-in-transit security van arrived to stock the local ATM. All around us hundreds of busy shoppers, oblivious to the scene before us, walked this way and that. Once again I noticed that many passers-by wore the kinds of T-shirts, with brand names like Shoprite, Boxer Tobacco and Lion Matches printed on them, that one seldom sees white people wearing in the suburbs.

Out of the van and two escort vehicles stepped a number of giant guards armed with semi-automatic rifles, holstered handguns and bulletproof vests. We hadn't seen any skollies about so we'd joined in the exercise by planning an imaginary hit of our own. The caramel-coated ice creams we were licking away at were the perfect cover, I thought as I watched the security personnel looking nervously this way and that, with their backs against a vehicle or wall. They had good reason to be jumpy; cash heists had been an increasingly high-profile crime in the country for a number of years.

The security van in front of us prompted Foamy to mention Colin Chauke, a former member of Umkhonto weSizwe who'd turned his military talents to committing a crazy cocktail of heists. A daring escape from the Pretoria Central Prison on 5 December 1997 had made the gangster, in his late twenties, a household name. He'd been awaiting trial for his alleged involvement in a multimillion-rand robbery from a cash depot, also in Pretoria, in October of that year.

Although his reputation as the suspected mastermind behind a number of heists – worth in the region of eighty million rand – would never be proved in court, he was eventually sentenced to fifteen years in jail for his role in the Pretoria theft. Only 2.2 million rand of the stolen money was ever recovered, possibly leaving more than ten million rand in his control. Up until his capture on 19 January 1999, the fugitive played a veritable game of cat and mouse with the police. Chauke even sent a Christmas card to the headquarters of the Pretoria police at the end of 1998 in response to their earlier public promise to have him behind bars by then. Sighted at a birthday party for the then ANC Deputy Minister of Environmental Affairs and Tourism, the late Peter 'one settler one bullet' Mokaba, he'd left the premises before the police arrived.

Colin 'Chookie' Chauke eventually died in late 2003 at the Kalafong Hospital in Atteridgeville, north of Pretoria, reportedly handcuffed to his bed. The gangster's funeral was attended by some three hundred people. Although it was said he'd recently agreed to a battery of medical tests, including one for HIV and Aids, the official cause of death was given as TB (tuberculosis). Chauke, who'd converted to Islam shortly before being convicted, succumbed to the disease on a Friday during the holy month of Ramadan, a sense of timing that Muslim scholars believe automatically earns one a ticket to enter the gates of heaven.

The security guards, who were climbing back into their vehicles, were performing the most dangerous job in South Africa, according to a documentary I'd seen.

Halfway through our hour's walk home it began to rain again, in that soft, soaking way which is also so typical of Cape Town. The wind had died down, though, so the journey wasn't that bad. By the time I was safely home I needed only to take a bath in my egg-shaped plastic tub and change my clothes.

The previous day Tshidi had banned me from the house for not cleaning up after myself in the kitchen, which meant I was relegated to cooking and washing in my cramped room. The accusation had been delivered without any kind of concrete evidence and Foamy had told me on the walk from the shop that Tshidi's anger had more to do with me inviting Molefe out for beers over the weekends than my own sloppiness. His explanation of her behaviour had not been confined to the definition he'd painted of her as a deranged woman who guarded her husband in a madly jealous manner; he and his family believed she'd bewitched Molefe, turning him into a kind of faithful zombie. And this wasn't the first time she'd done it. Foamy had heard rumours that she owned two other houses in the townships that she'd tricked ex-husbands into handing over during their divorces. He complained that since Molefe had married her, she'd forbidden him to have any contact with his parents.

Although I found it hard to relate to stories of Tshidi and her evil *muti*, I'd heard them before from certain neighbours and patrons at Vovo Cash Store. Foamy and Frederick, the little Burundian refugee who lived in the second room inside, had recounted a variety of creepy yarns to me the previous Sunday. The more I made faces and described their tales as bogus, the more tales they spun, as if their sheer quantity would convince me into recognition of the dark spirit world they appeared to believe in.

In a mix of a scene from Aladdin and Frederick's unique belief system, one such tale involved a gentleman he had seen jetting over the hills of Burundi on a carpet. The high flyer was not necessarily on an evil mission into a neighbouring province or state, Frederick told me soberly, but could even have been heading for Europe to wrap up a business deal, for instance.

'Do you think people like that need to take aeroplanes? Or go in submarines? There are witches who have meetings under the sea,' he declared solemnly.

Not to be outdone, Foamy followed up with a gory tale of his own, from his hometown in the Free State. 'Nightmare on Foamy Street', as I soon called it, involved a village family who had lost a loved one. The girl, murdered by a relation who had not been identified as the killer, had returned from the dead on numerous occasions to haunt the family with the truth. With blood oozing from her chest where the knife had been pegged days before, she would wave her arms frantically in the air, screaming and shouting at the culprit in order to reveal the truth.

Having never been one for Freddy Kruger movies, I'd tried to change the subject by inviting them to join me on a trip to Harare, home of the shebeen with the cheapest *umqomboti* for miles around. Two litres of the creamy traditional Xhosa beer, drunk out of a large tin can, cost just two rand.

The invitation was a terrible mistake.

'Do you know why I didn't drink any of that beer the last time we went there?' Foamy asked me.

'Why?'

'Have you never wondered why that beer is so cheap?'

I hadn't. 'Something to do with attracting customers?'

'Exactly,' he said, with an unusually sombre expression.

'First they attract customers by making the beer cheap. The thing is' – he leaned closer to me, fixing me with piercing eyes, just slits – 'once you've drunk the *iyeza* – the *muti* – in the beer they've got you under their spell and you'll keep going back for more. Then, when they have enough customers to make a fat profit, they'll push the price up a bit and you won't mind, because by then it's too late.'

'What kind of *muti* do you think they put in the beer?' I asked, thinking that because it had made me feel happily mellow it must have been a healthy additive.

'I don't know,' said Foamy. 'Only *they* know what they put in the beer.'

'Okay, but give me an example,' I persisted.

'Maybe when they make it in the big container they stir the ingredients together with an arm,' he said.

'What's wrong with that?' I laughed. 'Even if the guy doesn't wash, the dirt from an arm won't make you sick.'

'I don't mean a live arm,' Foamy whispered hoarsely across to me. 'I mean an arm stolen from a morgue.'

The expression on my face was enough to keep Frederick and Foamy in stitches for some time, making me wonder if they'd been serious. But I had the feeling they *did* believe it, because I'd heard a similar story at work. One of the black reporters had had a tip-off that nursing staff at a particular city clinic were suspicious of one of their colleagues, who apparently often disappeared from her duties for extended periods of time. Witchcraft was suspected. Most of the journalists present that day had mocked the reporter, with more than one hinting that the nurse's motive probably had more to do with laziness than magic. When the news editor told the black reporter to investigate the story, he refused on the grounds that even he was fearful of uncovering her intentions.

Whether Foamy and Frederick believed the stories or not, I never went to that shebeen in Harare again, even if it was only – as I told myself – to prove the *muti* ineffective.

'We don't believe in magic,' I had murmured to them, as the laughter died away.

'Who is "we"?' asked Frederick.

'White people.'

'When white people came to Africa they had very powerful magic,' he said. 'Many of them still believe in it today. Just think of the Bible story of Jesus walking on water. And later he floated up to heaven on a cloud!'

The kettle heating water for my bath boiled for a second time, and I was brought back to the task at hand. Foamy, who was experienced in these things, had advised me in great detail on how to bath in a bucket, an explanation that had seemed simple enough. After pouring the contents of the kettle of steaming water into the tub, I used one of the buckets I'd just purchased to fetch cold water from the outside tap. The liquid in the bucket then the right temperature, I stood with both feet in it, taking the facecloth from the table. Dipping it in the water, I held it over my right shoulder, squeezing it with my left hand in order to allow the water to run down my back and legs. Foamy had proudly explained that, after many years of practice, he could wash every part of his body without spilling a single drop of water on the floor. My unpractised hands, however, had already dribbled a thin vein of water that crept slowly towards my bed, a king-size mattress on the floor, already damp in places from the leaky roof.

After I'd wet myself on the front and back, from my neck down to my legs, the cold air gushing under the door hit me, resulting in a highly sensitive arrangement of goosebumps all over my upper arms and legs. My teeth chattering in time to the convulsions of shivering that shook my whole body, I quickly smeared myself in Sunlight, arguably the most popular township soap.

I'd never noticed the warming effects of soapsuds before, but as I spread the lather I was given respite from the icy draught. I checked the paper covering I'd bought the soap in, but it said nothing about adding insulation from township elements. Subconsciously I delayed the next step – rinsing the suds away – by entering that world visited by most people in the shower or bath, where time loses its hold on us and one minute feels like twenty and the other way round. Coming out the other side I grudgingly washed the soap off by repeating step one. The process of using my freezing hands to squeeze sufficient water to rinse the foam from my limbs seemed to take for ever, so that by the time I was finished, the cosy warmth provided by my huge beach towel was nothing short of bliss.

I got dressed and switched on the frying pan. The chicken pieces, which had been Foamy's idea of a quick meal, were almost completely defrosted, so I walked to the main house to call him. Back in my room, working nimbly with his fingers, he showed me how to rub the chicken skin from the birds' feet.

'They will be too tough if you don't remove this rough skin,' he said of the well-defined chicken feet, as he lifted them up to my face so I could see them a little more clearly than I'd wanted to.

I'd already counted them, soon confirming that for every two chicken feet there was a head and a heart, which in my mind increased the chances that the organs and limbs came from the same bird.

With a pot of steaming rice now standing to one side, Foamy rinsed the electric frying pan out and sprinkled sunflower oil over its bottom. Salt, pepper and Aromat spice followed, with my suggestion of a sprinkling of herbs being greeted with a perfunctory, 'The herbs that the chicken ate are still in the meat, Steve.'

Although I would never turn away food of any sort, the assorted pieces produced a little prickle of foreboding as Foamy bundled them into the pan. The fact that the feet sported rather long, dirty toenails, that the heads still had their eyes and beaks, and that the aortas dangling from the hearts displayed an impressive level of elasticity as they hopped into the pan, didn't help.

'*Eish*,' Foamy sighed, with the eye of the hunter fixed on the pan. 'This is going to be good. Do you mind if I have some too?'

'You can have as many as you want,' I said, a little too eagerly.

Probably the simplest meal I've eaten, the body parts were nothing less than scrumptious, with the hearts and heads best of all. The feet mainly consisted of gristle, bones and fat, a little too fatty to be classified as tasty. Once cooked, the hearts were a dark purplish-brown, an off-putting sight only until the organ was in the mouth, where it taunted the taste buds delightfully. Eating the heads was a little more complicated, but Foamy showed me how the beak served as a utensil for placing the cranium and its filling into the mouth.

These more obscure parts of the chicken, which I had never thought of eating before, marked my introduction into an eating culture that does not waste what can be consumed. Meat is a sign of status in the Xhosa culture, which means the more affordable forms of it, like the intestines and stomach, are often considered better than no flesh at all.

Later that night I prepared myself for bed. The raucous hammering of the rain on the corrugated iron roof above me was not just a pleasurable sound to fall asleep to, but called for a careful repositioning of the buckets I'd bought earlier that day. Once they were satisfactorily in place there wasn't much space for my body on the mattress, but this no longer seemed such a terrible thing to me as I lay there with a satisfied belly and heavy eyes.

Tsotsi

The faces looking up at me, as I stood sweating just inside the doorway of the house I'd fled into, appeared as surprised to see me as I was to see them. But while their expressions quickly became sullen, mine remained stunned. It wasn't just the Mandrax pipes strewn about on the floor around them, or the burn marks on the carpet. There was a lot more involved here than just the slight whiff of 'buttons' in the air, mixed with the thickly sweet stench of marijuana: it was the faces themselves. For starters, all of them were scarred. At a quick count I guessed there were seven or eight, and there was no doubt in my mind that they were hardened gangsters. They all had that sluggish expression typical of Mandrax smokers after a series of hits, but it was the one in the wheelchair who held my attention the longest. With a filled, unlit pipe in his hand, he said something in slow, monotonous tsotsitaal, while his neighbour, sitting on the floor like everyone else, lowered a handful of matches. I heard almost no words, but the match-carrier translated.

'Close the door behind you,' he said. I obeyed nervously.

Then the man in the wheelchair spoke again.

'Wat is hier aan die gang, my bra?'

This time I understood. It seemed strange that I should have to explain my behaviour to people like this, but my options were limited.

'I've just been chased from across the railway tracks,' I wheezed, short of breath both from having run some distance and from fear. 'Three tsotsis followed me from Siphokazi's Tavern.'

Immediately the man with the pipe, who was obviously paralysed from the waist down, shouted something in the direction of the kitchen. An agile-looking chap about my age came around the corner, edged me to one side, opened the door and went out into the night. Suddenly very sober, I took another good look at the room and its occupants, most of whom appeared to have forgotten my presence and had resumed their conversation in deep, low tones.

In Khayelitsha, as with most underground cultures, there are two types of tsotsi: the small-timers and the real gangsters. The men in this room belonged to the latter group. There were no yellow overalls with prison numbers scrawled on their front and 'Not Guilty' on the back, not too many earrings, and most of the heads were without the characteristic woollen hats. They were dressed, I realised, inconspicuously.

'Hlalaphantsi,' said the only man who had addressed me up until now, but I struggled to see where he wanted me to sit. Except for his wheelchair there was no furniture in the room, so I squatted down in an empty space by the door.

I'd come from Siphokazi's Tavern, a second-choice local. It was less than a kilometre from my home, and with a younger crowd and a jukebox it was quite a different scene to Vovo Cash Store. While the jukebox had my two favourite Mapaputsi songs 'Life' and 'My Love', the standard of pool was the best I'd come into contact with in the area so far. The only thing that spooked me about going there on my own was the trail over the railway tracks, where not even the tall lamp posts of the township cast any light.

The three skollies were following me long before I'd reached the tracks – they made no attempt to remain unseen. The faster I'd walked, the faster they'd followed, until finally all of us had broken into a sprint. There had only been one house in the street with lights on, and I had burst straight in. Now I was regretting it.

The younger man who'd hurried outside returned. 'They are gone,' he said. '*Hoe oud was hulle?*'

I told him they'd seemed about seventeen or eighteen.

'Those are not tsotsis,' he snorted scornfully. I nodded eagerly.

I don't remember much about that confused, frightening night, but I remember a moment of clarity as my new protectors handed me the pipe. I had never done it before but that night I smoked buttons. For most, Mandrax is a one-way street. For me, that night, it was my ticket to freedom.

Although crime is often a point of discussion in Khayelitsha, it is certainly not the obsession it is for many in the suburbs. One also gets the sense that the scale between the good

An iLitha Park house with a satellite dish, with Endlovini shacks in the background.

Crossing the train tracks in TR Informal Settlement.

A typical view of Site C streets.

Ta-fumsa chats to Mama Mbeti at her meat stand in Site C.

The sedate Ngqangqolo Street – my second home in iLitha Park.

Chatting to Ta-fumsa on a quiet afternoon at Hlehle's Cool Spot.
(Photograph: Denzil Maregele)

Repositioning a smiley to burn off its wool (above). The dish is named for its characteristic grin (left).

A vegetable store in iLitha Park, alongside Khayelitsha station.

citizens and the criminals is tipped firmly on the side of the good. I'd just covered a series of cases of vigilantism in the area for the newspaper where I worked. According to a Xhosa-speaking expert from the University of Cape Town, they had their roots in general disgruntlement with the police and the courts, which often released suspects on bail, or dropped charges because of a lack of evidence, creating sufficient anger to trigger the attacks. This take on events seemed to be confirmed by a story told to me by an iLitha Park friend of mine.

The saga had begun after her mentally ill cousin Oscar, who regularly suffered verbal and physical abuse at the hands of his stepfather, had disappeared one night. Wanting to find him as quickly as possible, the boy's mother had phoned my friend to ask her to go to the police to report him missing. Her arrival at the police station, she said, had been met with apathy so total that it bordered on scorn. One of the officers had laughed at her after she'd told them her story, and none of them had seemed interested in explaining to her the processes she needed to go through to declare her cousin a missing person. My friend had been deeply disillusioned by the experience, and the next day she had come to my room in Ntlakohlaza Street to ask me for help, hoping that my status as a journalist and a white man might encourage the police to do more.

But my intervention wasn't needed: she soon received a phone call from Oscar's mother reporting that the boy had been brought home by a stranger who had managed to convince Oscar to overcome his terror of his stepfather and to give the good Samaritan his mother's address. When he got home, they saw that his feet were bloodied and raw: he had walked up and over Sir Lowry's Pass in a desperate attempt to get as far away from his stepfather as possible.

At the scene of each vigilante attack I'd covered in Khayelitsha I'd found every resident tight-lipped about the incident; and while they had had much to say about the inefficiency of the police and the courts, no one had admitted to noticing a thing on the day the suspected tsotsi had been stoned, beaten or burnt. A friend of mine, Chris, claimed that the attacks had been carried out at the behest of one of the local kangaroo courts and I listened to his tale, as he was something of an expert, having once been brought before such a court by his girlfriend. Although he never told me the precise reason why Ziyanda had done this, I suspected that it had something to do with his failure to pay damages to her parents for making her pregnant, a custom in the Xhosa culture. A Xhosa man who impregnates an unmarried woman (as long as it is her first pregnancy) is expected to pay damages in the region of five cows. Or, if he doesn't have cows, the equivalent in cash.

I had never been able to track down any of the kangaroo court judges or other officers of the courts. Only once, when Chris and I were sitting on the train to town together, had I seen a judge. Chris had pointed out a well-dressed man, who looked to be in his fifties.

'His name is Peter,' he'd whispered to me, but no further introductions were possible. Chris, whose fear of the man was intense, would have none of it.

On the other side of the law, the tsotsis in Khayelitsha are not nearly as well organised as the gangs in the traditional coloured areas, where ranks are given to members of the different organisations that fight for drug territory. In Khaya, small groups of tsotsis, made up of two or three friends, usually head for the suburbs or rob locals late at night. They know very well that doing the same by day would attract the violent outrage of law-abiding citizens in the area, a backlash which has on more than one occasion resulted in the loss of life or limb. By following a fairly simple set of precautions, like not talking openly on one's cellphone too far away from home, many residents manage to prevent being the easy target of theft.

Another thing I'd learned from my friends was that one should not 'keep all one's eggs in one basket', meaning a few notes of the smallest denominations should be spread throughout one's pockets. Since muggings are usually carried out in a hurry, it would be unlikely that the perpetrators would manage to find every note, leaving at least sufficient cash for the victim to go home by taxi or train.

In Khaya everyone had a story about crime, and one that I was told struck me as a perfect example of the sort of dark humour – often touchingly true to life – that everyone around me displayed.

An elderly gent (the story went) was walking to the iLitha Park station one morning when he was confronted by three tsotsis. The thugs, who were armed with knives, helped themselves to the old man's wallet, his monthly train ticket, and the leftovers that his wife had carefully packed for his lunch. Penniless and humiliated, the old man stood in the drizzle as his assailants turned and began to hurry away; but no sooner had he started walking off than one of the tsotsis hurried back, and once again lifted his knife.

'What are you doing, old man?' he asked.

'I am going home,' the man replied.

'And why are you going home?'

'Because I do not have a train ticket,' the man mumbled miserably.

The tsotsi looked shocked. 'And how much is a ticket?' he asked.

The man told him, and the tsotsi immediately opened up the stolen wallet, took out the amount needed and handed it to the old man. Then he pointed to the station.

'Go to work,' he said. 'You must go to work. Not just for you and your family, but also for us!'

Harare

The morning after the Mandrax incident I tried to recall Vuyo's directions to her home in Harare: 'Cross the road to the right of the clinic and follow the path through the field,' she had explained.

It was more easily said than done, especially after my nauseating evening smoking buttons with the tsotsis. I was waiting for a small group of women to approach the gap in the wall surrounding the iLitha Park side of Harare. I always felt safest with the mamas, as I called them; a section of the population that I'd noticed combined a protective motherly nature with a no-nonsense approach to young troublemakers.

A few weeks before I had worked late and had been forced to take the last train to Khayelitsha. The time on my cellphone told me that I had ten minutes before the train left and I had jogged down St George's Mall at a pace that soon developed into a sprint. This was in reaction to a particularly nasty group of street children who, armed with fish knives, had chased me all the way to the station entrance. I might have been out of breath as I jumped on to the first coach, but if hadn't been for those kids, I realised as I stood doubled over and panting for breath, I probably wouldn't have made the train.

There were around ten commuters in my carriage, three of whom, sitting directly opposite me, began rudely to interrogate me. Their earrings and woollen hats made me think that they were small-time criminals, but I was frightened nonetheless because their conversation was liberally laced with the word *umlungu*. Just as we were approaching the Site C station, one of the two mamas sitting next to me leaned forward and said a few angry words to them in Xhosa. They got off at the next station and went on their way.

Although I had the feeling I was giving in to paranoia by following this group of women into Harare, there was certainly no reason to take any chances. There were plenty of people around on a Saturday afternoon, but with payday for most having taken place recently, there were sure to be some skollies about.

Still, conscious of the 'eggs in one basket' rule, I had ten rand in my back right pants pocket, ten rand in my front left, and various coins in a number of compartments in my jacket. It was unlikely, I thought as I entered through the gap in the wall, that a quick hand brushing over a pocket would pick up the presence of a single note. The most noticeable thing that I carried on my person was Vuyo's chocolate, a small Cadbury Top Deck, milk chocolate on the bottom and white on top, the symbolism of which had caused Zane and me much mirth. If that was taken from me at knife or gunpoint, he said, the story alone would ensure that Vuyo would hold me in the highest esteem.

'If you live through it, my friend, then she is yours for sure,' he'd chuckled.

Zane's laughter was not unusual. It is not uncommon for Khayelitshans, and even South Africans more generally, to try to cope with crime by joking about it. And although Zane himself claimed to have changed his ways, he still now and then committed petty theft. Most recently he had stolen from one of his girlfriends, a particularly fat woman who lived on the other side of the railway line. The first and last time I had met her had been a few Saturdays before, when we'd arrived at her house uninvited. The woman – whose body mass was probably not much less than a Cuban cow – had that special kind of Xhosa face that exudes a beautiful mixture of confidence and strength. From the steady stream of neighbours who arrived with cash and left with beers I could tell that once again Zane had chosen a girl based on her ability to provide him with freebies.

When Zane introduced us, his new lady filling a two-seater couch with her gigantic form, I found myself unwillingly trying to picture the physical hurdles Zane would be confronted with in trying to have sex with her, given that she was almost as tall lying on her side as standing up.

The day had progressed into an orgy of drunkenness, with the big lady inviting two of her middle-aged friends around so that I would at least be able to choose between the two of them for my bed that night. Once it became clear that my plans for the evening did not involve undressing either of them, one of them left in disgust. However, a few minutes later she returned with her youngest daughter in tow. While the four of us sat awkwardly in the lounge, Zane and his lady left for her room, which adjoined the lounge where we were sitting. A moment later she reappeared and waddled to the toilet. Two or three minutes passed before she returned, waddled back to the bedroom, and shut the door.

And that's when all hell broke loose.

I had never seen Zane naked before, and hadn't ever wanted to see him naked, but whether I wanted to or not, there he was, naked as the day he was born, flying backwards through the lounge, with his gargantuan lover holding him by the throat, her tiny night-slip straining at the seams as she screamed at him.

'You thief! You *thief*!' she shrieked, in a voice resonating from somewhere deep in her cavernous belly. 'Voetsak! Voetsak!'

A moment later Zane wriggled free of her vice-like grip, and as he and I fled through the garden, his lover hurling his clothes after us, I couldn't help but notice the pile of Castle quarts lying on the dusty soil outside his (now ex) girlfriend's window. My friend, it seemed, had seen her visit to the toilet as an opportunity to drop out of the window a few of the many quarts she kept in a fridge in her room.

My intentions, when it came to Vuyo, were much more honourable. Once through the gap in the wall, I turned right on to a sandy road. The houses on both sides of the street were small, but as neat and freshly painted as those of iLitha Park. From behind me I could hear kwaito music and, looking over my shoulder, I saw a shebeen on the corner, outside which a few men were sitting on beer crates.

'*Molo mlungu*,' a few of them said.

'*Molweni*,' I replied, waving at them.

'*Uyaphi?*' one of them asked.

'I'm going to my ...' I proudly touched each side of my chest with my right hand.

'*Oriiight*,' he said, to much laughter.

Turning, I noticed a lone bakkie standing outside the first house on my right. It wasn't so much the pig that was lying on the back of it, as the way in which the animal was tied down, that attracted my interest.

Not wanting to draw too much attention to myself, I slowed just enough to notice that the creature had been tied down with a long rope that was connected to a series of metal loops on the open back of the vehicle. It was an enormous animal, taking up well over half of the space in the back of the bakkie.

I made my way along the road which curved to the left, taking the first turn in the same direction. Three youngsters standing at the corner looked at me inquisitively.

'*Ndifuna icuba?*' one of them asked.

'You are too young to smoke,' I retorted.

Vuyo's directions were good. As the road curved to the right I turned left into a narrow thoroughfare between two shacks, after which her home was in sight. I crossed a small field and a road and found myself at her gate. The trip had been easier and shorter than I'd thought.

Vuyo's mother's shack was of the genre that makes one wonder why anybody would need a house. Superbly built, the shine of the corrugated iron that it was made from suggested it was brand new. It was also large, easily the size of a government house, with trim little windows and a garden fence.

'You made it,' said Vuyo, as she walked to the gate from a

door at the side of the house. 'How are you?'

Noticing a flattering change in Vuyo's hairstyle – from short to longer extensions – I suddenly felt very well. She looked far more beautiful than I'd remembered.

'They took all my money, but I managed to hold on to this,' I joked, handing her the chocolate bar.

We entered the house and moved through a spacious, impeccably tidy kitchen into the lounge.

Obviously the person who'd erected the shack hadn't heard of a spirit level, but I found it fascinating walking downhill towards my seat next to the television; I had the distinct desire to cover the distance again.

Although I might have been too frightened to visit if I had known Vuyo's mother would be there, the conversation got off to a lively start, not least because we all hailed from the Eastern Cape. South Africans have more in common than they think, although minutes later we launched into an animated debate over one of our differences. When Vuyo's sister made tea, her mother expressed shock at my request for only one teaspoon of sugar.

'I really think it is a black thing to use so much sugar,' I said.

'No,' replied Vuyo. 'It is a white thing to take only one spoon.'

Later that afternoon as I waved goodbye to Vuyo standing at the gate, I realised that the visit had been a pleasant break from my usual routine. I had arrived there – as I had in Khayelitsha months before – as a visitor but as it always is with family, I felt instantly at home.

My stomach was growling with hunger, but I noticed that the bakkie was gone. And so was the enormous pig. All that remained of it were heaps of bones in the garden across the street. There was the sound of lively chatter from the house, but a solitary small boy remained outside at the smoky fire. He was chewing on a chunky rib.

'*Ndifuna inyama, nkwenkwe*?' I asked him for meat.

'*Iphelile, bhuti*,' he replied.

Evidently the pig was gone.

Smileys

Being a regular South African, I've always loved meat. But in Khayelitsha, where animal flesh is so strongly interwoven with culture and tradition, I'd developed nothing short of an obsession for it. Every weekend I headed for the meat shacks, to provide my stomach with the greasy lining needed for the beer to come. Although my cholesterol level was on my mind now and then, the delightful taste of township meat pushed these worries away from the moment at hand. In Khayelitsha no part of an animal is wasted. The fact that what is minced into salami and croquettes in the suburbs is eaten here in its original form produced a contradictory response in me. For while the thought, not to mention the sight, of feet, heads and intestines may not be a pleasant one, most of these body parts are considered delicacies by locals. And the deliciousness of their taste soon overrides any notion of queasiness.

Mzondi and I had a tradition, something we both looked forward to. Each payday we gathered a few friends and headed down Ntlazane Road to celebrate with a delicious sheep's head. This was not supermarket meat, neither in price nor taste, but a far superior flesh. The sheep's head, or 'smiley', as it is called in Khayelitsha, cost sixteen rand, and with a loaf of bread and a litre of Coke, the total cost of the meal was about twenty-five rand. The name 'smiley' evidently comes from the expression that is fixed on the sheep's face with the final bleat that comes out of its mouth just as its throat is slit.

Mzondi had sent a young boy down the road to purchase the Coke and bread; his reward was that he could keep the few cents change.

Leaning forward from my low position on the torn antique sofa, I cut through the base of an ear with an ancient steak knife. A few hours before, the ear had been all furry and soft; now it was bare and sinewy. A red-hot iron rod and a bed of steamy coals were responsible for the metamorphosis.

'Steve, that is really your favourite,' said Mzondi, taking the knife from my greasy hand.

He cut into the soft cheek, sprinkling it, as I had done with the ear, with a large pinch of orange-coloured spices from a white dish on the table before us. He then wrapped the flesh in a slice of fresh brown bread and bit into it hungrily.

Today's lunch promised to be even more filling than usual, for there were only three of us – instead of the usual four – seated around the decaying wooden table, where the meat had been placed on a sheet of the *Cape Times*.

Now it was Zane's turn to dig in. Gouging out a white, fatty eye and expertly removing the dark brown lens in its centre, he covered it liberally with flavoursome spice before popping the juicy titbit into his mouth. One wouldn't usually associate a meal of this calibre with the kind of place we were sitting in; the three crumbling couches were standing on uneven, dusty ground in a windowless shack, built haphazardly to contain a business focused on the sale of only one product: the smiley.

There are many people in Khayelitsha who live on the proceeds of a limited selection of goods. While some ride the trains offering commuters single cigarettes from their shirt pockets, there are others who sell cool drinks from buckets filled with melting ice, or a small assortment of chips carried in open cardboard boxes. This informal economy puts food on the table for thousands in the township.

In the case of the smiley, which it is said takes considerable experience to boil to perfection, it seemed only right that this was the sole focus of attention of the little old lady whom we patronised so regularly. She would warm the already cooked smileys by turning them this way and that on the lightly glowing coals. Although the skulls, with their eyes still in, may well be a disturbing sight for those with sensitive stomachs, they would still prefer it to the scene that had greeted us earlier.

Eager to partake of our favourite meal, the three of us had arrived just after eleven in the morning, a few hours too early, as the first batch of the day was usually only ready at 2pm. As we'd walked up to the shack, I'd noticed to my stomach's dismay that a dozen or so smileys were not only packed on a raised wooden table all facing the street, but they still had their wool on. I battled to tear my eyes away from the spectacle, made yet gorier by the veins and blood sticking out and oozing from the sides of the beasts' necks. As the young boy ran off to buy the Coke, bread and beers, we watched the old lady's husband, who was equally tiny and had a grey grandfather's beard, put the heads in the open fire. Most of the wool burnt off, he removed them and singed off the remaining hairs with a red-hot iron rod. Most people have smelt burning human hair, and this was equally overpowering and repulsive. Wherever the red-hot rod was applied, the head turned a chalky black, until not a single piece of white flesh remained.

Once this had been done, the heads were boiled in a massive cast iron pot. The wait was made easier by the beers that we drank, but it was still a lesson in patience, something I'd learned to master over the past few months.

One of the few things that moves quickly in Khaya is a minibus taxi; the rest unfolds at a pace that is unlikely to result in even the slightest stress. Whenever I visited a friend close to a mealtime, there was no question that I would be fed, although it was the *when* that bothered me at first. A young boy would inevitably be sent on a slow walk to a store some distance away, while other delays to the cooking process, like the purchase of electricity units, or conversation with a stream of visitors, were not uncommon. This often saw me caught in a maniacal grip of hunger, sometimes at a point close to hysteria. Besides the benefit of a lesson in patience, there was another, more obvious one. By the time the food, usually accompanied only by a spoon, was handed over in a bowl, my hunger was such that absolutely anything tasted like it had been prepared in heaven.

I never mastered the art of cooking simple township dishes, like chicken, rice and pumpkin, for I never managed to escape the feeling that the person who had given me the recipe had kept one particular spice a secret. And I could never quite decide whether the meals that others had prepared were really tasty, or just seemed that way because they had taken so long to arrive.

Apart from the taxis, there is another thing in the township that moves at a rapid pace. Eating meat at shacks like the one we frequented was a communal process. There were no separate plates for participants in the feeding frenzy, for that was what it was, always completed at great speed. If you didn't chew and swallow quickly you were bound to lose out. Saying things like, 'I want the ear', would be greeted with a blank look from one's companions, because each part of the head belonged to every one of us, and which part one got depended on the dexterity with which one grabbed the communal knife. Besides, with a sheep's head, each part of which is delicious, it is hard to come up with a favourite portion. While the brains are juicy and tender, the gums and cheeks are tougher, but no less tasty.

The only time I had eaten meat more tender was with my friend Tarzan, while on a visit to a tavern near Crossroads, another of Cape Town's black townships. There we had ordered a pig's snout, which arrived cooked to perfection. A friend of Tarzan's had shared the delicacy with us, cutting thin slices from the juicy snout with his pocketknife. Even the tasty chunks of sheep liver that I had eaten on numerous occasions, soaked in fat on the braai grid by a mama a little way down Ntlazane Road, could not compare with the succulence of this meal.

In Xhosa tradition, the sheep's head is usually the preserve of the older men, whose wisdom is said to be enhanced further by its consumption. Today, with one eye gone from the head, courtesy of Zane, I dug my index finger in behind the other, gouging it out and reaching for the spice.

'Hey, Mzondi, did I tell you about the businessman I met

at a press conference at the Mount Nelson Hotel?' I asked, slipping the eye into my mouth.

'Was he white?' Mzondi asked, using both hands to break the jaws of the head apart with a loud cracking sound to reveal more tender white flesh.

'Yes. I was covering a conference,' I repeated, still chewing on the eye.

My two companions nodded their heads to show they were listening. I swiped at a fly that had perched on the tip of my nose.

'He asked me where I lived, so I told him in Khayelitsha.' I reached for the knife. 'Anyway, the first thing he asked was what people in Khayelitsha eat,' I said, cutting into the flesh below the ears.

'Did you tell him we don't eat anything?' joked Zane, whose hands were now shining with grease from his hands-on approach to the meat.

'No. I told him that this Friday I was going to eat a sheep's head,' I said.

'Okay.' Mzondi nodded his head slowly.

'So he said he had eaten sheep's brains at the ... I think he said the Mount Nelson, but it could have been another hotel. Do you know how much he paid for it?'

'A hundred rand,' answered Zane.

'No, it was quite a bit more than that. And you should have seen the envy on his face when I told him we pay sixteen rand for the whole head. You know what he asked me next?'

'No,' said Mzondi, wiping his mouth with the back of one hand.

'He asked me if we get the brains in the deal.'

'*Eish*,' said Zane, between fits of laughter from both of them. 'Maybe next time we should scoop them out and sell them to the hotel!'

Very soon, all that remained of the head were the fleshless jaws and a set of finely sculptured, tiny white bones from the brain area.

I'd never got used to the sight of the yellow teeth and I regularly asked the lady of the shack why she hadn't brushed them.

While Mzondi wrapped the bones in the newspaper over which we had eaten, I headed for two buckets standing on a low table just inside the shack door. After I'd used the mix of warm water and soap in the one to wash most of the fat off my hands, the cold water in the other and the clean cloth concluded the rinsing.

'Tonight we must find you a lady,' said Mzondi, looking at me seriously. 'After a smiley you can go on all night long.'

I'd been told before of the aphrodisiacal effects of a smiley, a belief in Xhosa culture, but I didn't even feel up to leaving my seat, which I'd returned to, let alone having sex. Licking my lips and breathing the lazy sigh so often induced by the consumption of meat, I recalled a trip on a train a few days before, when I'd noticed a small flock of sheep grazing in a little field in iLitha Park. In the past I had always thought of the animals in terms of their cuteness, without consciously thinking of their connection to the neat braai packs at the local supermarket. But a completely different thought had crossed my mind that time on the train. Looking hungrily at a very specific part of a sheep, I'd made a mental note to buy a smiley some time soon.

Kefu's Place

As the end of June arrived and the clouds over the Cape Flats thickened, bringing with them incessant, drenching rain, change of a more personal sort lay in the weeks ahead. My twelve-month stint at the newspaper was drawing to a close, which would herald the start of my final half-year of journalism studies. I also began to find myself drawn away from the local shebeens into other, no less important, aspects of township life. Except for Frederick, the little Burundian who stayed in the main house, and John, my friendly Ghanaian barber, I had not befriended any of the *makwerekwere* who lived in the area. This was to change in the coming weeks. Also, I hadn't made many female friends but this, too, was to become a thing of the past.

Mzondi introduced me to a charming young single mother named Lisa, just the kind of friend I had been yearning for.

Because it is frowned upon for 'decent girls' to frequent taverns in Khayelitsha, I hadn't had much opportunity to come into contact with women, which meant that I was developing a somewhat one-sided view of the culture and society I'd become part of.

A chubby girl with a round, handsome face, backed up by a strong voice and lovely sense of humour, Lisa had asked Mzondi to introduce us after she'd heard stories about me from a number of neighbours and friends. Because iLitha Park is relatively tiny compared to other areas of Khaya, Lisa's home was no more than ten minutes away from my own; a quick walk along Ntlazane Road in the direction away from Harare, before a brief stroll up a side street towards the Lookout Hill. One Saturday evening, after a quick visit to Mzondi's ex-girlfriend and their children, who lived a few houses away from Lisa, we'd gone to visit her. Mzondi and I planned to go to a shebeen called Kefu's Place later that night, so it was a short call. We could hear her booming laughter and lively chatter from outside her front door, which she opened with a flurry of vigour and charm.

'So this is the *umlungu*,' she cried, bubbling over with laughter.

'Can you believe it?' she said to two girlfriends sitting in her lounge. 'There is a white man living among us!'

With her zest for life, incredible confidence and out-spoken nature, I liked her instantly. Lisa was the epitome of independence, a woman with the spirit to go wherever and say whatever she pleased, buzzing around the township in her blue Corolla without a care in the world. The front door opened on to a tiny lounge, with an adjoining kitchen, also small, stocked with a tall fridge and a two-plate electric stove. Further back in the carpeted house were two little bedrooms and a bathroom. Lisa's daughter Sandiswa was the image of her mother, with a friendly, Oprah Winfrey-type face, and an innocent expression that hid a rather naughty nature. Equally plump and healthy looking, the ten-year-old stared at me from the floor, where she sat with a variety of drawings, one thumb in her mouth, the fingers of her other chubby hand gripping a crayon. She must have been responsible for the rainbow smudges on the lounge carpet.

Lisa, I decided as she asked me question after question, had that natural inquisitiveness not uncommon in women and journalists. While I was explaining that I lived across the road from the municipal building, for some reason called 'Stocks 'n Stocks' by the locals, I realised that I had changed significantly since I'd left the suburbs. There, when a black person had asked me where I lived, I'd always been a little suspicious of their motives, inevitably giving a rather vague description of my address. Now, no matter who asked, my explanation was complete to the point of revealing the house number.

I was finding it hard to decide which of Lisa's friends, Sandisiwe or Nosizwe, who were on either side of me on the couch, was the most attractive. While Sandisiwe (also a journalist) had a petite body and sharp facial features set off by lengthy hair extensions, Nosizwe, a student from East London, was a lot taller, with full lips and widely spaced eyes, an exact formula for beauty.

Whenever I met black people from East London, the first thing I noticed was the intense suspicion with which many of them regarded whites, something that stemmed from the fact, they said, that many of the white people who live in that city are racists. Even odder for me, coming from a group – English-speaking white South Africans – who I'd always viewed as largely exempt from blame for apartheid, was that a number of black people told me they preferred Afrikaners to us. They knew where they stood with Afrikaners, because they were often more straightforward about their dislike of blacks. English-speaking whites, on the other hand, concealed their racist sentiments by putting on a show of liberalism, while now and then letting slip a sentence or two that gave away their patronising feelings of superiority.

Lisa was telling me that she worked as a secretary and events organiser for a scientific laboratory when Mzondi rose from where he'd been sitting on the armrest of the couch.

'Why are you leaving so soon?' asked Lisa, springing energetically from her seat.

'We're going to Kefu's Place,' said Mzondi, in Xhosa.

'*Uyasithetha isiXhosa, bhuti*?' Nosizwe asked me if I could speak Xhosa.

'*Kancinci*,' I replied. 'Only a little.'

'If you live here you must learn it,' said Lisa. 'You have no excuse. But I can see that you are drinking too much, which is why you forget. What do you want at Kefu's Place?'

'I like to dance,' I said.

'*Eish*,' sighed Lisa loudly, somehow mixing laughter and speech. 'Does this white man have rhythm?' she looked questioningly at Mzondi.

'He does,' he replied, a little too politely, I thought.

'I don't believe it; that is very unusual for a white,' she boomed.

'If you come with us tonight I'll show you,' I shot back.

'I will never go there,' she replied. 'Tomorrow I am going to church.'

Lisa attended a church in the building next to the local police station, across the road from Kefu's Place.

'Why don't you come with us?' asked Sandisiwe.

The thought crossed my mind that going anywhere with her would be fun.

'Are all the girls as pretty as you?'

'*Eish*, Mzondi, this *umlungu* is a womaniser,' said Lisa. 'You go to church for God, not women,' she chided, releasing a sudden snort of laughter.

'I will be there,' said Sandisiwe, confidence radiating from her face.

'Maybe next week Sunday,' I said, not prepared to commit myself; I hadn't been to church in years.

'Okay, I will pick you up at half past nine,' Lisa boomed, not leaving any opening for dissent.

'All right,' I said, making a mental note to go out before then.

My only experience of Christianity in Khaya so far had been on the trains, where my morning trips to town were regularly punctuated by beautiful singing from fellow commuters. While most taxi drivers played traditional church choir music only on Sundays, the singing in the trains occurred on any day of the week. Usually still in a state of half consciousness from the drinking of the night before, I never failed to marvel at the strength of a conviction that is able to carry such fervour for God. With one banging out a beat on the inside wall of the train, another twenty or more women would sing traditional church choir songs with a passion I'd only ever seen for kwaito music in the shebeens. Sometimes I was so moved by the musical talent of these women that I felt an almost uncontrollable urge to jump up and add a verse of my own, but I considered, probably quite wisely, that my weak voice would only serve to dampen their efforts. By the time I walked into work, I had a big smile on my face and two or three powerful tunes playing in my head.

Then there were the train preachers, most of whom screamed verses and their interpretations of them at the top of their lungs. This drove me up the wall, especially when I was trying to read a book, or catch up on the news. Ironically, I would often find myself deep in prayer, begging our Lord to call the pastor to alight from our carriage at the next stop. But such was their perseverance that they would often carry the service through the full fifty minutes, from one of the Khaya stations right into town. Perhaps it was because they'd done this on so many occasions before, or they'd had the audacity to time the sermon but, whichever it was, without fail they would close in prayer, even asking the newly reborn to come forward to receive a personal blessing, as we rattled slowly into the city.

I preferred it when they spoke Xhosa, because then the words of the message, most of which I could not understand, did not interfere with those of my book. But when it was conveyed in English, I would find myself endlessly rereading the same sentence of my book.

These preachers were not always left to deliver their sermons in peace. An irritated commuter sometimes had the courage to complain loudly to his fellows about the racket. Once, when my cellphone rang, I asked the preacher if he could keep his voice down before I answered it.

'This is an important call from Nelson Mandela,' I'd said, to hearty laughter from most of the other passengers.

I'd regretted the comment instantly though, because the man actually waited for me to finish the call, after he'd blushed a particularly bright shade of red. After I hung up, his voice was softer and his tone had lost some of its previous vigour, making me sorry that I had hurt his feelings. During the last ten minutes of the journey, he urged us to put our lives in God's hands by coming 'to the front'. I seriously considered heeding his call.

Looking across at the church from outside the strong security gate of Kefu's Place, I decided that I would go with Lisa after all. Not only would it be an important personal experience, but it would also help to tone down the impression I'd apparently given my white and coloured colleagues and friends that township life unfolded solely in the taverns and shebeens.

But while church, evening television-watching (often with a whole family squeezed on to a single couch, glued to the set) and other forms of entertainment were a major part of township life, it was somehow at the watering-holes that I would end up, and none of them was quite as magnetic, at that time, as Kefu's Place. Perfectly safe, supremely comfortable, and stylish too, it offered its clientele a chance to drink and to dance in another world. Ambience was guaranteed.

After a long, thorough body search outside the gate, which had been unbolted by one of Kefu's two sons, who were always well dressed, Mzondi and I headed for the bar. Passing the restrooms on our right and heading down the long corridor to the bar area, I could already hear Hugh Masekela's magical voice singing the passionate lines of 'Chileshe'. Now I've always been afraid to ask my friends what Mr Masekela is singing about in that beautiful song, and it is something I have decided never to do. I would not want to risk losing the dream that it represents for me. His is a voice that can improve on the sound of any instrument on earth, although with something they can never offer – complete freedom and independence of rhythm. His passion soared over the June clouds, higher and higher, into a summer deep inside, until delightfully cold shivers ran down my spine.

I've played that song a hundred times since then, in Europe, Asia and Africa, but in those faraway places it only served to make me desperately homesick for Khayelitsha. Listening to it in Kefu's Place, I was at home. I wasn't the only one who felt this way; I could see it in the dreamy, glazed eyes of the few patrons who were already there.

Even Kefu's second son, who worked the bar with a sway and a hum that went perfectly with the tunes he played, had an absent-minded smile on his lips. What made this young man an exquisite barman was not the efficiency with which he served, but rather the patience and timing of each approach to a customer. He would lean forward over the polished wooden bar counter, a little to one side of your chair, the expression on his face neither expectant nor demanding. It was up to the guest to make eye contact first. At this point he would nod a greeting, put his head a little to one side and listen carefully, as if your words were a particularly pleasant part of a song.

Kefu herself was a most attractive host. There was a touch of traditional pattern in the long, flowing dresses she wore and she ran the show without having to say more than a few words. A glance in the direction of one of her sons, or her boyfriend, was all that was required for the recipient to happily fulfil his task.

Even the drinks offered at Kefu's Place, which cost a bit more than in other taverns, were chosen to go with the African jazz and pleasant ambience of the place, with most patrons sipping away at a creamy Amstel lager, or a variety of good brandies.

The semicircular bar counter was bordered by a cosy dance floor on one end and a comfy lounge on the other. In the latter, the softly cushioned benches surrounded two tables, and one could watch a large sports bar-type television set, which was hooked up to satellite.

We'd arrived a little before nine, so it took some time for the establishment to fill up. Once again I felt underdressed. Many of the men, most of them in their thirties and forties, were wearing either suits or were semi-formally dressed, while I had combined faded jeans and a faded green leather jacket. Mzondi, on the other hand, almost always dressed neatly. Tonight his smart black shirt was tucked into dark belted pants, and he wore shiny brown shoes. I'd never seen his hair grow longer than crew cut length and he was always clean shaven.

Soon a few old acquaintances began to arrive, among them a chubby taxi boss who always gave me a big hug, and an older man who never stopped smiling. The latter was somehow related to Kefu and had in the past bought me a number of beers. Next Molefe and Foamy came walking down the passage from the entrance; my landlord had somehow managed to escape the possessive claws of his wife. Sitting down on bar stools on either side of us, they ordered a nip of brandy. While Foamy's happy demeanour was as reliable as his brother's sourness, evenings at Kefu's Place usually wiped a little of the pained look from Molefe's face. But as usual this evening he remained reserved, possibly the result of what he knew was in store for him when he returned home: a terrible scolding from Tshidi in Sotho. Her suspicions that he cheated on her when he went out with us were totally unfounded – in fact, Molefe would hardly look at another woman, although the speed with which he averted his eyes when he noticed that he had accidentally done so, appeared to be more from fear of his wife than anything else.

◆

Later that night, I had company.

It felt good to have such a pretty girl close to me, and I launched into a long conversation with her, not a word of which I would remember the next morning. She spoke near perfect English, so it must have been an interesting chat. It was also punctuated by brief spells on the dance floor, where by now a fair number of couples were slow dancing sensually. I've always loved petite women and this girl had a bum that was a bit of a contradiction to the general smallness of the rest of her body. I spent an entire song exploring it with my hands, to happy smiles from Foamy and the two other girls watching us from the table.

Now I know it is perhaps not all that decent to be doing this sort of thing in a public place, in front of loads of people, but I hadn't expected to be shot for it. For suddenly there was an R5 semi-automatic rifle pointed at my legs, behind which stood a short, stocky and entirely unfriendly soldier in camouflage battle gear. Obviously he wasn't impressed by evidence of my perversion. Raising my hands, I moved away from the girl as I realised what was going on.

This wasn't the first time it had happened. While most other shebeens religiously obeyed the informal agreement between police and owners that they close before ten, Kefu only shut up shop once the armed authorities arrived to do it for her. Every time they burst in through the glass sliding doors at the back of Kefu's house, I felt a mixture of anger and disgust. Why they needed close to twenty soldiers and police officers to break up the party I would never understand. Probably because of the thorough body searches and classy clientele who visited Kefu's Place, I had never seen or heard of an incident of crime there, so the authorities must have had another agenda.

I'd recently covered a large shebeen owner meeting for the paper, where it emerged that the main point of contention between them and the government was the order to formalise their businesses by buying liquor licences. This would drive the prices up, which the owners believed would lead to a decrease in sales.

What annoyed me most about the invasion of soldiers and policemen was the look of blind anger on their faces. It seemed to say, who are you to be partying on a Saturday evening while we have to work? This must have been a contributing factor to the gusto with which they carried out their task. I felt it criminal that they could spoil such fun, particularly when it was not even halfway towards its climax. Looking at the time on my cellphone, though, I saw that it was close to midnight.

As I became part of the mass of bodies being shoved down the passage towards the narrow front gate, I suddenly remembered my leather jacket. It had been a gift from a friend and was one of the few items of clothing I'd owned that had sleeves long enough to fit my arms. Seeing Foamy in the throng of people a little way off, I shouted to him.

'Foamy, have you got my jacket?'

'No, I looked for it and it wasn't there,' he shouted back. 'Shit.'

By the time we met up outside, the three girls were no-where to be seen. Feeling that our treatment at the hands of the soldiers and policemen was unacceptable, I decided to take my frustrations out on them.

'Someone stole my jacket while you were throwing us out,' I said to a police captain standing nearby. 'You are meant to be officers of the law, but your actions have resulted in a crime.'

Most of the officers involved in these busts knew me and my friends quite well by now. On many occasions, in the company of one or two black reporters who I'd met for a drink at Kefu's Place, we'd pissed them off by pulling our notebooks and pens from our pockets and asking for official statements for news stories. Although I'd seriously considered writing a story on what the experience was like from the point of view of the patron, our questions had usually resulted in an angry reaction. Asked his name and rank, an officer had once replied, 'My name is *Poephol*, but my rank is none of your business!'

'Steven, leave these capitalists alone,' Foamy called with his characteristic sarcasm. 'We'll find your jacket. Maybe one of those girls has it.'

'Ja, but we don't know where they live,' I moaned, moving quickly away from the captain, whose facial expression suggested he was about to make an arrest.

'Don't worry,' said Foamy, heading unsteadily towards a group of cars whose drivers and passengers were leaning drunkenly against their doors. They were obviously afraid of driving away with so many police around.

'I think that one of these guys knows them,' Foamy finished.

After being sent this way and that, interrogating a number of people on the way, Foamy returned.

'I know where they live,' he said, pointing to the left of

the Lookout Hill. 'Just over there, which means we both might get lucky tonight.'

Fortunately the rain had stopped, although the bright light cast by the tall lamp posts took much away from the beauty of the stars. With my leather jacket gone, I was caught in a frenzy of shivering, so I upped the tempo and we moved quickly through the quiet streets.

When I was younger I'd done a lot of hiking, usually at high speed, a habit I'd later introduced to my everyday life in the city. But since my move to Khaya, this uniformity had been disrupted, resulting in my developing two very different walking speeds. While in Khaya I strolled along the pavements and down the middle of the streets at a very slow pace, when I reached the city this pace quickened to close to a run. I thought I now understood why many of the black folk in my hometown had walked in the streets, rather than on the pavements. It must have been because in the streets of the townships there was hardly any traffic, making it unnecessary to walk on the pavement.

I had developed the same habit, although when I alighted from the train at Central station and headed for work I resorted to my old rapid pace. I would weave swiftly in and out of crowds, rush up and down escalators and indulge in my old love of jaywalking. This exciting momentum, pumping adrenalin into my bloodstream, continued unabated until I got back on the train in the evening. But sometimes during the day those who greeted me on the city streets would remind me of the reality of my other life. For example, there was the Zulu family who played the drums and danced together in St George's Mall in the city centre of Cape Town. I had seen them on the train on their way to work. Then there were the Xhosa newspaper sellers and the beggars who worked the area around the newspaper offices and who would regularly stop me in my tracks by greeting me by my Xhosa name, Luvuyo. And of course the clerk at my bank, who discovered we both lived in Ntlakohlaza Street: we had tried to shake hands under the bulletproof glass of his cubicle.

After about forty minutes of this self-reflection as Foamy and I walked briskly along the dark streets, I began to wonder whether Foamy actually knew where we were going. I didn't have a clue, having never been this far into the back of iLitha Park. This was obviously the rich part, where residents had built on proper rooms, instead of the usual crumbling additions or shacks in the backyard. Here and there, smart cars stood inside automatic security gates, while the gardens, although devoid of greenery, were clean swept and neat. Finally, in a street I'd never been to, Foamy slowed down in front of a corner house.

'This is where they live,' he said. 'First let me look in the windows a bit and then we'll knock on the door.'

As Foamy crept around the house, which was bordered by a wall only on one side, I waited in the street. Although the lights were on in at least three rooms, including the lounge, which I could see from where I was standing, most of the curtains were drawn and there was not a sound from within. At length, Foamy returned to the front of the house and whispered to me.

'I'm going to knock on the back door so they think I am someone they know very well. Then I'll go in and confront them about the jacket.'

I followed him around the side, where he cautioned me to stay out of sight.

'*Dumela ausi*,' I heard him say in Sotho to the person who opened the door.

After it was closed behind him, I became aware that a protracted conversation was being carried out in low tones in various parts of the house. Shivering from the cold, I disregarded Foamy's advice and knocked on the back door. He didn't seem surprised to see me and continued speaking to the girl who'd let me in; I recognised her as one of the three from Kefu's Place.

'I've already searched all the rooms,' he said. 'Your jacket isn't here. But we will go and ask another guy who was also there if he saw anything,' he added. 'He stays just down the road. You wait here,' he motioned to a smart leather couch.

Too tired to study my new surroundings, I removed my shoes, lay back and drifted into a fitful sleep, with flashes of jackets and girls bobbing around on the insides of my eyelids.

Just as I was about to fall into a deep sleep, the image of my warm bed at home shook me awake. Bugger the jacket, I thought to myself; I was going home. Anyway, I thought selfishly as I opened the back door quietly and crept out into the night, Foamy would do his best to find it.

It wasn't until I turned up the gravel lane at the side of the house that I saw Foamy 'doing his best'; I couldn't believe my eyes. There, next to the garden wall, was a picture I will never forget. I couldn't tell it was him from the top of his head, but there were the running shoes I'd seen on his big feet earlier that evening. They were pointing up from behind and on either side of the girl, who was rocking up and down on his hips. Foamy, who had his pants around his ankles, where the steel of his belt buckle made a clinking sound to the rhythm of his hips, slowly twisted his neck, until his head reached what seemed an impossible position, the kind of thing I've only ever seen in a bird.

'We couldn't find that guy's house,' he croaked.

Pastor Xola

I awoke surprisingly early on the Sunday morning I was due to attend church with Lisa, excited that I would be meeting new people, even if I was a little apprehensive about staying awake through a Xhosa sermon. However, as is so often the case when one has plenty of time, I dawdled away the minutes, sleepily placing bunched newspaper pages at the bottom of the door to keep out the bitter cold. I'd somehow managed to stay away from Vovo Cash Store the previous evening and my body appreciated the break. So satisfied was it with the lengthy ten-hour sleep that it persuaded me to climb back into bed. Waking up a little later and seeing the lateness of the hour, I'd had to rush my bath in the tub; an easy feat, because of the cold. Then I dressed as quickly as possible in the neatest clothes I could find in my messy cupboard.

From Vovo Cash Store, with a glass of beer in my hand, I'd often seen the local churchgoers, dressed smartly and fashionably, heading for their places of worship. Some, I'd noticed, actually wore uniforms, and I later found out that they were members of South Africa's largest church, the Zion Christian Church.

I went as far as shining my suede boots until they were barely recognisable as the grotesquely scarred and scratched shoes I'd worn before. I hoped the strong smell of the polish on the outside would do a bit to overpower the strong, acrid odour on the inside, but I knew the chances were small. I'd bought the boots before my move to Khaya, but if I'd known then what I knew now – that when suede gets wet the water goes right through to the socks – I would never have made the purchase.

With the minute hand of my little pink clock close to nine-thirty, I finished tying my laces and stood up to go and wait outside. As I opened the door, Lisa, Sandisiwe and Nosizwe were already walking up the driveway. The three of them looked stunning in brightly coloured, expensive-looking outfits, with shiny necklaces, earrings and bags to match. Sandisiwe's jacket looked like genuine leather, and the other two girls were also immaculately turned out. Edging her way past me without a word, Lisa took in the interior of my room in one, sweeping glance.

'*Eish*,' she said, hugging her arms to her body, 'this room is freezing.'

Looking at the bucket, which I'd returned to its traditional place on my bed, she asked whether the roof leaked.

'Badly,' I replied, glad that someone had noticed.

'Steven, you need to find a proper room,' she said. 'This is not a healthy place to spend the winter.'

I nodded in agreement.

'I'm going to find you another home. Come, we are late.' Lisa led us to her car with an air of authority.

Her daughter Sandiswa was sitting on the back seat, her thumb still in her mouth. It was a very short distance to the church, one that I thought unnecessary to cover by car. But I was grateful for the body heat and company, even if the two older of the three passengers in the car spent most of the ride sending text messages. Lisa, meanwhile, had a new batch of questions to throw at me, often not waiting until I'd finished answering one question before firing another at me. The phones were switched off and deposited in the little handbags as we pulled into the church parking lot, where members of the congregation were already standing together in groups, shaking hands and chatting. Up and across the road I could see Kefu's Place and I lamented the theft of my leather jacket. It would have been perfect for this outing.

Judging by the cars parked alongside ours, some members of the fellowship were quite well off. As we stood outside the church, the old feeling of being out of place overwhelmed me again. This time, however, it was not just because of my colour, but also stemmed from the attitude I'd developed towards religion in general. Of course, I told myself as I shut the car door, religion as espoused by the apartheid Nationalists was perhaps not the best example by which to judge it. Besides, the segregated churches of my youth had nothing to do with these folk.

Hoping fervently that I wouldn't be recognised for what I was – a regular visitor to most of the shebeens in iLitha Park and beyond – I smilingly shook the hands of those to whom Lisa introduced me. Compared with many of the churches in the suburbs, whose congregations I'd heard were ageing rapidly, this was an extraordinarily young crowd.

The youthful and vibrant Pastor Xola made the biggest impression on me. At once charming and sincere, Xola combined a faithful and undoubting belief in God with a wit and intelligence that was a pleasure to come into contact with. Below average height and leanly built, he had the charisma of a great orator and the humility of one who is prepared to live and die for his beliefs, without any expectation of recognition from others. He later told me, after I asked him if he'd completed an education in theology, that although he had passed all the final-year exams at the Cape Town pastoral college he'd gone to, he hadn't received his graduation certificate. This was because he'd refused to attend the graduation ceremony. An informal agreement at the college that required the proceedings to be held in rotation at a traditionally white, black and coloured suburb over every three-year period had been ignored in his final year. It was the turn of Khayelitsha to host the ceremony, but because the white and coloured students complained that their families would be too frightened to attend, the venue was changed. The only Xhosa student who was to graduate that year, Xola boycotted the event in protest over what he saw as the ignorance and prejudice of his Christian fellows. There was no anger in him when he told me the story; on the contrary, it seemed he had simply felt it necessary to take a stand against what he deemed to be their hypocrisy.

His shining personality and positive outlook on life made Xola a powerful preacher. Instead of focusing – in the English and Xhosa that he mixed – on the brutal message of sinner and hellfire, he delivered a lesson on love. There are too many people, from a wide variety of religions, who fail to see the importance of their leader's personality in the shaping of their beliefs. It is often the impact of his or her personality on the sermon being delivered that has one leaving a place of worship feeling either condemned or renewed. With Xola, the latter applied.

The rest of the service closely mirrored those of the more charismatic and forceful happy-clappy churches in the suburbs, although there was the added strength of natural African voices and rhythm. Most of the hundred or so seats were occupied.

The church interior was arranged in a semicircle around a slightly elevated stage at one end, where three women and a young man led the lively singing, in a way not dissimilar to black congregations in the American south (as seen in movies). Although I've always preferred the more traditional Xhosa gospel pieces, I soon picked up the more modern tunes sung there that day, but I was careful not to be heard. My seat in the back row meant I could get away with only a gentle swaying of the hips, rather than the rocking and jiving happening closer to the front.

I was quite surprised at the amount of naked skin revealed by skimpy skirts and tops and, once again enraptured by a culture where the image of the female bum is larger than life, I averted my eyes, concentrating instead on the words of the songs.

At the end of the service when Xola asked all those who required blessings to move to the front, I was embarrassed to find that I was one of only a handful of people who remained in their chairs. However, I made some commitments of my own, although they were unrelated to matters of the soul. I'd just finished the last week of my twelve-month internship at the paper, and strengthened my resolve to achieve the best I could in the final semester of my journalism studies. Also,

I would take Lisa up on her offer to find another room for me, since I was tired of my landlady's unfulfilled promises to fix the leaks in the roof. After all, I wouldn't be covering any more stories on flooded informal settlements this winter, a task that had left me feeling too guilty to relocate from a room in much better condition than those I had seen where men, women and children were scooping bucket upon bucket of water out their front door.

When the collection plate did the rounds, to the rhythm of the last hymn, I was frustrated to find my pockets empty, but Lisa was kind enough to hand me a coin. The service over, we headed towards one side of the church where a number of tables, decked out in white cloths, were laid with coffee and tea. It was there that I stumbled upon a youngster who regularly watched me drink gallons of beer while playing pool in Vovo Cash Store.

'Steve,' he whispered in my ear, 'please don't mention it.'

I agreed, of course.

I remember my first visit to the local church not only for the impressive pastor and bad coffee, but also for the meal that followed. An invitation to Lisa's home for lunch, with Sandisiwe and Nosizwe, would have been stupid to decline, since if other Sunday meals I'd had in Khaya were anything to go by, I knew the food would be delicious. I have yet to find out what secret township ingredient is able to make something as plain as chicken, rice and pumpkin taste so good. Perhaps it would be safest to lay the credit at the door of *umuti*. But on this particular Sunday at Lisa's place, I decided to thank the Lord.

Makwerekwere

It's not every day one gets to say the word 'nigger', especially if you're a white man. Even Eminem reportedly only began to use the word in his raps after he'd cautiously asked the permission of the most prominent black rappers in the US. I, on the other hand, never had to ask: I was forced into using the word. For there was a Nigger in my very own local shebeen.

Political correctness in the South African context – even plain decency – would demand that you try not to notice the race of the man across the pool table from you. You would never allow yourself to think that he walked like a nigger, spoke like a nigger, dressed like a nigger, or was black as only a nigger can be. And if you were pressed to say the word, you would almost certainly say, 'You are *not* a nigger.'

And that's when Nigger would say in his African-American

accent, 'Yes, my brudder man, I *am* a nigger.'

But this was no gangsta rap 'nigga', short and aggressive, or the drawling 'nigr' of a racist Southern redneck. No, Nigger said it his own way, and said it best, pursing his lips and endlessly drawing out the first vowel:

'I,' he would say, 'am a niiiiiigar, man ...'

Nigger's real name, if ever he had one, was as obscure to me as most of his thoughts; besides, it would be hard to believe that one who appeared to have no past or future could ever have had a name other than the one he went by now. However, the fact that to Nigger all those he met on a daily basis were niggers too, goes some way to putting this all in perspective.

Early one afternoon, a couple of days before I went back to my studies, Nigger and I were playing pool at Vovo Cash Store. I had taken to spending my evenings writing in my journal, on those few occasions that I wasn't drinking or sinking balls. Nigger's habit of keeping to himself had made me curious.

'What's your name?' I asked him. The other three patrons, the only other people in the place, ignored us, sitting on their beer crates on the cement inside the open garage door.

'Nigger,' he replied.

I wasn't sure I'd heard him properly. I asked him again.

'Nigger,' he repeated, handing me the cue.

'I'm Steve,' I said, as I realised he hadn't asked.

He nodded his head almost imperceptibly.

'Your shot, my brother,' said Nigger, and pointed a middle finger at the pool table.

'Where are you from?' I asked.

'Kenya.'

'Did your father name you?' I asked respectfully, feeling

awkward about having to call someone Nigger.

'No, I named myself. Your shot,' he said again.

I played a solid ball and missed.

'Why did you name yourself Nigger?'

'Because I'm a nigger,' he said, leaning over the table to shoot.

'But what's your real name?'

Nigger motioned with his hand for silence. He missed a striped ball, and placed the cue on the table. He spread his bare arms.

'Look at me, man,' he said, opening his hands to reveal his pinkish palms. 'What do you see?'

'A person?'

'No, man!' he cried, attracting the attention of the three patrons on the beer crates. 'What do you see?'

'A man?'

He invited me to try again.

'A nigger?' I guessed.

'Yes, man,' he said. 'That is why I am a nigger.' Although there was only a tiny hint of a smile on Nigger's face, the three Xhosa men laughed loudly. 'Your shot,' he said, and handed me the cue.

I have always enjoyed the company of silent types, those who leave one wondering what they are thinking, and Nigger was as silent and tricky to read as the best of them. I'd noticed him in Vovo Cash Store a number of times, but I'd never heard him express a single opinion, raise his voice in anger, or lament a defeat in a pool game. His routine was always the same. He would arrive, lean against the wall, and watch a few rounds. Every so often he would buy a beer, called Jesus Juice, from Steve, his wife Thandi, or daughter Yoliswa. One evening, as Thandi floundered around in the fridge looking for his favourite brand, Nigger offered some advice.

'You must look slightly to one side of that bottle with the red label, half close your eyes and you will see the words "Jesus Juice" written on it.'

Nigger always wore the same white vest. It was difficult to imagine why. Perhaps he had never noticed that he was no longer in the Kenyan climate. Maybe he liked the look – an oversized top sporting hundreds of little holes, like netting, and a basketball player's number on the back. The number was red, with a black outline. Nigger probably wore other clothes besides the vest and a pair of huge black pants that tapered into expensive-looking snow-white running shoes, but I certainly can't recall them.

So there Nigger would stand, up against the wall; but after a number of pool games had passed he would dig in his pants and fish out a one rand coin, putting it at the back of the queue on the table, and then return to his wall, lean back and wait. It seemed to be a warming-up process of sorts, but if it was, it wasn't very effective, because Nigger was certainly not very good at the game. It was surprising to me, since I'd always thought that, as with rifle shooting, a muscular upper body gave one a steady hand.

And Nigger had a muscular upper body. In fact his build was massive, a fact that went some way towards disguising his short stature. His upper body was so huge that he was getting close to the stage when he would need to spread his arms to have them participate in the act of walking. While it was impossible (because of the baggy black pants) to see the size of his legs, even his neck had thick cords of muscle coiling from his upper chest.

Even more surprising than his weak performances at pool was his way with the other patrons. Despite looking fierce, even dangerous, Nigger greeted all questions or approaches with a friendly word, while his beer, which he drank straight from the bottle, was handed without protest to anyone who asked for it. Put simply, he didn't seem to have any friends, and he also seemed not in the least bit perturbed by this.

Of course, there were other loners who arrived at and left the shebeen on their own, but there was one main difference between him and them: Nigger was a *kwerekwere*. Derived from the way other African languages sound to the ear of a black South African, it is a derogatory slang word for foreigners, those migrants or refugees from north of the border who are often treated with a great deal of suspicion in Khayelitsha. I found it strange that I, on the other hand, had been taken in and accepted immediately. It could have had something to do with our shared nationality, but I suspected that the effectiveness of apartheid ideology in entrenching inferiority played a role.

For people like Nigger, life in Khayelitsha is not easy. Not only are there large cultural differences between them and the locals, but there is a general feeling among many Xhosa men that the *makwerekwere* steal their girls and jobs. More to the point, the outsiders impress their girls with smart cars, sometimes bought from the proceeds of drug dealing or other kinds of crime. Nigerians are considered the prime suspects in this. I myself had been approached on the street by a group of BMW-driving Nigerians in iLitha Park a short while after my move there. The driver had very seriously explained that they needed 'a respectable-looking white man' to pick up a suitcase at the airport. My laughter, which had burst out before I could choke it back, had been met with a look of genuine surprise by the three large men; but they got the message and drove away.

I could see that Nigger was respected by the patrons at Vovo Cash Store, but it was a respect that he had worked hard to attain. Zane and my other friends liked recounting how Nigger had managed to overpower small groups of tsotsis armed with knives. One tale doing the rounds was that he had wrestled a gun from a youngster who'd broken into his house while he was asleep. The next day he found out where the gangster lived and returned the weapon, although the motive for this strange act remained unclear.

It seemed odd to me that so many of my black country-men displayed xenophobic attitudes towards other Africans, especially since most were based on prejudices they them-selves had experienced under apartheid. Was it prejudice based on fear of the unknown? Or was it purely a competition for scarce resources? It was a debate I didn't want to have. Sometimes a single event can help us overcome our differences. The event was small and vague, but it changed everything: Nigger and I became friends.

Thabo

After a year of adrenalin-charged work in the field, returning to my old classroom at Peninsula Technikon made me feel I'd gone back a few years in time. However, there was also an obvious sense of change in the air. Whereas before I'd sat in class with largely naive, immature students, I now found myself among reporters who'd spent twelve months on the beat at most of the country's best newspapers, radio and television stations. The change was remarkable, with most of my fellows sharing my mixed feelings towards the pleasure of our meeting up again, and the pain involved in a return to the bureaucratic lethargy ingrained in most education facilities. Some familiars were missing, my former classmates having achieved so outstandingly during their internships that they had never returned, coaxed instead into staying on at their companies. There to fill some of their empty seats were a

few new faces, those from the year behind us who had been .
unable to find internships, or had decided to delay them for
a year. Among them were two Khayelitsha residents, both of
whom have remained good friends of mine over the years.

Fumanekile and Thabo are complete opposites. While
Thabo's character, bold and outspoken, was clear right away,
Fumanekile's rough exterior hid a nature that was soft-spoken
and kind.

Nicknamed Ta-fumsa, Fumanekile's late arrival for the
first day of class caused something of a stir. This wasn't only
because of the casual way in which he entered the room, but
also because of his gear. His revolutionary beret pulled low
over his eyes, matchstick in the mouth, off-green jersey and
faded khaki pants probably stirred up a number of clichéd
images in our minds that day; but the impression that stuck
in mine was that this was a man who had just purchased
his whole wardrobe at a shop named *Tsotsi*. I can't speak
for my classmates, none of whom were white, but I know
I was waiting for him to pull out a pistol, remove the old
green beret from his head and walk up and down the aisles
ordering each student to drop their valuables into it. Instead
Ta-fumsa slumped down into a chair, to the muffled chuckles
of the class.

Thabo, on the other hand, had the innocent eyes and face
of the cute little boy in the film 'e'Lollipop'. He was cherubic
– until he opened his mouth. And that point usually came
pretty soon: he talked incessantly. And what came out of his
mouth was so abrasive that it seemed difficult to match the
face with the mouth.

The media world is outspoken, and it wasn't long before
we were all in the computer room, loudly sharing our
experiences as interns; it was here that it emerged that I lived

in Khayelitsha. The reaction from all the Xhosa students in the class was one of approval, but I recognised the blank stares on the faces of most of the coloureds. It was the same expression I'd seen so many times on faces of a somewhat lighter complexion. The black attitude was that I had broken a rule that should never have been there to begin with, but the coloured students could clearly not begin to grasp what I was doing. Who in their right mind would want to live in a filthy, dangerous place where poverty and disease were the order of the day, a coloured student in my class asked me. 'Me,' I replied, thinking it would take too long to explain.

Being from the same township, it was natural that Ta-fumsa, Thabo and I would catch the same train home. As we stood together at the Technikon train station, where the wait was always long, the three of us were immediately at ease in one another's company. Thabo was curious about why I had moved to Khayelitsha and bombarded me with cocky questions, but Ta-fumsa was far less probing and stood with his books tucked under his arm, matchstick between the lips, happy just to be listening.

Fumanekile did a lot of freelancing for *City Vision*, one of the two community newspapers that were distributed to the black townships, and it turned out that we shared a mutual friend, Tarzan, its editor-in-chief. Although Tarzan had been a year ahead of me at the Technikon, I still saw him about once a month, at the black journalists' braai in Gugulethu, an all-black affair I'd been invited to for the first time a few weeks after my move to Khayelitsha. It seemed that Lukhanyo, the colleague who had circulated the email announcing that I was 'black on the inside', had been the driving force behind the invitation. As official arbiter of blackness, he had also been the natural person to approach me in the office to tell me that he and the other usual attendees had, after much consideration, decided I met the criteria demanded from those who organised the braai.

(I wondered at first why it was called the 'black journalists' braai', but after attending a couple I realised that it was simply an attempt by the black hosts to address, and perhaps ease, the fear they perceived in their coloured and white colleagues every time the idea of having a good time in a township was mooted.)

Thabo, who had never attended the braai, had just spent three months in the Netherlands as part of a student exchange programme. I had been invited by Aletta, my Dutch girlfriend, to visit her there after I'd finished my studies, but as a resident of Khaya, Thabo's stories about the Netherlands and its people seemed a much more colourful alternative.

'I'm telling you Steve, those people are so boring,' he said, with a thick Xhosa accent that rolled the 'r'. 'When a friend takes you out to drink, he goes home after just three glasses. Glasses, not quarts! And after he has invited you, he expects you to pay for yourself.' He shook his head in utter disgust. '*Eish*,' he chuckled as he recalled it. 'And if there are five of you, each one of you must buy a round of drinks. I mean' – the smile had been replaced by a look of scorn – 'I am an African. And the allowance I got was very small.'

'But you must adapt to their culture when you are there,' said Ta-fumsa, smiling.

'You are wrong,' Thabo replied earnestly. 'Because I am poor, they must adapt to mine. But after I taught them that they must pay for me I was not invited out so much any more. These people very quickly saw what I was doing, because every time I would wait until everyone had bought a round and then, when it was my turn, I would start yawning. *"Eish,"* I would say, "now I am very drunk and I must go home to sleep. In South Africa we go to sleep much earlier than this!" I'm telling you, Steve, they were very angry, because those Dutch people love money too much. And when I told a girl I loved her, she said to me, "How you can love me after being in Holland for only one day?" What is that?'

'But there are differences even between the cultures in our country,' I protested. 'If you told a white woman from here so soon that you loved her she would probably respond in the same way.'

'Ja, *mlungu*,' he retorted, 'but you live in Khaya now. You must change your way of thinking.' He snorted and moved on. 'Who was that Xhosa girl you were talking to in the passage this morning?'

'Her name is Vuyo,' I said, not wanting to share any more than the essentials. More than that, I had managed to push her out of my mind for some weeks, and didn't want to get back into the habit of thinking of her almost constantly.

'She is a fashion student,' Thabo said, knowingly. *'Eish*, but that one is beautiful. How long were you talking to her?'

'Maybe twenty minutes,' I replied.

Thabo looked amazed. 'What do the two of you talk about for so long? I could see in her eyes that she is yours – you must chow her before she loses interest!' Thabo's laugh, deep inside his chest, was as abrasive and noisy as his banter, but the fun was contagious. Ta-fumsa, smiling broadly in spite of himself, shook his head slowly.

'Thabo,' he said, 'you know that there are no white people living in Khaya, so you must see Steven as being a black man.'

'Eish,' our friend retorted, 'this guy is not black.'

Although I tended to agree with Thabo, I told them about the time I had felt closest to being black. Mzondi and I had been assigned to cover the launch of an art fair in the Gardens, which always meant plenty of free food and drink. After the speeches, a few notes scribbled in our notebooks, we tucked into the whisky. The gathered guests began to unwind: in an hour the party was in full swing.

Mzondi and I had made advances towards a couple of girls – he was forever handing me telephone numbers on the mornings after wild parties at shebeens, telling me that 'she really loves you, that one, you must call her!' – but at last I found myself with a particularly charming girl. The way her lips moved and her hair fell around her face conspired to leave me unable to do anything but worship her, but luckily I had been drinking a lot and discovered that I was a million times funnier and more witty than normal. Mzondi had sidled off to hunt on his own, and the girl and I were alone.

Flirtation turned to innuendo, and soon innuendo turned intense, and she was describing the layout of her flat, slowly leading me towards the bedroom. The details were getting dangerously specific, and I realised that fairly soon we were going to have to deal with certain practicalities. Like where she lived. I asked her.

'Tokai,' she said, sending goosebumps down the inside of my thighs. She was coloured and she spoke the Queen's English with devastating effect. 'And what about you?'

'Khayelitsha,' I replied.

'Benny!' she cried, suddenly seeing someone almost completely behind her, which required her to spin around and rush headlong into the distance. Benny, I saw, was way out of earshot, and moreover he had been standing there for some time. A back-up plan for when things go badly wrong.

The train pulled up at the Technikon station, and we jostled our way on board, steadying ourselves with the overhead straps. My story was done, and Thabo picked up his tale of the African in the Netherlands.

'People felt very sorry for me there,' he said with a chuckle. 'One time a street person even gave me money!' It had been in a corner café in Amsterdam, he said. 'I was struggling to count all the euro coins in my hand, to buy some potato chips. *Eish*, when you are used to our cents it is difficult to count those things.' Our friend's confusion had been mistaken for poverty by the old white man, and he had offered to help. 'In front of all the people there he offered to help me, handing me a five euro note. I paid with it, of course, but *eish*, it was embarrassing.'

As we clattered along, it seemed that Thabo had finally run out of things to say, and so he passed the time by looking at me and shaking his head vigorously.

'*Eish*, a white man in Khayelitsha!' He gave me another look as we got out at Bonteheuwel station to catch our next train. 'Aren't you afraid of all these blacks?' He threw back his head and laughed uproariously at his joke. 'White man, you must hold on to your money!'

'Ta-fumsa,' I said, as we began climbing the concrete stairs that crossed the line to the other platform, 'is this guy always like this?' My friend shrugged, as he and Thabo piled into the NikNaks I offered them, both taking extremely generous helpings from the tiny packet I had bought minutes before on the platform. I looked at the few remaining chips in the bag. I'd become quite used to this over the past five months, and had soon learned that generosity went both ways. We boarded the Khayelitsha train as it pulled in from Cape Town, but Thabo wouldn't let the joke go.

'Hey, white man,' he crowed. 'Where are you going?'

'You know where I'm going.'

'You are going the wrong way,' he cried. 'The suburbs are that way.' He pointed back towards Table Mountain, cackling with delight.

I asked him quietly to stop making a spectacle of me in front of the other commuters in the carriage; but over the course of the following months I would realise that this was a part of Thabo's character that was unchangeable. The more signs of irritation one displayed, the further he carried the teasing. The only effective approach was a counter-attack.

'How old are you?' I asked him.

'Twenty,' he replied, cautiously.

'Oh, so you still have to go to the bush.' I looked at Tafumsa, who was grinning widely. 'It is not right for us to be talking to an *nkwenkwe*,' I said, using the word for an uncircumcised boy.

'*Hayi*, man,' Thabo said softly. 'What does a white man know about the bush?'

Ganja, Beans and Pumping Iron

'Who do you rent it from?' I asked Nigger, as we entered his house.

'It belongs to me.'

Our conversation – if you could call a series of grunts a conversation – had taken the form of a question and answer session, something that, when carried out between neighbours for many minutes, starts to feel more than a little awkward. I had asked the first few questions to get us chatting, but Nigger's terse (though polite) replies served only to confirm the impression that I was supposed to be minding my own business.

The house I'd been asking about, and that Nigger said he owned, was so sparsely furnished that it was, to all intents and purposes, totally empty. His bedroom and lounge had only one item of furniture each; in the former lay a tattered single mattress, in the latter a stained, lopsided chair. The kitchen, in one corner of the lounge, was not quite so bare, with two cheap-looking pots standing on a rusty, two-plate stove. Out of both of the pots came fitful bursts of steam, filling the room with the starchy smell of beans.

'Yo, take a seat, man,' Nigger said finally, beckoning me towards the chair which left no space for him to sit. He went down on his haunches against the wall, but he was up again quickly to help me to my feet. The chair had collapsed to one side, and I had gone over it in a slow-motion backward somersault. Righting the chair, Nigger carefully adjusted each of the four bricks beneath it.

'It's fine now. Take a seat, my nigger,' he said again, moving back to his position against the wall, facing me with his hands clasped around his knees.

He was wearing the white basketball vest, the baggy black pants and the spotless running shoes, although from close up they were a little more frayed than they'd seemed around the pool table. The chair faced the longest wall in the lounge, as if a television was about to be produced out of thin air.

'The television was stolen,' Nigger said, reading my thoughts.

'When?'

'Two weeks ago. Those skollies up there took it.' He waved vaguely into the dark street, but I knew the house where three dodgy-looking youngsters lived. They had frequent visitors, and from the sluggish way in which they moved, I guessed they were Mandrax smokers.

'How do you know they stole it?'

'I know, man,' he answered. 'One of them has a sister that I had sex with. She was working as a spy for them.' He looked gloomy. 'I'm telling you, man, you can't trust these

Xhosa women – they are thieves and liars.'

'You can't say that about them,' I objected.

'I can,' Nigger replied. 'That's why so many of their men beat them.'

I decided to ignore his observations, and looked around. Immediately I spotted a narrow bench, tucked away neatly next to the door of Nigger's bedroom, and next to it, a single weight bar: this was the secret to Nigger's muscular torso. The bench was rickety at best; the legs and the plank on top that served as the seat were held together with a complicated arrangement of twisted and knotted dishtowels.

Clearly, I thought, this man is an athlete in training. Nigger obviously took his health seriously. But then he reached under my chair and I had second thoughts, because he pulled out a large transparent bag of dagga, cigarette papers and box of Lion Matches from under my seat.

'You smoke?' I asked him, rather pointlessly.

'All day.'

'How do you lift weights when you smoke? That stuff always made me lazy.'

He shook his head. 'It makes me powerful.' He held up his hand, his last three fingers raised. 'There are three things that I will never stop,' he said. 'Ganja, beans and pumping iron.'

'Beans make me fart,' I offered.

'Listen, man,' he said, a rare smile baring a set of teeth more yellow than mielie kernels. 'What is it that gives a car power?'

'Petrol.'

'And what sound does the petrol make when it comes out the car's backside?' He patted a buttock. 'What goes in must go out,' he said, looking pleased with himself. 'And the louder the noise,' he said, illustrating his point by blowing air noisily between vibrating lips, 'the better the fuel.'

I decided that I would continue to avoid bean-petrol, and changed the subject.

'Do you like living here?'

'Where, in iLitha Park?'

'Yes.'

'You know something?' said Nigger, conspiratorially. 'I like iLitha Park, but I don't like these Xhosas.'

Unable to get a click out on the 'x', he'd said *Kosa*. It was a more honest attempt than that regularly made by our Nigerian head of department at the Technikon, who always managed to get out a click of sorts, although the period of silence, as he adjusted his lips to accommodate it, before the 'osa', was extremely long.

'These Kosas are not normal niggers,' said the Kenyan.

'What do you mean?'

'Look, man,' he said, with a sweep of his arm, to illustrate his cleaned out house, 'they steal whatever they can. It is better to live here with nothing, like they do, because they will steal whatever you have.'

'I have not been robbed since I came here,' I told him.

'How long have you been here?'

'About five months.'

'Maybe they are scared of you because you are white.'

'If you had friends here maybe things would be different.'

'I don't want friends here, because I can't trust a Kosa,' Nigger said with finality.

Although it would have been rude in terms of township etiquette to bring up the matter right away, I'd had a specific reason for embarking on the short walk past Vovo Cash Store to Nigger's house. The next day I was moving to another part of iLitha Park and I needed someone to help me carry my bags. I'd declined Lisa's offer of the use of her car, because that would have meant waiting another day. I was impatient to leave the discomfort of a damp mattress and cold, draughty room behind and get off to a new start.

Lisa had been appalled when she'd first seen my home, and she soon persuaded me to move.

'How much do you pay here?' she'd demanded.

'Three hundred rand.'

'Do you eat inside with Tshidi and Molefe?'

'No.'

'*Eish*,' she hissed. 'At Nowie's place you will pay fifty rand more, but she will also cook for you.'

As she drove me to the wealthier part of iLitha Park, which Foamy and I, in search of my leather jacket, had walked through a few weeks before, Lisa described my new landlady.

'She is in her late thirties and she is very beautiful. She has two daughters, one is very small and the other one, Babalwa, is seventeen – you must leave her alone because she is too young for you.' The small houses sped by: Lisa drove the way she talked, quickly and confidently. 'I told Nowie we were coming,' she said.

Lisa had met Nowie in less than happy circumstances, but all seemed forgotten now as she cheerfully told me the story. A couple of months earlier, Lisa's friend's boyfriend had disappeared for a fortnight – after clearing out his girlfriend's purse. The dodgy fellow had finally been tracked down to

Nowie's place where, it turned out, he had spent his days drinking beer and his nights in the arms of his mistress. The affair had ended with a settlement between Nowie and the man's girlfriend, with Lisa in the role of mediator, and the devious chap had been banned from both their homes.

From outside the house, which stood midway up the steep Ngqangqolo Street, I could see my old room and the iLitha Park station, perhaps a kilometre away over houses and dusty fields. The homes on either side of the lane were not of the government variety, being larger than the mass-produced shoeboxes and each uniquely designed. We passed a garage shebeen, not unlike Vovo Cash Store, and I glimpsed two men with a small audience bent over a pool table.

'This is not much different from the suburbs,' Lisa said.

She was right. The whole area exuded a more sedate – or was that sedated? – atmosphere than any other part of Khaya I'd been to before. Cars outnumbered pedestrians and I began to wonder if I would miss the friendly chaos of Ntlazane Road.

Nowie, I thought, was not so much beautiful as well-groomed: apparently there had been a good settlement when she ended her marriage to a township taxi boss.

She had the thin, stiff, inwardly pulled lips I'd seen on many of the faces of white people in Uitenhage, a look I'd always thought came from hundreds of years of cynical conservatism. The picture that greeted us as Lisa and I walked into the lounge made me think of a magazine concept of an irresistibly cosy home for the new black middle class.

Flanked by her two daughters, Babalwa and the younger Pamela, Nowie had her bare feet, beside which lay two fake snakeskin shoes, resting at the foot of an oil heater, a luxurious illustration of comfort and warmth. The furniture was brassy

149

and looked uncomfortable, with the creamy brown carpet being its only saving grace, taking away at least a little of the image of artificial wealth cast by the shiny golden-coloured knobs that flashed signals from various vantage points on the hideous lounge suite.

After we'd exchanged names and pleasantries, I was introduced to Thabiso, who had opened the door for us. I saw her for what she was straightaway: a single-minded woman with the good grace and manners so characteristic of Xhosa women. Thabiso, Nowie explained, lived in the shack behind the house.

As I sat in the lounge and listened to Nowie talk, the feeling that washed over me – that this happy little nest was in dire need of a subservient man – was never fully to disappear in the months ahead. The look in her eyes suggested that she had had a design for me long before we'd met. I felt myself under the full weight of a pressure that would never express itself in words, but I was certain of its presence. In spite of Nowie's sweet smile and soft tone of voice that evening, I got the indelible idea that she was holding something back. Of course I could not be sure that it was of a negative nature, but my bad experience with Tshidi had made me cautious. In fact, this element of suspicion had nothing to do with Khayelitsha, since I had had my fair share of bad experiences with landladies and landlords in the suburbs, and I would be a liar of the most despicable calibre to suggest I was never to blame.

Because one can never predict what nature of personality clashes may unfold between two people who have yet to get to know each other well, there was nothing to do but throw caution to the wind, take the leap and hope for the best. Besides, a fully furnished room, with bed, cupboard, TV and a newly sealed roof for three hundred and fifty rand, was nothing short of a bargain at the price. Add to that the fact that Nowie would be buying my food, cooking it and washing my clothes, and it was hard to see what could go wrong.

After I'd spent about the same amount of time with Nigger and Nowie, compared with her, I thought as I tried not to move around too much on his lopsided chair, Nigger seemed an even harder nut to crack. After a prolonged period of silence and unresponsiveness, I asked him whether he had work.

'No, my friend,' he replied, taking another drag on his juggernaut-sized joint. 'When I need money I pray to God.'

'What do you mean?'

'If I run out of money,' Nigger said, moving his lips up to touch his nose after inhaling another large pull of marijuana smoke, 'in the night I kneel over there,' he pointed the joint in the direction of the weights bench, 'and I pray to God for money. Then, in the morning when I open the door, there is usually twenty rand lying on the step outside.'

It was difficult to know whether Nigger was having me on, or just hiding a darker truth about where he obtained his money. This kind of talk, for me at least, was not far distant from the realm of dementia, so I told Nigger I needed to go home and sleep. He stood up and walked quickly to the stove.

'No, my brother, first you must eat with me. I have cooked beans and rice. Good food,' he said, 'healthy.'

Since this would save me the trouble of having to cook for myself, a task I never enjoyed, I decided after all to make an exception to my 'no beans' rule and accept the offer.

'Thanks,' I said, before broaching the real purpose of my visit. 'Listen, Nigger, I was wondering if you would help me move tomorrow.'

'You're moving?' he turned his head from where he was dishing up the food.

'Yes.'

'Where to?'

'Ngqangqolo Street,' I pointed in the general direction. 'Up there.'

'I know that road,' said Nigger, motioning that the food was ready. 'It is a good place; it's very quiet up there. I'll help you move,' he added, in a way that suggested he didn't have too many plans.

As I arrived in the makeshift kitchen he handed me a plain white plate filled with steaming beans atop a large mound of rice, before sticking a spoon into the side of the rather intimidating portion. I headed back to the chair.

'Just wait,' he said, walking after me with an open bottle of sunflower oil.

It would be downright rude to complain about a meal received as a guest, but I came close to saying something about the dangerous quantity of cholesterol-inducing liquid he poured over my plate. Having done the same to his own plate of food, Nigger once more took up his crouching position against the wall.

'Smoking makes me hungry,' he said, digging into his plate, 'and beans make me pump iron.'

Although I was not particularly hungry, I was surprised to find that the simple combination of legumes and rice was extremely appetising.

'Why are you moving?' Nigger asked me, covering his

mouth, which was full of food, with the back of a hand.

'The roof leaks badly and the owner's wife has been talking and talking about ...'

'I know about her,' Nigger interrupted. 'Her neighbours say she's a witch.'

'Do you believe that?' I asked him.

'No, man,' Nigger replied, smiling as he chewed his food. 'But she's a bitch. I know because that Burundian guy who lives there ...'

'Frederick?'

'Yes, man, Frederick,' he took another spoonful of gooey rice and beans. 'He came here the other day to ask if he could move in with me. He has too many problems with that lady.' Nigger swallowed and scooped another generous spoonful from his plate.

'This food is good,' I said, to a light nod from Nigger. 'So Frederick will be living here with you?'

'No, man, I told him he can't come here. This is my place,' he said, taking in our surroundings with a slow movement of his eyes.

'I didn't know he also wanted to leave,' I said.

I was quite thankful to hear this because, as it so often is when one is a participant in a feud, I'd begun to wonder whether I wasn't perhaps the person with the problem. Foamy and I had regularly been on the receiving end of Tshidi's wrath after we'd spirited Molefe off to Kefu's Place. For Foamy, who had to sleep on a mat in the lounge, life had become particularly unbearable and the fact that he hadn't found a job hadn't helped. When I'd told him the previous day that I was moving, he'd had similar news about himself.

'I phoned my father yesterday and told him I am coming home,' he'd said, with an improvement on his habitual smile.

It seemed things had come to a head if Frederick, Foamy and I were simultaneously leaving Tshidi in the position she probably wanted to begin with, where she could downsize on the large dosage of *muti* she was rumoured to be giving her husband on a daily basis, because she would have him all to herself.

'I mean, imagine if I need to water the garden and Frederick is sleeping in my room,' Nigger said.

I hadn't noticed a garden outside the little house, so for a moment I looked at him in astonishment. Far smaller than the typical government homes in the area, and with a flat roof, I certainly hadn't seen a hosepipe lying on the lawn. Nigger didn't seem the type to mix gardening with weightlifting.

'There are many gardens to water here and the job keeps me very busy,' said Nigger, triggering the beginnings of a vague understanding on my part. 'When one of the women in the neighbourhood asks me to water her garden I won't be able to do it in front of the Burundian,' Nigger added, smiling as the recognition of what he was implying came over my face.

'Ah,' I said. 'How many girlfriends do you have?'

'I don't have even one,' said Nigger, taking the empty plate from my hand. 'I lived for a long time with a Kosa girl. Then one day I went to the shop and when I came back she was gone. With my television, stove, money ... so all I do is water their gardens. After that they must go and never return.'

Having placed both plates on the tiny sink alongside the stove, he made his way, with quick strides, to the other side of the lounge, where he lifted the weight from the floor and lay down on the bench. He hooked his legs under the sides of the contraption, which creaked dangerously under his mass. After sucking a deep breath of air into his lungs, Nigger's chest expanded as he began jabbing the air with the weight. But for the minuscule hint of red in his very black face, one could easily have been fooled into thinking that what he was gripping in his hands was in fact made of plastic. This was the first time I had seen his face so transformed. Before, no matter whether I'd looked at it from the front or the side, I'd always felt that Nigger had a face that was very difficult to describe. Perhaps if anyone in Hollywood had ever believed there would have been profit to be made from a movie featuring a black Superman, then Nigger could have played the lead role. For while his features were rather nondescript, his look as a whole was a black version of Clark Kent.

Now, with his cheeks puffed up and his eyes bulging from the strain, he was almost unrecognisable. I didn't count how many times he pumped the weight, but when he was finished some time had passed.

'Beans and ganja,' was all Nigger said, as he prowled this way and that across the room, beating his chest and biceps violently with his fists.

Later, after Nigger had put his hands to the bar to enable me to do some weightlifting of my own, we walked down the road to Vovo Cash Store. Each of the three girls who passed us was greeted by the same expulsion of air from my friend. It wasn't because of the beans that we'd eaten, but Nigger's first step in the garden-watering process.

'Phewww …' he would say, coughing into his hand.

Embarrassed, I wondered how we must have looked walking the streets – the short, massively built *kwerekwere* and a tall, thin white man. As we crossed over an empty plot and reached the pavement of Ntlazane Road, a police

155

car answered my question. We narrowly missed being hit as it screeched to a halt on the pavement where we had been standing just seconds before. Nigger's hands were up in the air long before mine.

'Lift your arms,' one of the two black officers shouted at me.

The other, who'd alighted from the passenger side, was already working on Nigger. After they'd given us a brisk, full body search, they drove off.

'Motherfucking Kosas,' said Nigger.

The Snort

The routine I had developed in my new home was certainly not of my own design. In truth, however, it would have been quite contrary to my own, instinctive wishes for maximum comfort and limited responsibility on the home front, to have fought against the helpful and friendly current that had swept me up in its arms. While Nowie cooked dinners fit for a king, Thabiso came in and out of her shack at the back of the house to make my bed, wash my clothes and scrub the dishes. It had been just three weeks since Nigger and I had carried my meagre belongings from my old room in the dead of night, but already I could see a healthy swelling around my waist and a rosy chubbiness in my cheeks.

I had not even bothered to tell Tshidi and Molefe of my imminent departure, instead asking Foamy to convey to them a curt farewell. It had been an entirely different affair saying goodbye to my good friend Foamy, who was due to depart for the Free State two days later. We'd laughingly recalled the good times we'd had together, among them the occasion on which he had taught me to cook chicken feet, hearts and heads and our countless visits to Kefu's Place, one of which had ended with me staring confusedly at the toes of his shoes jutting up in the air, his hips straddled by a pretty Sotho girl.

'I'll write you a letter after I arrive back at my father's house,' he said, since he didn't have a cellphone. 'I'll ask Molefe to give it to Steve at Vovo Cash Store so he can pass it on to you.'

It made sense that we keep in touch, not least because we had spent so many hours sharing our experiences as relative outsiders to Khaya, where the Xhosa culture reigned supreme.

As we waved farewell to Foamy, Nigger and I could barely see him from under the huge mattress we carried atop our heads. My new living space was fully furnished, and I'd seen no need to ask Lisa to transport the mattress there when Nigger so obviously needed it more than I. The two of us had already carried everything else up to Nowie's place an hour before, so it was our second journey of the night. After placing the awkward load in Nigger's lounge, we made our way to Ngqangqolo Street. Nowie had invited my Kenyan friend over for dinner.

Nigger had become a regular visitor, one who arrived at unpredictable times and sat quite silently watching television with us, his lips only moving when a question came his way.

Living in such close proximity to a Xhosa family was not only delightful for the way I was so quickly accepted, but I soon reverted to being something of a child, as if I was being pampered for the very first time.

I also became aware of certain cultural differences between myself and my new family, noticing the stern, yet silent respect that was shown towards various members of the household. Nowie was revered as the head of the home while I, being the only white person, was seen as the key to an understanding of white people as a whole.

Little Pamela's shyness in my company soon began to abate when I joined in some of the games played by her and her friends. Babalwa, at seventeen, quickly regarded me as an endless supply of knowledge. I was sorry to disappoint her so often; failing on numerous occasions to explain a particularly difficult mathematics equation or science experiment she'd been taught at school. Having fairly recently arrived at the age where she had begun to attract the attention of boys, who regularly set her cellphone ringing or waited discreetly for her down the road, Babalwa was well aware of her beauty and had developed a way of moving and an eloquence that suggested she might be a bit of a tart. However, it soon became clear that she had inherited her mother's quick, yet quiet intelligence and good humour, perhaps without the cynicism that so often comes with age. Not wanting to be thought uncouth, I decided to refrain from asking Babalwa about the pinkie on her left hand, which appeared to have been sliced off at its first knuckle. But I soon began to mimic her thick Xhosa accent, which went so beautifully with her chubby lips and huge brown eyes. On my return from the station on weekdays, she was the first person I saw each day, her slim body leaning up against the seat of a couch and bored eyes staring blankly at a page in a school book on the carpet before her.

'Hau aah yoo?' she would ask, looking up as I walked in

the door.

'In what way do you mean?' I would reply, faithfully following her prompt.

'Physicaally, emotionaally and psychologicaally,' Babalwa responded, as if the words belonged to her language rather than mine.

This never failed to produce hysterical laughter from both of us.

There were other small differences in my new accommodation, each peculiar and new to me. The smell of the house, which I'd experienced in homes all over the township, had embedded within it a rich earthiness that I have only ever been able to describe as 'the township smell'. It was neither pungent nor obtrusive, but it was there nonetheless, as foreign to me as an olive, or glass of red wine consumed for the first time. It is hard to know what the source of this smell is, but far easier to come to terms with the fact that research into the subject would probably not be seen as a worthy part of nation building in the new South Africa. Also, I have never had the opportunity to sniff white and coloured people (and their homes) through the nose of a Xhosa person.

What I do know for sure, however, is that it wasn't long before both my room and I must have begun to smell the same as the rest of the house and its inhabitants, because soon I couldn't discern it at all. While I didn't ponder too long on the issue, I developed the idea that the odour probably had something to do with diet, hair products and Sunlight soap.

The township snort was a very different kettle of fish altogether. Although at the time I would have put it down to culture and called it, as I had with the smell, 'the township snort', in later years I heard it almost daily in the Netherlands and most other parts of northern Europe as I sat down to dinner with friends, walked down a pavement, or waited for a bus, tram or train.

I am sure that if the folks at the Oxford Dictionary were pushed to pen a definition for it, this is pretty much how it would look: 'A short, sharp, powerful intake of breath through the nose, in order to engineer a nauseating and thorough clean-up of the nasal cavities, throat and brain.'

Wherever and whenever I have heard it, it has never failed to induce a reaction in me so ghastly that I have been forced to retreat quickly to a quiet place nearby to battle with the demon of nausea. It is not so much the sound itself – and all the images of snot and phlegm it conjures up – but the suddenness of its arrival that makes me start. Notwithstanding the many times I was exposed to it in the company of Nowie, Thabiso, Babalwa and Pamela, among most of my other Xhosa friends, there was one particular occasion when I heard it in class that I shall never forget.

Thulani, a very capable fellow student who had been one of two peers to join me for our internship at the newspaper, was sitting in front of me that day. Although not usually cause for any concern, a brief pause in the lecturer's speech, I realised afterwards, had been the signal for the tremendous intake of breath through the nose. It was so loud that I considered diving for cover; Thulani's unbelievably rapid, ferocious snort actually shook my desk. It was not so much the snort itself, but the contrast of its thunderous sound with the relative silence that preceded it that later stuck in my mind. After a yelp of terror from me, he turned around with a look of innocence that only magnified my disgust. I sat there, retching in silent horror, while our lecturer continued with her line of thought.

Apart from such minor irritations, my routine at Nowie's house began to echo that of my youth. With the mother of the house once again taking care of my every need, I would take long baths, lying back and staring into space for minutes at a time, only leaning forward every so often to add more hot water to my pleasant reverie. Since my room was nestled in between those of my new family, it was always warm, which meant that for the first time in months I was not forced to race for a towel after bathing, shivering and cursing the cold.

The dinners of pap with red meat, chicken bought still flapping outside the iLitha Park station and a variety of beans meant that I saved much of the money I would otherwise have spent on snacks, meat and takeaways. Now I developed the habit of purchasing a single item of fruit, usually an apple or orange, from hawkers who rode the trains I took to the Technikon. In addition, I often bought one of the little, see-through packets of peanuts they sold. Mzondi, on one of the many days on which he accompanied me to work, had been astonished to see me eating the nuts with their shells still on and deftly taught me how to remove them in the local way. Rubbing a group of them together between the palms of his hands, he intermittently blew quick gusts of air at the pile, which would send the shells flying, until eventually the brownness of the nuts was entirely replaced by a new and inviting paleness.

I noticed rather happily that Nowie and her family used toilet paper, accustomed as I had become to regularly having to toss a page of newspaper, after reading it from top to bottom, into the bowl beneath my bum. I'd gone through a variety of publications in past months, but the most popular, probably because they were free, were *City Vision* and *Vukani*. While rubbing various parts of the page together to soften them, I would inevitably think of a good friend's joke. Tarzan, the editor of *City Vision*, had emailed it to me.

In the throes of that particularly special sexual ecstasy created by oral sex – the joke went – John and Nosizwe were pleasing each other simultaneously.

'Hey, Nosizwe,' John paused for a moment.

'Yes, John,' replied Nosizwe, huskily.

'Did you know that last year President Mbeki spent five hundred million rand on the treatment of Aids patients?'

'No, John,' replied Nosizwe, her voice unsteady.

After around thirty seconds John turned his head slightly to one side.

'Hey, Nosizwe,' he said, temporarily dragging her away from her bliss. 'Do you know that Trevor Manuel has been offered a very good position at the World Bank?'

'No, John, I didn't know that,' replied Nosizwe, a little put out by his conversation at a time like this. 'This is all very interesting, John, but why are you telling me this now?' she asked.

'Nosizwe, my baby,' he said, 'the front page of *Vukani* is stuck to your bum.'

On my new train route to the Technikon I often met up with fellow journalism students, like the charming Noluthando and the lovely Nolizwe, at the Bonteheuwel changeover, or as they embarked at Site B and Site C stations. Whether in the company of friends or not, the trip presented a fashion show the likes of which I had never witnessed before. While the guys were dressed in pants and shoes of a quality that left me feeling like an ex-MK cadre who had forgotten to remove his gear after 1994, the women, with their shapely bodies and sexy walks, often caused prolonged gawking on my part. Cellphones rang all the time, their owners talking loudly over the clanging of the train wheels. Also unusual on the train, especially for one who had never seen this in his local shebeen, were the lively conversations between the sexes, all of them aspiring professionals on the way to cementing their careers.

On weekday mornings Nowie would accompany me down Ngqangqolo Street, providing little stories about her employer in Claremont, whose house she cleaned three times a week. Or she would complain about John, my Ghanaian hairdresser, with whom, to my amazement, she had a relationship of sorts. I was surprised at the way Nowie spoke about him far more than by the fact that John sometimes actually slept in my new house. I have always been suspicious of the motives of women who share with me details of their relationship with another man, so it wasn't long before I got the hint. The feeling I'd had during our first encounter turned out to be true; it seemed Nowie was gunning for me. Since I was certainly not attracted to her, and she was ten years my senior, I regarded this as improper behaviour and did my best to cut it short.

Then one evening a distinct feeling of being trapped came over me as Nowie, sitting at my side in front of the TV, launched into a conversation about *muti*. My experience of Tshidi's hold over Molefe had certainly led me to look upon the practice with less cynicism, but this didn't mean I wanted to discuss *muti* at length. Nowie's mother, I'd been told by Lisa, was a sangoma, but I'd felt secure in the knowledge that the dreams that call one to the healing trade aren't necessarily hereditary. Feeling increasingly unsettled, I'd listened as the conversation between Thabiso, Nowie and Babalwa moved in the direction of love potions. Nigger sat silently, his eyes glued to the television screen.

'There is a lot you can do if you want someone to fall for you,' said Nowie, lifting an edge of her skirt from where it had been resting on one of the gold-coloured knobs on the couch.

'Yes, there is lot you can do,' echoed Thabiso, adjusting the volume of the television set to mute.

'Reaaally, it is true,' said Babalwa.

'If you love a man,' said Nowie, looking at me in a way that suggested she had considerable experience in this field, 'there are many things you can do.'

I shifted my gaze to the window: night had fallen.

'There are many women who go to the sangoma for special herbs,' she continued, oblivious to my discomfort. 'But there are also other ways.'

'There are many other ways,' said Thabiso, nodding her head up and down vigorously.

'One of them is to add the saliva from your tongue to the herbs from the sangoma,' explained Nowie, glancing at me again.

'Excuse me?'

'You take a knife and scrape a few coatings of saliva from your tongue and put it in his food,' said Nowie, sticking out her tongue, and drawing an imaginary blade down its length, 'and in a few days he will be yours. You can tell him to do anything and he will do it.' She clapped her hands twice for emphasis.

My empty plate on the dining room table caught my

eye. Feeling a great wave of nausea rising from the depths of my belly, I wondered how the person who usually prepared my food could say something as disturbing as this. I'd never been opposed to herbal remedies and traditional cures, but the idea of eating a mouthful of chicken and rice with a few millilitres of saliva mixed in left me with a terrible sensation of revulsion.

Peering over at Nigger I saw that he was smiling widely, although it was hard to discern whether he was reacting to the stupidity of the story, or its accuracy. Even if the former was the case, it would have done nothing to allay my fears that I had possibly, over the course of the several evenings of my stay thus far, swallowed a couple of cups of saliva. Perhaps I was overreacting, I thought, as I recalled some of the wonderful meals I had guzzled down; surely a person doing something so revolting would never tell her victim of her plan, however obliquely. The only meal I hadn't enjoyed had been the pap and *ithumbu*. While the latter – the intestines – didn't taste bad once on the plate, as they boiled vigorously away in the pot for hours, the house would be filled with the unmistakable pong of faeces.

I'd spoken to Xola, the minister at the local church, about my dislike of the dish, an opinion he had reacted to at length. He told me that meat was a sign of status in the Xhosa culture and that most families would do everything they could to have meat on the table in the evenings, even if it was in the form of intestines, feet, or stomach lining. But it was that smell of faeces that had given me the courage on two occasions to decline my dinner on account of a tummy ache.

With regard to her saliva-spiking tale, I decided not to pass unfair judgement on Nowie. I nevertheless recognised

166

what I saw as a definite pattern in her words and actions; I was by now convinced that her design for me was one that would eventually see me trapped under the covers of her bed. Therefore, each morning that I knew she was working I stole quickly and quietly from the house before she could join me for the walk.

Luvuyo

My move from my room near the station to Ngqangqolo Street heralded a new and unexpected revelation. Even my new local shebeen, Themba's Tavern, was affected by the sedate atmosphere of the surrounding streets. I began to get an idea of what it must feel like for someone accustomed to living in a township to move into the suburbs. While I am sure that for many who choose to follow this route, the privacy and relative quiet must at first feel like a godsend, I very soon became bored and I missed the contagious friendliness on the streets around Vovo Cash Store. There, we had all greeted each other on a daily basis, but in my new territory there were some pedestrians who walked by me without showing any real enthusiasm for returning my greetings. The physical cold of my old room had been replaced by a relative iciness on the streets around my new home.

Themba's Tavern – owned by a tall, undoubtedly wealthy and handsome taxi boss, who was always formally dressed and jovial in a reserved manner – was a disappointment. Pool games unfolded in relative silence and, no matter how hard Nigger and I tried to introduce some spontaneity to its vibe, the tavern reminded me of those many nightspots in Cape Town that one never feels comfortable visiting alone. Only one of its patrons made an impression on me: a wrinkled old man whom everyone called Madala (grandfather). With his mischievous sense of humour, Madala would somehow manage to keep up a running commentary through each and every pool game, commenting on each player's attire and what he usually proclaimed were his non-existent skills. Sips from a glass or beer bottle were described as, 'He takes another sip', while lighting a cigarette towards the end of a game was interpreted as, 'The *mlungu* has become nervous'.

I often wondered how long it would take Madala, who was the grandfather in a family that lived in the street behind mine, to realise that his humour and jovial character would never have any effect on the businesslike and gloomy mood that we were to no small extent the victims of.

So it wasn't long before I began to crave the easy familiarity and untidy comfort of Vovo Cash Store. It was this longing that had taken me there one Saturday afternoon. Although I am the type who is easily overcome by teary nostalgia, I was still surprised that it had taken me only a couple of weeks to miss the place. Everyone was there: Zane with a matchstick in his mouth and the smart, light brown jacket I had given him; Biza, who always managed to park his car so close to the garage door that its bumper appeared to be touching the pool table; and Steve and his pretty daughter Yoli, who was serving the many familiar faces arriving all at once. Little groups had begun to form around the clusters of quarts assembled, as always, on any available space – atop the white plastic table, on the floor, or in the dust to one side of Biza's car.

It was a mild winter's day, an exception to the rule of miserable winter weather, and ordered for the right day exactly. The little groups weren't adhering to strict rules of participation, with various members of the noisy huddles sometimes leaning backwards, or to one side, to listen in on the discussions of their fellow customers. Now and then someone would agree or disagree with what another was saying, producing a feeling that everyone here counted; each man could have his say. Most had completed a week of hard work, had bosses to complain about, sons to brag about, wives and daughters to be proud of. Zane and I kept our eyes on our one rand coins, at the back of a long queue on the side of the pool table. I'd cut short a plan to go to town, deciding rather to get up to date with the friends I hadn't seen for far too long.

Tubby and Happy, two local tsotsis who somehow always managed to sniff me out when I had money, had just left the spot where they had been waiting for me across the road, after which Steve had given me his usual lecture through the bars above the beer counter.

'Why do you always give those guys money?' he said, in the stern tone of voice that always accompanied his regular, fatherly advice.

'It's only once a month,' I replied, 'and you know that we have to share with each other.'

'I know that,' said Steve, 'but those guys are skollies. Right now they are buying Mandrax with that money. Soon they will have smoked it away.'

I told Steve about the night I had narrowly escaped being robbed by them. Because Mzondi had to attend one of his many appointments with his lovers, I'd had to walk home from Kefu's Place on my own. This was nothing new to me and, besides, iLitha Park slept early, leaving the streets almost entirely deserted. With beer in my sails and that warm glow of contentment that the jazz bar never failed to invoke in me, I'd cut quickly through a few side streets, until I'd come out in Ntlazane Road. I always felt safe when I reached this point of the walk, since I was close to home and the road was wide and well lit, bordered on one side by houses and on the other by municipal buildings and land. I'd slowed my pace.

With most of the lights in the houses switched off and the odd sound of an accelerating car far away, I felt I had the streets to myself. It is at times like this that some of my more strange behaviour surfaces, seeing me skipping up and down, or clicking the top and bottom teeth on the right side of my mouth as my left leg moves over a crack in the tar. Although perhaps not an example of full-blown obsessive compulsive disorder, when I fail to get the timing just right, or accidentally touch the crack with the toe or heel of my boot, I require myself to take a few steps back and repeat the movement.

As I slowly neared the turn into Ntlakohlaza Street, with my room just four houses down, I noticed the three tsotsis. It was not just their habit of striking in the hours of darkness that backed up their reputation for being the lords of the streets at night, but also the speed at which they moved. These three, coming from the direction of my home, were lapping up the ground between us rapidly, with the silhouettes of their assorted hats extending up into the air above them. The swaying movement of their legs and hips immediately revealed the nature of their menacing trade.

They'd obviously spotted me, because they quite suddenly swung out across the road, heading directly into my path. I didn't have much time to think, but it was enough to know that fleeing would be a futile exercise and, in a strange kind of way, some form of admission of guilt – as if I had announced myself as a target. So I adjusted my direction quickly, showing them I was not afraid and planned to meet up with them earlier than they'd originally intended.

One of them, who was wearing a tall, black top hat, was mumbling softly to his two companions who flanked him on either side, in what sounded like tsotsitaal, his right hand reaching deep into an inside pocket on the left side of his coat.

Although there is no limit to the time one can spend wondering what one's reaction will be to staring down the barrel of a gun, when the possibility nears the point of becoming a reality, a combination of blind fear and raging adrenalin slows the whole process down, in much the same way as music slows after a sniff of glue. This in turn makes seconds feel like years. I had already entered this frame-by-frame progression by the time I noticed the one with the top hat removing his hand from his jacket; it was empty.

'*Au*, Slim Shady,' he said. 'You gave us a fright.' He extended his hand towards me.

'Shit, Tubby!' I shouted, my voice trembling.

I was unable to hide my relief.

'I should have recognised your hat. *Heita*, Happy,' I said, shaking his companion's hand.

I silently thanked God that I'd remembered their names. 'I'm Steve,' I said to tsotsi number three, who introduced himself as Tsolo.

'*Eish*,' said Tubby, turning to Tsolo and adjusting his top hat to reveal his eyes, 'This is not Steve, this is Slim Shady.'

'What does your name mean?' asked Happy, his permanent smile hinting at the origin of his nickname.

'Steve comes from an English king ...'

'No, man. Slim Shady,' Tubby cut in.

'Because I am a South African version, it has a different meaning to Eminem's,' I said, suddenly sounding quite expert on a topic I knew nothing about. '"*Slim*", as you know, means clever in Afrikaans,' I said, my relief translating itself into a sudden and uncontrollable flow of words. '"Shady" refers to my criminal ways.'

Clutching at their stomachs and laughing wildly, the three did a little jig in front of me. I couldn't help wondering what it would be like to be robbed by Happy, and then having to explain to a policeman that he'd been smiling rather pleasantly throughout. Still holding their bellies, they relieved me of a cigarette and went on their way.

After that I had felt almost indebted to them, so whenever they picked up the scent of cash on me and hung around outside the shebeen, I would go out, exchange a few pleasantries and give them twenty rand. Steve, who had made it clear to them and all the other dodgy youngsters in the area that they were not allowed to enter his establishment, did not let the story influence him.

'You should have beaten them up,' he said, 'not given them a cigarette. These *kwedinis* are not even men; they must still go to the bush.'

Knowing that Steve would never see it any other way, I agreed with him.

Returning to Zane's side at Vovo's, I noticed that he was still watching over our coins protectively. After placing the beers on the floor I saw that Nigger had arrived during my absence, taking his customary position against one wall.

'You want some Jesus Juice?' I offered him my glass.

'I don't drink from a glass,' he said, lifting a half full bottle of Black Label from the dusty ground at Zane's feet and taking a long swig.

Just then the solidly built Biza, who had the massive head of a bull, edged between us and the pool table. We had met awkwardly. I had written a piece for the paper about a teacher who had been suspended for allegedly sleeping with a fifteen-year-old pupil. He was that teacher, although he swore that he'd been set up and blackmailed. I would never know the truth and now we got along fine.

'Luvuyo,' he addressed me by my Xhosa name, 'do you have a *bhabhalaza*?'

'Yes,' I admitted. 'Last night I had quite a few quarts, but today's beer is helping.'

'There is only one real solution for a *bhabhalaza*,' Biza said, handing me a yellow tinted glass.

At the bottom of it about two tots of a foamless, golden liquid that I identified as brandy was swirling nastily around.

'No way,' I shuddered, pulling a face. 'You know I don't drink hot stuff.'

'You must,' he said, leaving me no choice but to enter that warm, reckless world of intoxication by hard liquor.

'We must sing today,' said Biza, loudly enough for all to hear. 'Luvuyo,' he smiled at me, 'you must start.'

My Xhosa name had actually been chosen some years before, during the three years that I worked for Volkswagen South Africa. It was there, in my position as a material handler and later a forklift truck driver, that I had made my first real contact with black people. This was also where I had had my first experience of the popular township game of checkers. Never managing to develop any real skill at the game, I was named after my happy, seemingly unperturbed reaction to my countless defeats during lunch hour. In truth, I had just become so used to losing that I really didn't care.

Literally translated into 'joy', the name Luvuyo had stuck. Many years later, finding myself in a township with thousands of Xhosa people, I had been designated a large number of new names. Covering a multitude of words in the Xhosa dictionary, their very different meanings reflected the diversity of the ways in which different individuals saw me. The names all had one thing in common, though; they were complimentary, except for the odd one given in jest, like 'he who likes to drink', or 'the one who is without a girlfriend'. To those who christened me with a new name, I always explained that I had been named Luvuyo many years before, so it had caught on again, until very soon I was reacting to it as though it had been given to me at birth.

Lifting my chin, I now launched into 'Asimbonanga', one of my favourite African songs. While in the original chant Johnny Clegg's lead singing is backed by a number of deep Zulu voices, our own version had one major difference: the lead singer was also white, but the chorus was sung by a large number of Xhosa men, in a vast variety of tones.

'*Asiimbonangaa,*' I stretched out the word.

'*Asimbonang uMandela tina, laphekona, laphehlelikona,*' the powerful chorus followed.

Looking around as I sang on, I saw that there was not a single man who had not joined in; even young Yoli was mouthing the words from the bar where she was serving a customer. In a scenario so typical of the Xhosa people, out of the twenty or so patrons, only one or two were unable to hold the tune, but even their voices, which were balanced out by brilliant harmonies from other, more skilful singers, added a mysterious and moving lilt to the rich melody. As I have said, I am easily overcome by tears and it was particularly difficult for me to get through the verses dry-eyed, and I had to concentrate all my efforts on keeping control of my emotions. Once before Zane had lectured me that 'an African man doesn't cry' and I could see him watching me closely. I always felt an incredible freedom when we sang like this, a practice that had become more and more frequent in Vovo Cash Store. As we reached the end of the chorus, Zane launched into my next favourite song, which he and some friends had taught me a few weeks before.

'Wena nawe Umkhonto, Umkhonto, Umkhonto weSizwe,' he began, as everywhere voices joined in with zest.

'Tina nawe, tina nawe Umkhonto, Umkhonto, Umkhonto weSizwe.'

A song for the old military wing of the African National Congress, everyone there that day was old enough to remember the words. For me, it was a song from a struggle I'd never been a part of, one that, if I closed my eyes and joined in the passion of my brothers, I could very nearly see.

'Uit die blou van onse hemel,' I started, just as the song ended.

Although there was quite a bit of laughter throughout, all my friends sang the words with an enthusiasm no less genuine to that shown to the earlier song.

A Criminal in the Family

'I really have the feeling that she likes you,' I told Nigger, who was standing up after yet another lengthy set of bench presses.

I regarded it as a miracle of sorts that the rickety old bench hadn't collapsed, knowing that the day it did, Nigger would probably require urgent hospitalisation.

'Do you think she's nice?' I asked, as he prowled this way and that about his lounge, patting and flexing his muscles.

'Yes, man, I will water her garden any time,' he replied, much to my delight.

'In fact, I am sure that she feels the same way about you,' I lied.

'She told you?'

'No,' I answered truthfully, 'but you can see it by the way she looks at your body.'

What I was doing was a fairly normal response to Nowie's flirtations, which had up until now been focused solely in my direction. The chief target on a variety of fronts, I had developed a defence strategy that included the few tools I had at my disposal. On a number of evenings I had adopted the manner of one who is distracted, fitfully joining in the conversation that unfolded in Nowie's lounge and regularly glancing at my cellphone with an expression of mild impatience.

'Are you waiting for a call?' Nowie asked, the first time I put my plan into action.

'Not really,' I replied, relying on the natural curiosity of my female companions.

'Is it a lady?' Babalwa asked.

'Mmm ...' I said, absent-mindedly.

'Come on, Steve, you can tell us,' said Thabiso, who was by then leaning forward on her couch and looking intently at me, quite blatantly inquisitive.

'Well, actually,' I said, thinking the time was right, 'there is this girl Vuyo. She is studying fashion at the Technikon. She lives in Harare.'

'Is she very beautiful?' asked Babalwa.

'Very,' I said, looking from her to Nowie, who seemed not in the least bit interested.

'You must bring her here so we can meet her,' Nowie said, moving her gaze from the television to me. 'Tell her she is welcome here any time.'

I was not expecting a phone call from Vuyo at all. Although I had regularly climbed the stairs to the fashion class in the early afternoons to spend time with her and her friends, we hadn't made any further arrangements to see each other away from the Technikon.

Except for the soccer game, that is. Vuyo's uncle, who did promotional work for the Kaizer Chiefs football club, had, through Vuyo, sent me an invitation to join him and the family at the screening at a clubhouse in Nyanga of a live Sunday game between his favourite team, debatably the country's best, and the Moroka Swallows.

Since I had never been educated into developing a love for South African league football, my main reason for accepting his offer had much to do with my feelings for his niece. But the game was still two weeks away and, despite my need to love and be loved, which was intensifying on a weekly basis, I had managed to put my feelings for Vuyo on hold for some time in the hope that they would eventually fizzle out altogether. But sitting on the workshop bench in her class, where she stylishly cut and sewed material of different shades and patterns, I was constantly visited by a sensation of wonder at her devastating beauty, only lightly concealed by a simple pair of faded jeans and a rather plain T-shirt.

I always needed to remember, when in conversation with her, that there were things to say and questions to be answered which, if left unsaid, would have drawn her attention to the clearly palpable heat that I so readily succumbed to in her presence.

It was not without a stab of guilt that I was using her, without her knowing anything about it, to rid myself of Nowie's attentions. Whether or not I was interpreting the signals from the mother of the house accurately was not at issue. Rather, it was the irritation that began to build up in me as I gradually began to get the feeling that I had been latched on to by a lovesick puppy.

The partly fabricated story of Vuyo had helped to a certain degree. An almost appropriate distance had developed between Nowie and me, with my landlady's complaints about her boyfriend (and my hairdresser) John, dissipating almost entirely. Whereas before she had been loath to admit that John actually slept in her bed, often telling me she had banished him to the guest room, Nowie now no longer bemoaned the existence of their relationship. I felt happy for John, a straight-up guy who worked long hours snipping hair in his iron container, a good man who deserved better treatment.

Then, just when I had become convinced that I would be left alone, Nowie had said something to me that made me realise the need for a new approach to my problem.

'The day I find another man, anyone,' she'd said one morning as we walked to the iLitha Park station, 'I'll kick that *kwerekwere* out of my house.'

The smile that followed her words brought me quickly to my senses, leaving no doubt in my mind that nothing had changed. It had been a mistake to let my guard down and resume walking to the station with her; talking about Vuyo had done nothing to deter her advances. It was a natural reaction, I felt, to be driven to reciprocate Nowie's unjustifiable behaviour with a clever scheme of my own.

'I am sure that she likes you, Nigger,' I said again, above the creaking of the bench, as he lay back on it and gripped the bar in his hands, 'and Nowie is always portraying John in a negative light.'

'What do you mean?' he enquired, dropping the weight to his chest and turning his face towards me.

'She seems very unhappy with him,' I said.

'I don't care about that guy,' said Nigger, taking a deep breath and holding it, taking me back to the disagreement we'd had an hour earlier.

I'd told Nigger that it didn't make sense to hold one's

breath throughout a whole set of presses. Rather, I'd said, it would seem sensible to inhale each time he lifted the weight, providing desperately needed oxygen to his muscles.

'Does it look like my strategy isn't working, my brother?' Nigger had replied, touching a finger to his biceps and chest.

Over the weeks I'd come to know Nigger well. His habit of being vague slowly melted away as we earned each other's trust. I soon began to realise that he was engaged in some form of illegal business, although at first its precise nature remained a mystery. He always had what he called 'a deal' coming. The deals saw him disappearing for a day or two, during which time his neighbours would express their ignorance as to his whereabouts, saying only that he had been away for some time. Then, a night or two later, I would find Nigger standing with a bottle of Jesus Juice in Vovo Cash Store, looking as if he'd never left.

'I had a deal,' he would explain nonchalantly.

But as the weeks passed and I began to earn his trust, the nature of his deals gradually came to light. Most of the times that he accompanied me from his house to Ngqangqolo Street we would stop off at the home of two friends of his. Richard and Nick were Tanzanians, which meant the three conversed in Swahili, the widely spoken central African language and Nigger's native tongue. But here and there I would pick up an English word or two, until one day I confronted Nigger about my suspicions. Finally, he explained that he was sometimes paid to keep watch while his friends sat in a sewer under a street in Woodstock, from where they provided a bridge connection for international phone calls for a number of clients. Often up to their knees in faeces, the two would sometimes spend two days at a time breathing in the deleterious fumes that hung over them. Nigger's reason for giving me these details soon became clear.

'If you want to speak to your girlfriend in Holland, then they can organise it very cheap,' he said.

I'd turned the offer down, but saw the news value in what the three of them were doing. During my stint as a journalist, our brilliant crime reporter had published information that he had obtained from the police about this form of criminal activity, but my friendship with Nigger, Richard and Nick presented an entirely new angle to the story. I therefore asked my Kenyan friend if he would try to convince the two Tanzanians to let me interview them for a freelance piece about the work from the thief's perspective. After all, they had a fascinating 'job', one which saw them spending their days on ventures into manholes in different parts of Woodstock, and the task of organising a weighty list of clients, who paid rather reduced prices for links mostly to other countries in Africa.

I was also drawn in by the gentlemanly ways of Richard and Nick; they were both tall, good-looking guys who were always smartly dressed and impeccably well-mannered.

I had never before had a criminal in my own family, blessed as we were with superior resources when it came to education and the like, and had noticed how brilliantly the TV drama series 'Yizo Yizo' reflected the very different situation in the townships, where in many families having at least one criminal element is a raw reality.

I therefore felt that a close look at the minds involved in the theft of telephone hours, along with a moment by moment account of what the filthy work actually entailed, would enlighten readers to the personalities behind the trade. But Nigger's promise to ask Richard and Nick if they would let me interview them never materialised and I never got to know them well enough – our visits to their house were always very brief – to ask them myself. And of course it would not be in their interests to divulge publicly – and therefore to the police – the more intricate technicalities of their work.

Soon I began to unravel a little of the mystery behind Nigger's past. One day Nigger told me that he had been a drug dealer when he first arrived in Cape Town. Since for many of the illegal immigrants in South Africa the options available for making a living are limited to criminal activities, I wasn't at all surprised at Nigger's confession. The first time I had heard this kind of story had been from an Angolan who worked in the suburbs as a waiter at a popular restaurant and bar. He told me that although he had been granted refugee status, he had wanted to get out of the church hall where he stayed in town and earn a living. The way he did this was a shock to me; he had spent month after month giving gay white men blow jobs, or allowing them to do the same to him. Pedro (not his real name), who was not himself homosexual, had imparted this information quite lightly, although he had moved quickly on to more pleasant topics. Apparently one of his regulars was a restaurant owner who took pity on him and offered him the position of waiter at the establishment he worked at when I knew him.

The way Nigger spoke about his drug dealing days

suggested that they'd had less to do with choice than with the hard reality of hunger and the need for clothing. Selling cocaine from the petrol station at the top end of Long Street, Nigger had been in the lower echelons of the Nigerian syndicate he worked for. However, one particular thing that Nigger said about that time had a very unpleasant effect on me.

'I fucked a lot of young white girls,' he told me, going on to explain how easy they were once they were hooked on the drug he pushed.

My reaction to this really perturbed me. I was not only disgusted with the fact that he had turned some of his clients into sex slaves; it was also the racial issue. After much soul searching, I still found it strange that after all my efforts to clear my mind of all forms of racial prejudice, what upset me most about Nigger's actions had more to do with him having sex with a white girl than anything else. But then, I decided, this is the core nature of racism. If you are a white man and you see a black guy with one of 'your' girls, you feel your pride has been threatened in some way. On the other hand, a white guy with a black girl has never been that much cause for concern.

Quite a few white men have asked me whether black men actually do have bigger penises, to which I have always replied that I have never felt the inclination to measure them. But this kind of speculation plays a large role in the white racist's attitude when he sees a black man with a pretty blonde girl.

The reaction towards me in Khayelitsha, where friends would regularly ignore my protests that I was already in a relationship and attempt to find me a black girlfriend, made me feel still more of a racist bigot. My reason for turning down their offers may have been due to my desire to be faithful, but many didn't see it that way. Instead, it was as if having a black girlfriend would be my final act of acceptance. Ironically, as an actual resident of a township, I often felt I had more of a right to fulfil my daily quota of the racism embedded deep within me during my youth. And because I had shown such an interest in my black countrymen, they allowed me to get away with it. Since I had shown my willingness to throw off the baggage of the past, the racist jokes that I now and then told my friends were always greeted with strident laughter.

But my reaction to what Nigger told me was no joke, so I kept it to myself, wondering just how long it would take for me to develop a set of completely non-racial morals.

And while selling drugs, or exchanging them for sex, is certainly far removed from what one would regard as noble behaviour, I remained Nigger's friend. Besides, for him, having sex with white girls – no matter the circumstances – had probably helped him regain some of his injured black pride, otherwise I am sure he would not have mentioned their race. Who was I to judge a person and his circumstances when I could never hope to have the faintest idea of what it was like to be him?

Positive Beliefs

I could see by the way the youngsters averted their eyes shyly one Wednesday evening that the minister of the local church was breaking some of their culture's taboos. Before the devastating and sudden arrival of HIV and Aids, the traditional silence on sex between the generations had probably not been damaging at all, but Pastor Xola had obviously come to realise that this trend needed an urgent overhaul.

He had arranged a talk for some young people by Ruth, a nurse who was HIV positive. Ruth spoke with a strength that appeared to come from something far bigger than herself. I have always been astounded by the faith of those who look certain death in the face, even when that death will come, as it inevitably does with full-blown Aids, slowly and with excruciating pain. It was as though the disease itself, which at that very moment was unhurriedly chipping away at her

Vovo Cash Store, where I first met Zane.

Defying gravity – a double-storey shack.

The soccer field between iLitha Park and Harare, where Nigger and I were held up.

Too few toilets to share – this boy waits for his friend while he uses a path.

*Looking out from my favourite spot in the garden of the
shack where I lived with S'bu.*

*A view out over iLitha Park, with Harare and the Indian Ocean
in the background.*

Some of my friends: Zane's 'hola 7' (above left), Ayanda and Banana outside Hlehle's Cool Spot (above right) and Nigger after beans, ganja and pumping iron (below).

immune system, would one day come to acknowledge the idea of an immortal soul which could never be destroyed in the same way as the body. This was the assertion that shone from the face of our speaker. Whether it poured from the God that Ruth so convincingly believed in, or was simply a reflection of her belief, it was a powerful force.

'You don't only get HIV when the boy's sperm goes into the girl's vagina,' she said, putting one finger through the loop created by an index finger and thumb. 'There are also other ways that many people don't know about. When the vagina is dry' – a few of the sixteen, seventeen and eighteen-year-olds around me blushed, while a particularly young girl sitting next to me giggled shyly into her hands – 'this can cause bleeding, which may also spread the virus.'

Lisa, who had picked me up and brought me along to the youth meeting, cast me a knowing glance. Lisa's face was tonight graced with a religious austerity that I found surprising in one usually so mischievous.

As Ruth continued speaking, I noticed that the boys' reaction was rather different from that of the girls. Many of their faces revealed a youthful eagerness at having the opportunity to hear these juicy facts about sex.

The lecture, in the little church room designated for Bible study group, had been launched with hugs all round.

'You cannot get HIV by embracing someone who has the disease,' Pastor Xola had explained.

In his introduction he had told us that Ruth was HIV positive and, as we'd each given her a warm hug, I could see the delight on her face. Not an unattractive woman, her plumpness and healthy facial skin, which her hair extensions brushed gently as she leaned into each embrace, suggested that Ruth was fighting the earliest stages of the virus with an overdose of vitamins and healthy food. It wasn't long before she began to speak of the importance of eating vegetables and fruit, but first she told us her story.

Happily married, she had paid no attention to the stories that abounded in her Harare neighbourhood of her husband's infidelity. Initially believing that they stemmed from jealousy on the part of her female companions, she had continued to make love to him whenever they felt the need. A couple of years later her husband fell sick; his health deteriorated rapidly and very soon he was dead. The cause of his death, as is so often the case with Aids victims, was put down to tuberculosis.

'Deep down I knew it must have been Aids,' she said, touching a hand to her breast, 'but I tried to push the thought from my mind.'

Then one of the women with whom her husband was rumoured to have had sex with died too, amid silent speculation. In the months before her death she had not left her shack and had grown increasingly thin. Painful festering sores had invaded her skin, while her diseased lungs – so it was whispered in the streets around her home – had sent her into uncontrollable spasms of coughing.

'It was then that I knew I had to do something,' said Ruth with resignation. 'So I went for the test.'

Having been diagnosed as a carrier of the virus, she decided to make the best of a bad situation. Against the advice of her relatives, who were concerned about the family's reputation, Ruth began to speak openly about her predicament. The therapeutic spin-off of doing this, she explained, far outweighed the reaction of the few who avoided her. The fact that some of the women in her neighbourhood began to approach her in confidence for information on how the virus was contracted and detected, made her feel certain that she had done the right thing.

'If one person in each neighbourhood is truthful about his or her status, then the cycle of death will begin to slow down,' Ruth said. 'In my case, for instance, men in my area know that they cannot sleep with me without using a condom.'

As the nurse launched into a simple, but precise, explanation of how HIV is spread, something which I knew well from some of the research for stories I had written during my time at the newspaper, I looked over at Pastor Xola. Here was a man who was prepared to risk the possible wrath of these youngsters' parents and a culture that had not previously needed or wanted to be open about sex. My own relationship with Xola, which had reached a level of honesty and intimacy where we both spoke our minds, had become one which I valued greatly.

What made him different from many of those who worked in religion was that he was a realist down to the bone. While he believed that the ideals of Christianity would be best served by his congregation adhering to celibacy outside of marriage, he told me that insistence on this would have been to blatantly disregard the reality. Instead, he had decided to come to terms with the fact that a sizeable proportion of his fellowship would have premarital sex, while there were still others who would fall prey to HIV through the unfaithfulness of their spouses.

This was what had driven him to invite Ruth to speak to the church youth, whose coyness and blushes were a small price to pay for an education that could one day save their lives.

Xola's vision for his church was not only focused on the well-being of its members. His dream, one for which he was forever searching for funding, saw his fellowship one day actively involved in the community. He wanted to set up container clinics for the ill, while a well-equipped sports stadium was needed to entice the youth away from the negative influences of gangsterism and drugs. Impressed from the outset by his character and verve, I regarded his interpretation of Christianity – in which its leaders lived by example and did not resort to bribing non-believers into submission with messages of hellfire – as nothing short of revolutionary.

What never failed to sadden me, however, was the general reaction to his plans for Khayelitsha. I went to a meeting that he and his church elders had organised for business and social leaders from the Cape Town community. Food and drink remained untouched on the tables, and I could see only the familiar church folk standing in the hall. It was not only the fact that almost every single invitation had been ignored that made me livid, but the thick disappointment that hung in the air, where usually there was joyful song, dance and prayer. This affected me so much that I left as soon as I could. I bumped into Xola as I was walking out the door. At first it appeared that he was standing there in a futile wait for late arrivals, but his eyes, lacking none of their usual glow, told me I was wrong.

'We will just have to work harder at this, Steve,' he said brightly, 'and eventually we will get it right.'

As I shook Xola's hand, I felt humbled that I had so quickly lost hope.

'Are there any questions?' Ruth asked, bringing me back to that Wednesday evening youth group.

There weren't any questions, although it was difficult to gauge if this was because Ruth had covered the topic of HIV and Aids so thoroughly, or whether the young people were just too shy to ask.

Holding hands in a circle, we sang two melodious gospel songs before Xola led us in prayer.

Bulelani and Punky

I had never before been into the massive informal settlement of Site B unaccompanied, and I was feeling apprehensive. I hoped that my brisk stride as I stepped from the train carriage and the stern expression on my face would go some way towards hiding my fear.

Walking quickly up the stairs to the exit from the train station, I returned the greetings of a number of fellow commuters who nodded and waved at me.

Fumanekile's directions had been accurate, I thought as I walked towards a huddle of shacks. I could see the taxi rank from up here, with its lively bustle and the sound of honking horns carried on the mild afternoon breeze.

I could not know then that in a few years' time Site B would be my home, but there was something about the raw life and soul of the place that mesmerised me. I reflected on how my impression of Fumanekile had changed since he had walked into our class that first day back at Technikon, late and dressed to kill. Literally. The time I spent with him between classes had been enough for me to realise that here was the kind of person one seldom has the privilege of meeting in a lifetime. Sincere and open, his pride was never translated into arrogance, because of a humility that was not only self-deprecating, but made one wonder if he ever found any time for himself.

Since that day, when he was wearing a stereotypical tsotsi outfit, complete with matchstick in the mouth, my perception of Fumanekile had done a full about-turn. The wide gaps between his teeth and the revolutionary beret that was his trademark had become more representative of his honest, open and sharing demeanour than anything else, while the respect he showed those around him often made me feel I had a lot of work to do with regard to my sometimes abrasive and selfish personality.

Here was a man my age who supported a family of five on a few hundred rand a month, earned through his grandmother's work as a domestic in Fishhoek and his meagre income from a story or two written for *City Vision* each week. Fumanekile had on numerous occasions invited me to share a meal with him, after remarking that he thought I had lost weight. He had not fathered any children, in accordance with the reality that this would only have added to the already weighty responsibility he carried on his shoulders. His family was not a family in the conventional sense of the word. Apart from his grandmother, sister and nephew, there was a young boy he had unofficially adopted. Ruu had stolen from him 'only once', Fumanekile had explained.

'That time I beat him up properly, so he will never do it

again.'

Fumanekile neither smoked nor drank, although he did confess to having done the latter in earlier years. In line with his sensible disposition, I heard him on numerous occasions lecturing some of our more promiscuous male classmates on the necessity of wearing a condom during sex.

As I came to know him better and to appreciate his accepting and tolerant ways, I began to realise that Fumanekile's character was perfectly suited to the field of journalism. I never once heard him judge anyone and whenever the loud-mouthed Thabo and I gossiped about a classmate, he would just shake his head and smile, refusing to take part in our malice.

My friendship with Fumanekile had in a very short time taught me two important things – that looks usually are deceiving and that the Theory of the One Good Black is bullshit. The latter is the mindset that espouses the view that once Nelson Mandela dies, South Africa will be plunged into anarchy. Although I have heard some say that the chaos will only come when his successor, Thabo Mbeki, leaves office, the two sub-theories remain part of the larger one – that there are just a handful of black men and women in our country who, because they are able to think like whites, are holding everything together. Once they are gone, the natural African way of things will return, leaving the poor whites to try to pick up the pieces, or flee for their lives.

This way of thinking comes from ignorance and stupidity, a combination that ruled our land for almost fifty years, and one that very nearly ruined the lot of us. And if, as white people, we continue to keep a distance between ourselves and the black man, how will we ever get to know him? How can we pass judgement on someone we don't know? There are thousands upon thousands of Ta-fumsas and Madibas out there, but we whites ignore them and do our best to encourage them to become the thugs we so desperately fear.

As I continued on my journey into Site B I reflected that the dust in Khayelitsha had at least one positive function. It served to soften the smell of urine in one's nostrils which on many occasions, in other parts of the township, I had found nauseating. Or perhaps it was the smell of meat from the stalls across the road from the taxi rank that was diluting the odour.

My friend's directions from the station took me along a jagged track lined with informal clothing stalls and single-roomed shack cafés. A hawker, smiling gleefully, raised his voice when he saw me: 'Sunglasses for the white man, sunglasses for the white man!' But I was quickly out of earshot. Another held out a piece of cloth in my face, although one of his clients voiced her disapproval.

'But the white man is rich,' the vendor said in English.

'Utheth'ikaka,' I said over my shoulder in tsotsitaal. 'You are talking shit.'

Nearby stall owners (including the big-mouth), their customers and the pedestrians walking alongside me laughed, and when I looked back the wise guy waved enthusiastically.

I took the next left turn into a wide street. This was where Fumanekile lived. There were many people walking in both directions and local residents were sitting or standing outside their homes. The shacks were neatly built and from every second or third one came the sound of music – kwaito, gospel and reggae were competing for listeners. I stopped beside a shack, ducked down and put my head through the door.

'I am looking for Ta-fumsa,' I said. 'He's a journalist.'

After a brief look of utter surprise at the sight of a white face, the woman who was stirring a pot of pap in the dark interior replied.

'He lives over there,' she said, pointing an arm in the opposite direction from which I had come.

Confusingly, her arm had initially pointed in one direction, before moving slowly towards another.

'Can you ask someone to take me there?' I asked, still puzzled by the sweeping movement of her arm.

'Alriiight, okaaay. Thulani!'

A little boy who looked about seven years old came running into the room from the back of the shack. When he saw me, he clung to his mother's legs, peering at me from behind her skirt.

'Umlungu,' I said, pulling a face at the shy child, who suddenly beamed with delight.

'Umlungu,' he repeated the word, nodding his head and looking up at his mother.

After she had given him instructions, I took the boy's little hand in mine and asked him to lead the way.

The two steps down into Fumanekile's lounge meant that the street outside was almost at eye level when I sat down.

'Hey Stevovo,' Ta-fumsa said, as I leaned back in my chair. 'What should we do? Do you want to meet the tsotsis?'

First, however, we visited Vuyani's tavern. It was empty when we arrived, but soon filled up with inquisitive people. Fumanekile came up with the idea that I should hire myself out to township shebeen owners, since my arrival at their establishment almost always had this effect. It wasn't so much the nature of this conversation, but the place where it happened that amazed me. The two of us were sitting on a bright yellow Metrorail third-class bench. Now I understood why I so regularly walked into windowless train carriages that had also been stripped of most of their seats.

The slant of Punky's stylish hat, pulled low over his face, made it difficult to see his eyes. His large, square, golden-rimmed sunglasses hid the beginning of a lumpy scar that edged down his bulbous left cheek. The smoothness of the skin on the other half of his face accentuated the effects of the pale blemish, hinting at the existence of two very different pasts.

The chunky nose that protruded from between the two light brown lenses was pockmarked with blemishes which, as the weak light reflected off it, were of numerous shades of coffee. But the feature that dominated Punky's overall appearance was his lower lip. It brought to mind a documentary I had once seen on Botswana's Kalahari Bushmen. Having been transported along with a number of San families from their natural home to a new, hostel-like structure, an old woman had spent some time studying an outside tap. After it had been turned on for her she had drunk with her massive lower lip extended under the spout, gulp after gulp of a substance she had never before experienced in such abundance. Punky's bottom lip was no smaller, and protruded simultaneously upwards and outwards, leaving his face as an insignificant background.

'Slim Shady,' he said, smiling numbly from behind his sunglasses, the unscarred cheek twitching slightly.

His calling me after the Eminem rap song, I realised instantly, had to be more than a coincidence.

'We know each other,' he said with finality.

'Yes,' I said, leaning forward to get a better look at him.

Bulelani and Smiley (the latter's uncompromising seriousness hinted at more than a touch of irony in the humour of the one who gave him the name) hadn't moved an inch since we arrived, except to shake hands with us. They leaned back together against the cardboard lining of the colourful interior of the shack, which exaggerated the warmth of the strengthening spring sun. I could see from his long legs stretching back into the darkness that Bulelani was very tall and slender. The only light from outside came from the open doorway. Only a little of the rectangular shaft of light penetrated into the gloomy interior, rendering some corners unseen in the seemingly circular room. Two large posters of rap stars Eminem and Tupac adorned the walls on either side of me, where I sat with Fumanekile on one of the three beds. Eminem stood out from the cardboard more prominently in the weak light. In these surroundings, to the South African eye Eminem would have seemed as out of place as I must have. As I sipped my beer, I wished that Punky would remove his mysterious sunglasses and obtrusive hat.

The light shining off his abundance of jewellery, it was hard to see the poster of Tupac Shakur – he was rapping silently from a speaker behind me – clearly from where I sat.

Had I met Punky before? Feigning recognition would have been silly, so I would have to think a little while longer. Lighting a cigarette, I sighed heavily.

'You are the pool champion at Nyamezela's Tavern,' Punky said, in his slow monotonous Xhosa.

'Ah,' I said, 'so that is where I know you from.'

'You beat me three times,' he said, in broken English, turning to his friends on the bed. 'This *mlungu* plays like a black man. *Wena*,' he pointed at me with two fingers like a gun, '*you* play best when you are so drunk' – he rolled the 'r' – 'that you can no longer stand.'

'Were you wearing the same hat and glasses when we

played?' I asked, grinning at his compliment.

'No, my brother,' he replied. 'I have another hat, but you were wearing that black cap' – he pointed at it – 'and a pair of very dark sunglasses.'

'*Eish*,' I answered, 'I have beaten so many people three times it is difficult for me to remember.'

The three tsotsis, even Smiley, and Ta-fumsa threw back their heads and laughed at my arrogance. In Nyamezela's it was difficult to recognise anyone, since the many tsotsis who played pool there concealed their faces and heads in much the same way as the three sitting before me. The only person who had ever been willing to accompany me there was Nigger; Mzondi and Zane and my other Xhosa friends said it was too dangerous. I had heard the stories long before my first visit, tales of gunfights that had resulted in at least one death during the past year while some, it was said, had been left in wheelchairs.

On our numerous visits Nigger and I had never had a problem, which had eventually left me feeling brave enough to go on my own. I had religiously stuck to the shebeen's informal dress code, though: sunglasses that made it difficult to see the pool balls clearly in the dark interior and a heavy jacket with the zip half open. This combination of partial concealment of my identity and the hint of a concealed weapon had done nothing but earn me more than a few rude words from the tsotsis. My safety had remained unthreatened.

My fondness for the smelly, gloomy shebeen had more to do with the level of pool played there than anything else. I'd seen every kind of shot one could imagine was possible in the game and had, over time, honed my skills to the point where there was only one other man who ever managed to beat me. He was always there, in his bright yellow overall with the prison number below his left breast. On the back of the unsightly garment were the words, 'Not Guilty', while on his head he wore an orange woollen hat that stretched almost to the ceiling. As he leaned over the table to play a ball, I always wondered whether it contained a rifle that kept it from collapsing over his face.

'Eish,' I said to Punky, pouring beer from one of the quarts brought by the young boy he had sent to the shebeen, 'everyone tells me that place is dangerous, but the standard of pool is the highest in Khaya, so I can't stay away.'

Punky, who was casually stuffing big chunks of marijuana into a bottle neck, chuckled in agreement.

'Eh, eh, eh,' he said, dragging his next words out, 'but everyone there thinks you are an undercover policeman, so you have nothing to worry about.'

Having filled the bottle neck with a bulky, thumb-sized filter rolled from thick paper, Punky leaned to one side, where a scratched and unsteady chest of drawers stood at the top of his bed. Opening a drawer, he took a transparent bank bag from it. At first unable to believe my eyes, I quickly came to terms with the fact that there were probably well over a hundred Mandrax tablets crammed into it. Handing one to Smiley, who was wearing the expression of one who is being given a sheaf of papers labelled Top Secret, Punky stood up. After unfastening his belt and the top button of his pants, he removed his hat and sunglasses. The change in his appearance was revolutionary, making me sit back in surprise. His face was as cute and innocent as that of a character in a children's story; his eyes, except for their slightly dazed expression, were as innocent as a little black toddler's.

This reminded me of Zane and how he really looked the part of a bank robber, although his responses to my questions had perhaps been too quick and easy. After I had published his story, which ended with his comment that he had killed an Afrikaner at a Bellville bank because 'I hate the Boer', in the Cape Town-based magazine *Chimurenga*, the owner of my local shebeen, Steve, had disputed its accuracy.

'That guy is lying,' he said. 'You must not believe him.'

'What?' I had asked, shocked by the possibility that my friend had lied to me.

'A true tsotsi won't speak about his crimes to anyone but another tsotsi,' Steve said. 'Killing someone is nothing to be proud of.'

But Zane had stuck by the story when I confronted him later.

'It's true,' he'd said, but the mischievous grin on his face had suggested otherwise.

Punky, on the other hand, had indeed, according to my reliable friend Ta-fumsa, just returned from a two-year stint in Pollsmoor Prison. Although our meeting had been set up to ensure that those who lived on this side of the Site C station would know exactly who my friends were, ensuring my relative safety to and from my friend's shack, Ta-fumsa had cautioned me against asking Punky too many questions.

'Do you want to smoke first?' asked Punky, as he sat back on his bed.

'No, thank you,' I replied. 'Mandrax makes me feel stupid.'

'Sometimes that's nice,' Punky said, looking at Smiley, who was crushing the tablet, wrapped in paper, on the side of the bed with the heel of one of my quarts, covered at the bottom with an old dishcloth.

Checking that it was sufficiently powdered, he handed the marijuana-filled pipe to Bulelani who cupped his hands around the bottleneck, with the smallest opening against his lips and the largest sticking up towards the low ceiling of the shack. Where it had been broken, the bottle's edges were dangerously jagged.

Smiley took two matches from a box lying beside him and lit them. When he held the flames to the pipe, Bulelani's deep, long inhalation of air drew the flame through the marijuana and towards his lips like a magnet. Just when I thought he had managed to smoke all of its contents in one drag, Bulelani took the pipe from his lips and spluttered and coughed. He looked at me and smiled heavily in the gloomy light – a look that said he was halfway to wherever he was going. Smiley, meanwhile, had passed the pipe back to Punky, who was digging around in its top with the end of a match to prepare a permeable bed of blackened marijuana for the powder.

When this was done, Smiley sat alongside him and used a tiny makeshift paper spoon to scoop a portion of the fine particles of Mandrax on to the singed dagga at the top of the pipe.

'Are you sure?' Punky looked at me, smiling like a child offering his friend the first lick of his ice cream.

'I've got these,' I pointed at the beers.

'And Ta-fumsa,' Punky laughed, 'he has nothing but his thoughts.'

Fumanekile winked at me.

'This man is one of my heroes,' I said, putting an arm around him. 'He takes his responsibilities very seriously.'

After the three tsotsis had smoked the button they weren't the best company, but we stayed a while longer anyway, listening to their periodic slurs of speech, the jumbled words making sense only in the way little children's do. Before we stood up to leave, I decided to tell them one last story: my first and last experience of drinking my own urine.

The night before the urine incident had been one of those that Punky had mentioned, where I had hogged the pool table at Nyamezela's through a particularly fine series of victories. By my third and fourth games I was already so inebriated that in the sweaty, dark air of the shebeen I could only just make out the table and balls through my sunglasses. I navigated my way around the table by keeping a hand on its sides.

I had left the tavern after the mama shouted through the bars at the counter that she was closed for business. As usual, I had taken my last quart, by then half empty, with me up the road to Ngqangqolo Street, both for its remaining contents and its suitability as a weapon of sorts.

At home, hearing Nowie and John arguing loudly in their room – Nigger's name came up – I had struggled drunkenly with my key to lock myself into my quarters. Lying back on my bed, with the quart standing discarded on the floor alongside, I had tried my best to stave off the urge to pee. Finally coming to terms with the fact that my mind would lose the battle against my stronger bladder, I had stood up and unlocked the door.

Outside in the passage all was quiet, except for a disturbing sniffling from somewhere nearby. Pushing the toilet door open clumsily, I saw its source: Nowie was sitting on the toilet with her head in her hands. I quickly shut the door and crept furtively back to my room.

By now utterly consumed by the urgency of the situation, I again left my room, this time running down the passage to the front door. It was locked. Knowing it was not a good time to bother Nowie for the key, I succumbed to the realisation that I had only one option remaining: the window in my room. But even this would be a disaster, because just centimetres from the sill stood Thabiso's boyfriend's taxi, which was white and new, and didn't need a wash. Cursing, I rushed frantically around my room. And then I saw the bottle.

I fell asleep after noting with amusement that my bladder had held just enough to create a full bottle with a realistic head of foam creeping up the neck.

When I awoke the next morning I remembered almost nothing – apart from the advice of my friends regarding the best way to deal with a hangover: a long, long slug of beer. Needless to say, the café owner up the road made a killing on toothbrushes that morning.

As Ta-fumsa and I walked out into the bustling township, the air rich with smoke and meat, we could still hear their laughter.

Watering the Garden

'Hello, Steven,' Vuyo's sister Zodwa opened the door shyly one Sunday. 'How are you?'

'Ndiphilile sisi,' I replied, hiding my disappointment that she was at home. *'Unjani wena?'*

'I am also well,' she replied in Xhosa. 'Vuyo is in the lounge.'

Indeed she was, kitted out in a pink T-shirt and blue jeans, sitting back on a couch facing me when I walked in, her bare feet tucked under her on the tattered sofa. Once again I felt flustered as I regarded the natural beauty that shone from her flushed face, giving her the appearance of one caught unawares in a photo shoot.

'Molo bhuti,' she said, smiling up to where I stood. 'Sit down.' She gently patted the empty seat beside her. 'I'm watching the Teletubbies.'

I sat down, hoping that I had chosen the correct distance from her. With her sister still in the shack, I decided philosophically that it would be unwise for any part of my by now electric body to touch Vuyo's. She smiled at me, wrinkling her freckled nose, and turned back to her favourite programme.

Now I had certainly never absent-mindedly watched more than an episode or two of the Teletubbies, but I knew enough about the children's programme to know that it was broadcast some time during the week.

'I wasn't here to see the last episode, so I asked Zodwa to record it for me,' she explained, looking from me back to the television set, where a baby's face giggled and burbled gaily from the centre of a bright yellow sun. Vuyo smiled broadly at this, which I hoped didn't mean I had been invited to provide her with a toddler of her own. With my right hand, which was buried deep inside my pants pocket, I clasped and unclasped the three government-issue condoms that I had brought along. Although they were rather thicker than those for sale at petrol stations across the city, I had always been dismayed at how regularly they broke, so had upped the quantity I usually carried on my person. Besides, because of the effect the mere sight of this girl had on me, who could predict how many *rounds* – as my male friends termed them – we would need to fulfil our sexual appetite for each other? My only worry was that she would try to pressurise me into not using one, something I would not be prepared to do. Some of my male friends had told me that the preference for sex without condoms was not just their wish; their girlfriends often put significant pressure on them to do it 'flesh to flesh'.

'I'm going to visit Pumi,' Zodwa said matter-of-factly to Vuyo. I hadn't noticed that she had been standing just

206

inside the doorway watching the two of us, her eyes moving knowingly between our faces.

Vuyo pressed pause on the video machine and followed her sister into the kitchen, where the two exchanged words that I struggled to make out. When she returned she put the key for the back door down on the little wooden coffee table in front of us and pressed the play button without looking at me. Wondering just how important it was to her that she watch the episode right to its end, my thoughts meandered stupidly, only serving to delay the first physical expression of my feelings for her. Looking around the room, my eyes settled on the sloping floor, which was covered in a rather unsightly floral vinyl. I couldn't see Vuyo's shoes anywhere, so I decided that she'd slept late and had not yet been outside. The curtains had been drawn across the little lounge windows, leaving the room in a soft light, one which, I thought nervously as I avoided looking in Vuyo's direction, set the scene rather aptly for first-time lovers. Tearing my mind away from the thought, I studied the features of our state president on an ANC election poster hanging on the wall closest to the kitchen. The poster was obviously quite old, if its curled edges were anything to go by. In contrast, Mr Mbeki looked young and handsome, and I wondered what he would say if he were able to follow the events that were about to unfold before him in this shack in the new South Africa. A sudden gush of daft pride washed over me, replacing the fear I felt each time I attempted to pluck up the courage to kiss the woman beside me. The unanimous opinion of my friends had been that I first tell Vuyo I loved her, 'because then she will know that you are serious', but I had decided I would do whatever came most naturally to me.

Then Vuyo looked at me, and the meaning in her eyes was

clear, so I leaned forward and kissed her longingly. With one hand caressing her neck and the other around her shoulders, I felt her body relax all at once, a shift that had the opposite effect on me. This kiss had been a long time coming and it was with a sudden surge of excitement that we now fell down on the couch together, me above her, grasping at each other's pants and shirts.

'Don't smell my hair,' said Vuyo, using a hand to push the extensions behind her neck, revealing the slenderness and nakedness below her chin that I had loved so much on our very first meeting.

Although the comment might sound strange to one unaccustomed to running his hand through extensions, Lisa and others among my Xhosa female friends had told me that it was a difficult task to keep the artificial hair smelling fresh as the days after their attachment wore on.

With the greedy hunger now in control of every inch of me, I slipped my hand quickly inside Vuyo's shirt, softly kneading and rubbing her pouting, warm breasts with my right hand. Her hand on the side of my face was very cool, as was the rest of her body, except where I now had my hand, while Vuyo's scent had an earthiness that was different, yet new and inviting.

'Ndiyakuthanda sisi,' I whispered my love breathlessly into Vuyo's ear, as I tenderly kissed her cheek.

'Ndiyakuthanda,' she replied, almost inaudibly, although I could feel the form of each lovely syllable on my lips as we kissed.

From the way in which the channels and languages on the television set were changing I could tell, in some nether region of my mind, that the video and TV remotes were being given a variety of contradictory instructions from somewhere beneath Vuyo's back, but she hadn't seemed to notice.

I had kissed a number of Xhosa girls in my younger days, and each one of them had disappointed me with the shallowness of their kisses, all of which had been devoid of any kind of tongue play, but Vuyo was different; her moist, nimble tongue darted this way and that inside me, leaving me feeling like a time bomb set by some masterful terrorist who had never before erred in his evil intent. The unstoppable urge to be completely naked with Vuyo made me rip off her top, pants and my own clothes in almost a single sweep of one arm, until the only unnatural participants in the early afternoon romp were our lower body underwear, by now bulging and straining, as if in an attempt to express their need to escape the heated intimacy of their contents. My own underpants, which had in my instinctive core taken on the intrusiveness of a bird cage containing a massive white lion, or a beast that regarded itself as such, were the first to come off; they were discarded with one fling of an arm in no particular direction. In rural Xhosa terms, 'the bull had come home to graze' or, as Nigger, in a reference to the quite common job of gardener in South Africa, had put it, 'it was time to water the garden'. But before I could be shown the garden, even from a distance, and then be led towards it in a state of beautiful disbelief, there was a brain-rattling knock on the back door of the shack.

'Vuyo!' It was Zodwa's voice, bringing me back to Cape Town, Khayelitsha, Harare and a tiny, nondescript lounge.

No one had prepared me for this possibility, since once horniness has taken proper hold of the human body, the art of lovemaking comes as naturally as one's morning ablutions.

Zodwa had been away for well over an hour, I thought, looking at Vuyo and doing a rough and painful estimate of all the time I had wasted before kissing her. Even the expression on our state president's face, which earlier had seemed encouraging, now appeared to have taken on a look of disdainful disapproval.

'What to do now?' I asked him silently, before the commencement of another, particularly loud series of knocks.

'Vuyo!' Zodwa exclaimed again, in a tone of voice that made up my mind.

I dressed speedily, noticing sadly that my erection had shrivelled into nothing more impressive than an Eastern Cape earthworm suffering to survive through a year-long drought.

'Shit,' I said, more as an afterthought at the pathetic sight, proof that manhood is only ever a temporary thing, than out of any other emotion related to anger or dismay at Zodwa's sudden arrival.

'Wait,' said Vuyo softly, pulling her panties and jeans up to her waist.

After she had fastened her bra and drawn her T-shirt over her head, she looked at me and sighed, her beautiful face still flushed.

'Open the door for her,' she said, pointing to the key where it lay on the table.

It was a rusty old pistol, but the jumpy finger on its trigger didn't give me the luxury of debating whether or not I should run. The choice seemed obvious. My chances of survival would be greatly boosted by the shooter having to make a choice between two targets, Nigger and me. Furthermore, my brain told me, pistols have a very small range of accuracy. I'd also seen the odd gun misfire or jam in a gangster or war movie. But the live human target hadn't been me, and despite knowing with complete certainty that I should run, it just wasn't enough to get my legs moving: it was as if I had grown roots.

There we stood, Nigger and I, with our arms raised in the air, palms outwards, mine far higher than his (because, although the weapon was being moved constantly between the two us, each time it was aimed at my own chest it hesitated a little longer), me pathetically repeating the words 'please don't shoot' over and over again. I saw that my begging was only further unnerving the skollie with the pistol and so I shut my mouth and began to pray silently, hoping, as I do whenever I find myself in a tricky situation, that God would remember His lost sheep.

As if one blow to my ego hadn't been enough for the day.

Our first chance to make love had been noisily interrupted by the return of Vuyo's sister, who must quite clearly have seen from the mistiness in our eyes what we'd been up to. And yet she had hung around, moving between her room and the lounge, where she would now and then say something to my lover in Xhosa, inviting a half-hearted response from Vuyo's softened lips. Then Nigger had arrived, and I had resigned myself to the fact that, especially with the imminent arrival of Vuyo's mother from church, there would be no chance for us to finish what we'd begun.

Nigger had cut right to the heart of the matter, as we walked through the now familiar streets of Harare towards iLitha Park.

'Did you water her garden?'

'Nearly,' I replied, looking down at my feet forlornly.

'What is *nearly*?' Nigger asked, stomping over my

211

sensitivities with evident delight. His smile did not do much to improve my mood, although after that question he'd had the decency to allow me to indulge in a lengthy, undisturbed and sulky silence.

'Nearly,' he'd repeated sadly, as we'd crossed the road towards the iLitha Park soccer field but, I noticed gratefully as I looked sideways at my friend, the word was neither accompanied by nor followed up with an unkind smile or grimace. My pride had certainly been injured, and it was the instinctive nature of that hurt that left me feeling bewildered and confused. Had Vuyo asked her sister to return after a time, I'd wondered, and why had Zodwa refused to go away after not receiving a quick reply to her first knock? Surely she must have seen by the restrained expressions on our faces and the sweat on our brows exactly what she had interrupted, I thought, as Nigger and I headed up the embankment lining the left boundary of the soccer field.

Chewing on these thoughts, and looking back over my shoulder in the direction of her shack, I decided that I would return to Vuyo very, very soon.

And then I'd seen them.

My instant, awful realisation that they were the hunters and we were the prey had nothing to do with their attire. Every culture or area has a sizeable group of wannabe gangsters, usually young men who adopt the dress code of the real thugs and kwaito stars they have seen about them. But as this subculture is invaded by an ever-increasing number of youngsters, so the real heavies resort to dressing fairly normally, if they didn't always dress that way to begin with. For the heavies, it is a way of life, not fashion. Khayelitsha is no different. Standing outside a house or shack anywhere in the region, on the lookout for the characteristic dress code generally associated with tsotsis, one would notice that around eighty per cent of young men were wearing white, brand-name running shoes, nondescript pants and thick jackets, topped with a high woollen hat.

The real skollie would certainly not want to attract the attention of the police by heading out in the evenings in stereotypical tsotsi attire. Instead, just like the two who were now making their way swiftly up the embankment forty metres behind us, they are perhaps garbed in a smart, checked shirt and plain pair of pants, almost entirely covered by an open thin coat, in which a weapon, usually a gun or a knife, is concealed. The two who were closing in on us now had bare heads, making the zombie-like way in which they had their eyes fixed upon us extremely scary.

'Nigger,' I said quickly and breathlessly, as I began to up my pace, 'there are two tsotsis behind us!'

'Motherfuckers!' said Nigger, rather unexpectedly. 'Fuck them!' He stopped and checked them out. 'Let's fight,' he said matter-of-factly.

This course of action was probably the last on my to-do list, but by now Nigger was walking back the way we had come. I followed cautiously behind and to one side of him, noticing that the point where the four of us would meet up – apparently explosively – was well away from the first row of houses on this side of the soccer field. The game that had been under way when we crossed earlier was now over, with spectators and players nowhere to be seen. What the hell was Nigger thinking?

'What do you want, nigger motherfuckers?' Nigger shouted, as we came within five metres of the two tsotsis, both of whom were taken aback by my friend's unusual approach.

'Your money and your cellphone!' yelled one of them; and that's when his colleague produced the pistol, screaming at us to put up our hands.

Although Nigger's hands shot up faster than mine, my long arms, reaching for the sky, climbed to a far more impressive height. For a fleeting second I hoped with all my heart that Nigger would not attempt to run, and then this thought was swamped by the terrifying realisation that I had nothing to give them.

'I don't have ...' I croaked through thin lips. The gun barrel continued to sway from Nigger to me and back, as the other tsotsi began a frantic search of every inch of my body. 'I promise,' I tried again, 'I never walk with money or a cellphone.'

'Hey, fokof wena,' spat the man with the gun, his nasty eyes suggesting that he was deciding what to do next. 'Yiza,' he beckoned to his companion.

And then the two of them hurried away, back in the direction of Harare, as quickly as they had arrived behind us.

Nigger was incensed. 'Fuck you, motherfucking niggers!' he screamed at their shrinking forms.

It was my turn to yell. 'Don't shout at them!' My voice was shrill from relief that neither of us had been hurt.

For some time we walked in silence, privately replaying the few seconds of extreme danger we'd faced. I could hear my heart beating – from various parts of my body – while my hands were shaking uncontrollably. It was only as we began climbing Ngqangqolo Street, where little groups of youngsters sat here and there outside their homes, chatting away the afternoon, that I heard Nigger chuckling. I peered at him curiously.

'Hey, my nigger,' he said. 'Why did they only search you?'

'You know why,' I said, feeling whiter than ever.

War Zone

It had been a tough two weeks. For one, I hadn't contacted Vuyo since our last meeting. This was not because she hadn't called me, but because I felt an odd kind of humiliation that I had been stupid enough to open the door after Zodwa's sudden return during our few heated minutes together. Thabo, who had somehow got wind of what had happened, had done nothing to improve my general mood of despondency.

'Why did you open the door for her sister?' he asked me, in front of Fumanekile and a number of our other male classmates outside our lecture hall at the Technikon. '*Eish,*' he shook his head at the others in disbelief, 'this white man has a lot to learn.'

'What was I meant to do?'

'What is her sister's name?' Thabo had asked.

'Zodwa.'

'How old is she?'

'About sixteen.'

'So you stop what you are doing with Vuyo and get up to open the door for a sixteen-year-old girl?'

'She just kept knocking,' I replied defensively.

It was quite unusual for our group of friends to be discussing a topic such as this, but Thabo had not let up since class ended.

'*Eish*, but this white man is a *mampara*,' he said, shaking his head in disgust at my stupidity.

Since that last visit to Vuyo, another, rather more violent event had worked its way forcefully into my life: the inevitable and final resolution of the dangerous love triangle involving Nowie and her two men – John the hairdresser and Nigger. The blow-up had occurred the previous weekend, exactly seven days after Nigger and I had been held up on our way back from Harare.

While John's early return from his visit to his family in Ghana had surprised us all, it was Nigger and Nowie who were to have the greatest shock. For when the hairdresser entered his girlfriend's room that Sunday morning, it was to find my friend and Nowie midway through a particularly raunchy and noisy bout of lovemaking. Before John's arrival, I had been in that state of semi-sleep where the real sounds in the vicinity of my bed mingle confusingly, although not uncomfortably, with the dream images in my head. Just as the rhythmic pounding of my landlady's head against the wall between our rooms, and the variety of male grunts and female shrieks were becoming a background drumbeat in my dream, a third, familiar voice dragged me out of my stupor. The voice was John's, a loud staccato rattle of angry words, made ragged with betrayal and disbelief.

'... do this to me!' was the only part of that first roar I would later recall.

With that, my home had exploded into a war zone. Springing out of bed, I listened fearfully as a fierce physical struggle broke out next door. By the nature of the lengthy female cry that burst from the room, I knew at once that the Ghanaian had attacked Nowie with all his stocky strength.

'Don't do that!' Nigger shouted, and this was followed by a crashing, metallic sound that hinted that either he or John had been shoved into his weights bar, which had taken up permanent residence in Nowie's bedroom. It was then that I heard Babalwa's voice, the first thus far to take on a tone of reason.

'Don't fight,' she appealed to them in a voice that was strangely calm.

Opening my own door an inch, I saw her boyfriend, Sivuyile, making his way quickly down the passage towards the kitchen and front door, in his hurry somehow managing to pull a T-shirt over his head with each of his hands gripping a shoe, a sock hanging loosely from each.

'Sivuyile!' I whispered frantically after his retreating form. 'Please don't go!'

'See you later, my man,' he replied from the kitchen door, before disappearing quickly around the corner.

As I heard Sivuyile's car engine start up, John came hurtling down the passage, off balance and flying backwards with a look of shock frozen on his face; after him walked Nigger, thankfully empty-handed, but with a deadly expression on his features.

'I will kill you, my nigger!' he shouted at John, who by now lay sprawled on his back in the kitchen doorway.

'Don't do it, Nigger!' I cried, surprised at how ridiculous

and motherly my voice sounded. 'Leave him alone!'

'Steven!' screamed John. 'You were my friend, how could you do this to me?' he cried, guessing my role in the situation. My sturdy hairdresser stood up, the expression of hurt on his face so intense I was forced to look away.

Slamming the door of my room, I dressed quickly, realising that I would have to get help before Nigger injured the Ghanaian. After struggling to pull up the zip of my short pants with my trembling fingers, I fled down the passage towards the kitchen, where I arrived just in time to see Nigger crashing the kettle down, with the full might of his strength, on the Ghanaian's head. As the appliance made contact, its jug came loose from the handle, ricocheting off John's skull, and hitting the fridge door with an incredible, tinny crash. Nigger didn't seem to have noticed this, because he brought the handle down again with his right arm. This time, however, the action was lost down one side of John's head, which by now was bleeding profusely.

'Nigger!' I yelled. His crazed appearance gave me the scary feeling he wouldn't hesitate to divert his anger towards me.

But looking at me, he hesitated, a momentary understanding registering in his eyes.

'Get him out of here,' he said in an unnervingly calm voice, 'otherwise I'll kill him.'

Seizing the opportunity, I'd quickly helped John from the floor, where a puddle of blood from his head injury was smeared this way and that, the liquid made yet redder by varying strokes of whiteness where the floor peeped through.

'Come,' I said to John, looking at Nigger once again to make sure that the insanity of his earlier violence wouldn't return.

As I helped the Ghanaian to the front door and out through the desolate garden, he repeated the words he'd said to me earlier, over and over again.

'Steven, you were my friend,' he exclaimed, that pained expression once again on his face. 'My friend! How could you do this to me?'

His voice had become a pig-like squeal, making the guilt I had been feeling for weeks develop an acuteness that made me desperate to say something, however pathetic.

'You are too good for Nowie,' I said softly to John, as we stood in the street outside.

A fair number of our neighbours, young and old, had left their houses to find the source of the commotion. I looked at them apologetically, trying my best to make it look as if I had the situation under control.

'I will come back for him!' bawled John, as he struggled to break away from my grip. 'I won't rest until I've got him, that dog!'

'John,' I said gently, noticing an acquaintance from the shebeen down the road standing nearby, 'you need to go to the clinic for stitches. That will also give you some time to calm down. Wait here,' I said, in an authoritative tone and walked towards the man I'd recognised. 'Please take John to the clinic, my friend,' I said to him, having forgotten his name.

'Okay,' he replied, taking John by the arm and leading him down the road.

By the time I reached the kitchen I could hear Nigger trying to calm Nowie, who was sitting on a couch in the lounge. Holding a piece of toilet paper to her face, she was sobbing hysterically, her other hand covering her eyes.

'Let me see that,' I said, gently pushing the hand that held the toilet paper to one side.

Just under her right eye, Nowie's cheek was swollen a dull purple, although it was free of blood.

The next evening I carried John's belongings down to his hairdressing business, where I found him silent and sulky. Sitting mournfully on a chair in one corner of the room, he ignored all my attempts to lift his spirits. His two female employees were busy at work, trying desperately to cope with the evening rush. John had a long line of stitches down the top of his head, which was downcast as evidence of the recent blow to his self-esteem. Seeing John in this state, where he was too depressed even to work, left me feeling devastated, and I quickly said farewell. As I walked away I again heard the words he had used the previous day, 'Steven, how could you do this to me?'

I left without acknowledging his words, hoping he would think I hadn't heard what he'd said. But I felt responsible in no small degree for what had happened, so the words did not fall on deaf ears. Although Nigger had been my friend first, I had always respected John for his steadfast decency and honesty, and if there was one person in the love triangle that did not deserve his lot that Sunday, it was my hairdresser.

The Race Card

During the next few days my relief that the matter between the two foreigners and my landlady had finally resolved itself was uppermost in my mind. But I soon began to sense that the power shift from John to Nigger was not necessarily a positive thing for me. Not only did the Kenyan's music and television preferences begin to make themselves felt on a daily basis, but the way in which he strutted arrogantly around the house induced in me a feeling of despair. He no longer respected my place in the household, a subtle change that made me feel I was losing a friend. To make matters worse, Nowie would regularly persuade him to turn down my invitations to join me at one of the local shebeens for a drink and a game or two of pool. This left me feeling somewhat displaced on the home front and I wondered at the blatant selfishness that can so often overcome those whom one has initially regarded as faithful friends. Of course, I understood that their behaviour was an expression of their love for each other, but it was the suddenness of the change that surprised me.

Nowie's daughter Babalwa also showed signs of discontent, and evenings in front of the television set passed in an uneasy silence, one whose subtlety made it no less palpable. As at my previous home, I began to divert my attention away from Ngqangqolo Street to my friends Thabo and Fumanekile at Peninsula Technikon and to my old haunt, Vovo Cash Store.

It was at the latter that I received the disturbing news that I would never receive the letter Foamy had promised me. Dropping in for a beer one evening at Vovos, Frederick, my old Burundian housemate, informed me that Foamy had written a letter to me and sent it to his brother, my previous landlord Molefe, soon after his return to his father's house in the Free State. Frederick hadn't managed to find another place and still lived with Tshidi and Molefe. However, Molefe's jealous wife Tshidi got wind of the correspondence and apparently threw the letter away. I was upset by the news, because Foamy had promised to include his address and contact number in it. We had promised to stay in touch and, failing a visit to Molefe, which would have taken a great deal of courage, this would now be impossible.

But soon Fumanekile and Thabo, with their very different characters, provided me with a healthy balance of humble and outspoken companionship. While time spent with the quiet Ta-fumsa was usually away from watering holes, providing a pleasant respite from drunken talk and lofty ambitions, Thabo kept me partying. His adeptness at organising party funds at awkward times of the month was certainly his most admirable quality. With his humour absolutely devoid of any kind of decency or respect for racial, cultural and religious considerations, Thabo was a regular source of laughs. While in class he would bait lecturers and students alike, in the township he took on the confidence and doggedness of a *Drum* magazine reporter from the fifties. Added to this was a belligerence that often got him into trouble for breaking some of the age-old Xhosa customs. In addition to his advances towards various daughters of shebeen owners in Site C, which saw him regularly walking into Monday morning class with severe facial bruising, the youthful Thabo never allowed the fact that he had not yet been circumcised to inhibit his strong opinions, even in the company of large groups of men. He did not allow his own ignorance of the secrets that are passed on to *makwethas* during the circumcision rites to get in the way of healthy debate, even when he knew it would most certainly lead to a beating. When some of the men in his company asked him questions that only a graduate of the bush would know the answers to, the lengthy reply of the boy – for that was what he remained in his own culture – would gush with insolence and arrogance.

'I have been to the bush,' he would lie proudly in Xhosa, 'and I don't have time for this nonsense.'

Seconds later, thrown out of the establishment on his ear, with a slap from one or two of the men, he would stand outside hurling abuse at his attackers, his fists waving furiously in the air.

It was very difficult to decipher what, if anything, Thabo actually believed in or held sacred, because whenever he was in my company he would denounce Christianity and Western culture, regularly labelling himself a 'traditionalist'. However, whenever Ta-fumsa described himself as a traditionalist,

Thabo would shake with laughter. Many of the differences that existed between the individualistic Thabo and his very traditional parents were a direct result of the attainment of freedom for his people in 1994.

Lifting the lid from a pot of leftovers from the night before on three separate occasions in the space of just one week, I noticed that Thabo and his family appeared to be living on a diet of cabbage and mieliepap, a combination sadly lacking in nutritional value. My young friend had told me that the family's only income came from his father's work as a gardener for a wealthy Afrikaans family in Paarl, so the sight shouldn't have surprised me, but it did. I found it difficult to relate Thabo's intelligence and wit to this lifestyle, which had him living in squalor in a minute, corrugated iron shack, with only an ancient, smelly bed and a large, black bin for his clean and dirty clothes, in the front yard of his father's house. While he described his parents as being traditionalists, versed only in the Xhosa ways of old, he retained many of their beliefs, although his incredible grasp of the Western principles of material ambition and individualism made him a lethal mix of opportunism and feisty overconfidence. Not being one to mince his words, Thabo would regularly ask the coloureds who were studying with us why they had 'no culture', while in the company of whites he had no qualms about using what he himself described as 'the race card'. A prime example of this had happened on his trip to the Netherlands, where he had been a participant in a student exchange programme. An aid organisation had asked him to deliver a speech on the suffering experienced by residents in the many townships of Cape Town, to which he had instantly agreed.

'I'm telling you, those businessmen felt sorry for us – you could see the guilt in their faces,' he said to me, laughing gleefully. 'I told them I lived in a shack without any facilities, while white people in Europe lived like kings on money they had stolen from Africa!'

Not only had Thabo's emotional speech driven the businessmen to donate a large sum of cash to the aid organisation, but he had returned to South Africa with a few hundred euro for himself. Although his use of the monetary gift was no different from what many youths from wealthier homes would have done with it, the fact that Thabo was from a poor family made me feel sad that he had spent so much of it on booze.

'It was enough to party on for many months,' he told me, laughing at the stupidity of his Dutch benefactors.

Thabo's habit of taking the opposite view in any argument was backed up by an acute talent for opportunism, one that even his own family was not spared. He once told me how, during his first month of an internship for a local newspaper, his father had asked him to pay a visit to their house in Site C. At the time he was living in the Cape Town CBD and he knew beyond doubt the motive behind his father's invitation.

'You know how my culture works,' Thabo told me. 'Obviously my father wanted my first pay cheque.'

With his expert understanding of the Xhosa way of talking respectfully around the point for a considerable time, Thabo had gone to his father's house prepared for what was to come. After dinner, when his sister and mother had left the kitchen table for the lounge, understanding that the men of the family had a matter of great importance to discuss, Thabo's father had launched into his vague speech.

'You are my son and I am very proud of you,' he had begun.

The first of his clan to attain an education above the final year of school, Thabo was regarded as being something of an enigmatic genius by his relatives.

'You are your father's son,' his dad continued proudly.

'*Eish*, my friend,' Thabo said. 'My father spoke for a long time about how clever I am, but even before he came to the subject of money I hinted several times that I was earning very little at the paper. I also pointed out the high cost of rent in town, which meant that I barely had enough money left over for food.'

Thabo did end up contributing money on a monthly basis to his family, but he managed to reduce the amount considerably with his nimble tongue. And, judging by the way he ended the story, it appeared he had never felt even the slightest guilt.

'You know how cheap life is in the township,' he said to me, 'so eight hundred rand is actually too much money for the three other members of my family.'

Pink Pig

Alighting from the train at Site C station on a sunny afternoon towards the end of the year, Brown Pig and Pink Pig were equally confident this would be a birthday party to remember. The added year hadn't taken Brown Pig out of his early twenties, but had at least provided the first legitimate reason he had had to party for some time. The younger of the two by far, Brown Pig was a bad influence on his older friend, or at least that was the way Pink Pig saw it.

Both participants in the unfolding celebration, in the heart of spring, were walking with a bounce in their step as they headed towards Brown Pig's family home.

About an hour earlier Thabo had walked into my local haunt in iLitha Park with a plan that convinced me immediately to go with him to Site C. Every cent of the five hundred rand in Thabo's pocket, he explained on the train, had been deposited into his account as 'compensation from a Dutch friend'.

'Compensation for what?' I asked.

'What do you think, Pink Pig? Apartheid of course,' replied Thabo, his expression both amused and impatient. 'Those people gave us Jan van Riebeeck, so now they must pay up,' he added.

I found it difficult to believe his Dutch friend had fallen for it, although Thabo was notoriously persuasive. The two had apparently kept in touch since meeting in the Netherlands, although I now wondered how long the friendship would last.

Understandably, most people found Thabo extremely intimidating. Tackling prejudice head on, he'd often appeal to one's guilty conscience with a string of politically charged allegations, resulting in donations of beer, meat and money falling easily into the compensation category.

The fact that he always appeared to be on the verge of addressing a thousands-strong crowd through a loud hailer at a workers' rally didn't do much to smooth the rough edges from his personality. Short and thinly built, with a head a little bigger than one would expect from a body the size of his, the abilities of his oversized brain were unquestionable. It would be hard to imagine a polite Dutchman standing up to a challenge that contained unrelenting references to Jan van Riebeeck's arrival at the Cape in 1652.

Thabo had christened me 'Pink Pig' a few weeks before, in front of a large number of customers at a local tavern. He'd blurted it out during a heated debate on racial issues.

'As a white man ...' was all I'd managed to get to say, before he launched into one of his noisy speeches.

'Don't say you are white, you are pink!' Thabo retorted. 'A

pink pig, that's what you are!'

Predictably, Thabo refused to accept my response that if I was a pink pig, then it followed that he was a black pig.

'This is black,' he'd said loudly, fingering his leather jacket and cackling loudly. 'My skin is brown.'

At this point I'd joined in the laughing, neither of us caring about the attention we had drawn to ourselves from the other patrons in the dusty bar. It was in between songs on the jukebox, and our neighbours at the tables nearby had been listening to us for some time. The laughter seemed to come as a relief to them, which only made us hoot louder.

We followed the sharp curve in the road that led from the station to Thabo's parents' home, entering into that period of evening where dusk is a lazy hour or two away and life in the streets of the township has been charged with the electricity of homecoming. I was remembering the intense embarrassment that Thabo had subjected me to soon after we'd met on our first day of term. Rubbing the sleep from my eyes on a particularly crowded train early one Monday morning, I mourned the fact that I hadn't been able to find an empty seat. Standing with my hangover in the crush of commuters, I'd counted the stations as we'd pulled up at each of them, waiting in vain for someone to get up from a seat and hurry out the door. However, since most commuters from the townships on this route were headed for Cape Town's CBD or suburbs, the chances of my finding a seat were small. And even if I had found an empty seat, it would have been just a matter of time before I would have had to vacate it for a mama or tata. As the train progressed along its way, one could clearly see the benches age, while the younger ones among us filled the space between the bustling doorways.

It was two stops after the Site C station that the albino

entered the carriage. He was short and slightly built with a skin so pink that I thought my own complexion probably looked quite tanned. But a powerful, hearty voice arrested my thoughts.

'Hey, Pink Pig,' it boomed down the length of the carriage. 'Don't you greet your brother?'

Although I hadn't seen him get on at Site C station, I instantly recognised his voice. As uproarious laughter erupted from the passengers, I scanned the area between the other two doors further down the carriage, where the voice had come from. Then I saw him, his head thrown back as he cackled loudly. It was Thabo, of course.

A few minutes later, as the two of us waited at our Bonteheuwel changeover, Thabo refused to apologise for his behaviour.

'Do you know what the Xhosa word for albino is?' he asked me, grinning widely.

'No, I don't,' I replied, 'and what has that got to do with what you said on the train?'

'Inkawu,' said Thabo. 'And do you know what that means in English?'

'Albino?' I answered, sarcastically.

'It also means monkey!' Thabo said, screeching now, his hands clutching his aching belly.

My soft chuckling at this memory attracted Thabo's attention and he turned to me as we strolled down the busy, dusty street, lined with a sprinkling of disorderly shacks and houses, the cocky smile once again on his face.

'What are you laughing at?' he asked.

'I'm just thinking about that day on the train with the albino,' I replied, greeting the raised hands of those who knew my friend in these parts.

231

'*Eish*, Steve, when a black man climbed on the train in Holland we would greet each other, so why wouldn't you do the same here?' Thabo cried, before a wild spasm of laughter overtook him, one that would grow into hysterics within seconds.

◈

The dog wasn't very big, but the bellow that came out of its crocodile jaws was no less deafening on account of its size. My heart stood still when it hit me; a roar released at the exact moment that its jaws touched my ear, discharging with it a ghastly smell of rotten meat. In a state of sheer terror, I reacted instinctively, fending the dog off with my left arm and sending it skidding in the dust behind us. A typical township canine, with its faded, scruffy light brown fur and yellow fangs, the beast scuttled frantically back in the direction of the shack it had leapt out of. It had obviously had a bad experience with stones before, because by the time the rock left my hand, the creature was already well into the front yard of its home. My state of shock did not do much for my aim and I was well off the mark, the rock ricocheting off the uneven ground and leaving a dusty trail behind it as it hurtled towards the front wall of the shack. The sound of the missile hitting the corrugated iron wall was thunderous, although it was not loud enough to drown out Thabo's scream.

'Run!'

Thabo ran swiftly for one so short – his arms and legs pumping furiously and his head held back. I followed hot on his heels. At the end of the road we turned right, weaving in and out of the people walking down the middle of the road.

My friend eventually stopped outside his home, signalling to me to be quiet. There we stood, panting and heaving for some time. When we had collected ourselves enough to go over the events of the past two minutes Thabo's good humour returned to him, although I was still struggling to breathe.

'Hey, Steve, that dog is a racist,' he said, giggling hysterically. 'You are the first Pink Pig it's ever seen.'

He was right, of course; out of all the people walking along that road the mangy beast had picked me as the odd one out. My response was feeble, but it rang true, nonetheless.

'Thabo, at least I know now how black people in Uitenhage felt when our dogs barked only at them.'

'Yo-yo-yo,' said my friend. 'We are really in the new South Africa!'

A Friend like Sisi Lulu

'Look at that!' the little boy said to his friend in Xhosa as he pointed in my direction.

If I'd stood up to my full height alongside him his head would barely have touched my knees. His head was quite big for his body, with his full lips, button nose and inquisitive brown eyes adding to his childish innocence. His scrawny brown legs wobbled slightly under his big belly, while his arms rowed at the air to assist with his newfound balancing skills.

'A white man, *eish*!' exclaimed the friend, who was also not much older than four or five.

The friend had more chiselled features, giving him a wizened look. Unlike the first boy, the friend's belly was only slightly rounded.

Looking up from my book, I took a swig of beer from the

quart bottle on the grass beside me and fixed my eyes on the pair. I'd been sitting uninterrupted for hours on a hillock in the small open field opposite my home, so it had taken some time for me to register their presence.

'Let's have a look at him,' the first boy said. 'Come.' He confidently beckoned to his friend.

Walking up to me, they leaned forward and peered deep into my eyes.

'They are green,' said the friend, after some thought.

'And his eyelashes are red,' said the first boy, shaking his head in amazement.

Although normally I would have greeted the boys, I had the distinct feeling that this would put a halt to their adventure, stemming the natural flow of words that came from their mouths.

'Let's go closer,' said the first boy.

His friend nodded.

I'd been leaning back on my arms, the book in my lap with my knees slightly raised. After the first boy had perched himself on my left knee, his friend took a seat on the right. Leaning forward until I could see the elastic snot that moved rhythmically up and down with his breathing, the friend, whose inquisitiveness had now got the better of him, reached out and touched my eyelashes with his miniature fingers.

'You are right,' he said, with the certainty of a scientist. 'They are red.'

'What a small nose,' the first boy said, as he ran a tiny hand down one side of my beak. Thankfully, his own nose was clean. Then, pushing the tip of my nose from side to side, he turned to his friend. 'Look,' he said simply.

But his friend's attention was focused on the hair on my arms. Gripping dishevelled tufts in his tiny hand, he pulled them this way and that, looking at my face for a reaction. When none was forthcoming he lost interest and averted his gaze to my upper chest, which was visible above my vest.

'*Eish*, this white man has got hair everywhere!' he exclaimed to the first boy, who joined him in tugging at it. 'On his face, his chest, his arms and his legs,' he continued, before producing a long sigh. This was followed by a sharp intake of breath, which pulled the string of snot very suddenly up into his nose. Just as I became certain the gooey substance had been drawn in so deep that it would not come back out, it bounced slowly on to his upper lip as he exhaled.

'Is this mud?' the friend asked the first boy, who had also been staring at the moles on the bare calves of my legs.

'I don't know,' said the first boy, before looking once again into my eyes.

For a moment I thought he was going to ask me about them, but then I saw that his own eyes were fixed in an expression of wonder that never allowed for the possibility that I could speak.

'*Eish*,' the first boy said, shaking his head slowly from side to side.

'*Eish*,' replied his friend.

'What kind of sweets are you going to buy?' the first boy asked as they both stood up together.

They were looking at each other now.

'Chappies,' said the friend, and they left as quickly as they had approached me just minutes before.

'And don't forget the bread for your mother,' said the first boy as they walked towards the shop.

I watched the two little boys enter the shop, where they stayed for some time. When they came out they walked quickly past me. Only the friend cast me a fleeting glance.

'Have you ever seen a white man before?' he asked the first boy, but I never heard the reply. Instead, as the two little boys disappeared from sight, I marvelled at the naked interest they had expressed in me. I was a different colour to them and they had picked that up instantly. Their reactions, unlike those of many adults, had been untouched by fear or prejudice. And from the lack of anything derogatory in their observations, I judged that their parents, teachers and any other adults they came into contact with had probably never said anything negative about white people in their presence, or perhaps their young minds had ignored it if they had. How lucky they were, I thought as I cast my mind back to my own youth. And what a journey I had had to travel to lose just a small portion of the prejudices and fear I had harboured for black people for most of my life. I knew then that I still had a fair distance to travel.

But in less than two months I would be living in the Netherlands and I could never have known that it was there that I would learn the most important lesson of all.

Khayelitsha had been my home for a little over eleven months when, a few days before Christmas 2002, I sadly took my leave of the township. With a little persuasion, I got my mother to drive me from the southern suburbs, where I'd met up with her that morning, into iLitha Park to pick up my belongings. She'd been holidaying in the Mother City, staying with a friend. From iLitha Park we would drive to our family home in the Eastern Cape. A month later, I would catch a plane to Johannesburg, then another to Amsterdam – the journey to my Dutch girlfriend Aletta of a year earlier was about to begin.

My mother had good reason to worry about driving her car into Khayelitsha, and not for the obvious reasons of a white woman driving alone into a black township, as my living in Khaya had brought much light to the subject of life in South Africa's townships. Until a few weeks before she had been a member of a church volunteer programme for children in KwaNobuhle, Uitenhage's largest black township. She had stopped her work there abruptly when a young man from the township who was also involved in the programme told her he'd received a tip-off that a group of local tsotsis was planning to hijack her. Driving nervously out of KwaNobuhle for the last time, she'd noticed a group of young men following her in a car, but even if they were the men she'd been warned about, they did not stop her.

While it may not be a misconception that crime surrounds life in Khayelitsha, the statistics were very different from my daily reality. Most of my parents' concerns came from the media view of what a black township is. Perception is almost everything and, let's face it, black townships haven't exactly had positive publicity. My parents were anxious when I first moved to Khaya – they thought anything could happen to me. Obviously they asked why I couldn't conform and be 'normal'. And my father was worried about what potential employers would think if I applied for a job and they saw that my residential address was in one of the most notorious townships in the country.

But as time went on, my experiences, which I often conveyed over the phone to my parents, began to have as positive an effect on them as they had on me. They began to show a real interest in my life in Khayelitsha, and asked questions about respect in Xhosa culture, about diet, and what my friends were like. So, after almost a year, it wasn't too hard for my mother to imagine driving into the township one Saturday morning to help me move out.

In the days before my departure from Khaya I'd carried my belongings piecemeal from Nowie's house to Tata Hobe's where his wife, Sisi Lulu, who expressed great sadness at my imminent departure, mothered me to the very last. I must have put on close to three kilograms in those last days, as a show of respect for Sisi Lulu's chief philosophy in life, which seemed to be that the stomach is capable of digesting an amount of food far larger than itself.

I took a minibus taxi to Wynberg early on that Saturday morning so that I would be able to accompany my mother to the township. We turned off the N2 highway at the Spine Road exit. It felt strange being in a private car, accustomed as I'd become to travelling to and from Khaya in taxis and trains, and as we drove towards iLitha Park I felt a tremendous sadness at my impending departure. I knew I would miss Khayelitsha and her people, my perceptions of whom had changed so dramatically over the past year. I had by now come to regard the narrow, white, English South African identity of my early years as outdated and out of place in my life among my black countrymen and women. As a result of this change in the way I saw myself – and in much the same way as adolescents rebel against the constraints of their youth – I had moved to the other extreme, where white South Africans were anathema to me. I had begun to feel more black than white and more African than European, convictions encouraged by my Xhosa friends. One such friend, whenever I answered a question about white people with the habitual, 'as a white person, I believe ...' would shout, 'Voetsak, Steve, you are not a white man!'

My occasional trips to town hadn't helped. White people I encountered seemed unfriendly and alien to me, and unsuited both in skin colour and attitude to the African sun. Though this fitted rather predictably into the fear-of-what-one-doesn't-know category, it felt no less real. My township-style Bermudas and tsotsi gait were evidence that I had taken on the culture of my country's majority, while my ubuntu and the sharing and humanity that came with it had built up in me a disdain for wealthy individualists.

There had been so many times in Khaya when I had come within a hair's breadth of feeling truly African. My imminent trip to Europe, however, where my ancestors had come from at different times over the past hundred years, had prevented me from accepting that African identity. One grandfather may have fought in the Second World War for the Germans and the other for the British troops in North Africa, but they had Europe in common. I had lived for a couple of years in Austria as a toddler, but I couldn't even remember the bubblegum vending machine my older brothers sometimes talked about. Although I was going to the Netherlands to be with Aletta, I knew that my journey to Europe had far wider implications than anything to do with her. It was in Europe that I hoped to find answers to my questions about my identity and where I truly belonged.

'You know,' my mother turned to me as she drove us up and out of the Mother City along Sir Lowry's Pass, 'I really wish I had a friend like Sisi Lulu.'

Many of the white people I knew referred to Khayelitsha as 'that place'. The biggest compliment about my taking up residence there had been a passing reference to my 'courage'. Although her remark was based on my mother's very brief assessment of just one resident of the sprawling township, she could never have known the totality with which it summed up my experience of the place. I'd had hundreds of friends just like Sisi Lulu, people whose kind-heartedness had touched me deep down, leaving me a changed person. None of them had been judgemental or unforgiving when it came to my many character flaws, while each and every one of them had done everything in their power to make me feel loved and at home.

How much, I wondered as I sat alongside my mother with not a few tears in my eyes, would I miss Khayelitsha, which in English so aptly means 'new home'? Would I remember my time there only as a valuable experience that had gone some way towards changing my perceptions of black South Africans, or would this great black township have a lasting impact on my identity? I know the answer to that question now, but then, as we headed towards the Eastern Cape, the ancestral home of the Xhosa people, all I knew was that the only way I would find the answer was by putting considerable distance between me and Khayelitsha.

Homesick

The first thing I noticed in the Netherlands, a country whose citizens donate millions of euros to the Third World, Africa in particular, was that the buses and trains ran on time. I also noticed that the common man there was wealthy by South African standards, a decent salary for manual labour was taken for granted, and most people had the means to go on an overseas vacation at least once a year, due only to a confusing thing called an exchange rate, which for some reason favoured the First World.

I got a job the same day I started looking for one and was amazed to hear from a Dutch acquaintance that, a few years earlier, Holland had faced a crisis of not having enough workers to fill all the job vacancies. Although I was told that only around a thousand Dutch people were HIV-positive and that Amsterdam had fewer than fifty murders a year, I never quite got used to not having to be vigilant of those around me, now and then touching a hand to my money pocket to check that my notes were still there.

I made it through that first year in the Netherlands with ease. Every material thing I had ever yearned for walked right in through my front door, while my after hours work as a journalist involved such petty topics as bicycle theft and canal boat tours.

'Gee, Steven,' my good friend Candace, who'd studied with me at Peninsula Technikon, wrote sarcastically in an email after she'd read one of my stories on the Internet, 'you're really coming up in the world of journalism. Bicycle theft? Who would have thought it?'

After my first year in Holland, however, the novelty of the cushy life lost some of its initial allure. I began to miss the unique challenges that life in South Africa presents, like having to deal with countrymen, especially Capetonians of all colours, who regularly arrive late for appointments, and a mindset that demands from participants in any conversation that they fight vociferously for their talking space. Of course there are exceptions in both countries, but I noticed how my collection of South African kwaito, gospel and traditional music was growing. I soon became concerned that I was usually the only participant in the braaivleis I had in our tiny back garden, the result of the all-important Dutch agenda, which doesn't allow for such ridiculous and old-fashioned human traits as spontaneity. Of course, I knew deep down that I was judging a society based on my unique set of memories of my home far away. I began to understand how this could work in reverse for Europeans living in South Africa. But I began to dream of a place where a long, warm summer and a short winter was the norm, and not the other way around.

As the neighbours' complaints about the smoke from my braaivleis intensified, so I began to become – as we South Africans so regularly say – *gatvol*. I began to think back to what Thabo had said about his few months as an exchange student in the Netherlands, and it wasn't long before I began to feel South African. As the son of an Austrian father, and therefore a citizen of that country, as a youngster I'd always suspected that I would feel at home in Europe. From the time of my arrival in the Netherlands and during a quick visit to Austria, however, I rapidly became convinced that this would be impossible.

As the months passed, I began to realise the validity of Thabo's complaints about life in the Netherlands. What was more, I started to feel more and more patriotic about Africa as a whole. It was ironic that when, during the first months I was there I'd greeted some of the blacks I saw with the customary Khayelitsha greeting, '*Heita*, my brother', those dark-skinned Europeans would avert their expressionless eyes. This made me realise that home is indeed where the heart is, regardless of the shade of skin that covers it. My heart, I came to accept, was in the south of Africa. Where black consciousness would have struck a chord with a black man, an African consciousness began to take root inside me. At my one-man braais in Utrecht, Hugh Masekela, his voice refined by the earth and the people of his homeland, took me home as a kindred spirit. They were small things, but together they had a powerful effect on me.

When Mzondi wrote in an email that my old friends at Vovo Cash Store wanted me to write a letter for the wall alongside the pool table, I sent a list of complaints about the tedium of my new life. The well-oiled system of Dutch life appeared to be perfect, so I constantly felt deflated about what

I saw as the insignificance of my daily contribution to their society. I missed the feeling, especially among South African journalists at the turn of the millennium, that South Africa was heading somewhere, like Spain after Franco. Working as a journalist in Cape Town I'd always been aware that my country was at a crossroads, it was a make or break situation and my individual contribution counted.

Of course I was basing my judgements on my own set of references, but the reality was that after my first year there I ran out of interesting stories to tell my South African friends and family. I yearned for the spontaneity and relaxed atmosphere of my home.

I became embroiled in arguments with Dutch friends over the injustices their forefathers had meted out to 'us', bringing up Jan van Riebeeck, colonialism in general and the newer form of it, neo-colonialism. A strange fickleness saw me writing to Mzondi that black South Africans should open up to the idea that Van Riebeeck had perhaps left the Netherlands because he was sick of the weather and had run out of things to do indoors.

I imposed a one-man boycott on the Shell Oil company because of its despicable polluting of the Niger Delta and its shady involvement in Nigerian politics over the years. The latter spurred me on to mention to the Dutch the trade agreements that favoured the First World, the plunder of Africa's natural resources by Western companies and whatever else I could think of in the heat of the discussion. While working for a newly launched English-language newspaper in the Netherlands' most famous city, Amsterdam, I had a brush with the darker side of my continent. My undercover investigation of the Nigerian mafia's 419 scams saw me receiving daily calls from a criminal in Lagos who wanted me to fly to Barcelona, so he and his friends could get cash out of me in a city where I wouldn't know the whereabouts of a single police station. Finally my editor and I realised the story wasn't going anywhere, so the next time the Nigerian called I came clean and told him I was a journalist. His initial silence was soon followed by a snort of threatening laughter.

'Do you have any idea how much money I have spent on these phone calls?' he asked, his laughter ending abruptly.

'I also called you a few times,' I retorted lamely.

'Who gives you the right to waste my time and my money? Where in Amsterdam do you work?' the man asked, a dangerous tone of anger entering his voice.

I had the phone on speaker and the two other journalists in the office, Kaj and Armand, huddled closer to it.

'Tell me,' I said, 'why do you do this to people?'

'I do it because you Europeans have spent the last few hundred years stealing from us,' the man hissed. 'We may have a Nigerian government, but they are the puppets of the big Western companies that steal from us every day. They steal oil, diamonds and everything else they can from Africa,' he said, before continuing, except this time race featured in his justification. 'If white people are greedy enough to fall for something as stupid as a 419 scam, then they deserve what they get!'

With that he hung up. Armand, Kaj and I remained silent for some time, the three of us pondering the man's words.

'Even if people always come up with a justification for the bad things they do,' Armand said, 'it's hard to argue with the core of what he said. In a way he and his friends are just taking back a little of what has been taken from them.'

Although I'd always been taught that what was illegal was wrong, deep down I could relate to the man's words, whatever his motivation. The fact that I had to a small extent taken the Nigerian's side made me worry about the dangers of unconditional patriotism.

But in a way I knew that whenever I rambled on about Western injustice and oppression in Africa, I was blaming every European I met for my homesickness. I soon realised just how unfair I was being towards the Dutch people I knew, many of whom had gone out of their way to make me feel at home in their country.

I found the attitudes of the Dutch people I knew towards South Africa and Africa in general oddly contradictory. Almost every Dutchman who had visited South Africa, upon finding out my nationality, would inevitably say, 'What the hell are you doing living *here*?'

At the same time, there was a general attitude of resignation towards Africa's problems, a sense that it was a basket case and beyond help.

'We donated millions to Africa for decades,' said one friend, 'and the money went into a bottomless pit. It made no difference at all to the lives of Africans.'

There appeared to be no recognition of Europe's contribution to Africa's woes, a responsibility I felt they shared with a plentiful collection of African puppet leaders.

On those evenings alone in my little Dutch garden, the flames of the fire dancing to a raw kwaito beat, my memories of Khayelitsha were the strongest. Some of them were warped by South Africa's history of discrimination, but that took nothing away from their impact. I knew that in a house in iLitha Park, for instance, there was a photograph of me and a baby who had been placed in my arms by his mother. In the doctor's rooms a little way down Ntlazane Road there was a black practitioner who had treated me enthusiastically, listening to the white man's heart for a long time on his stethoscope, after greeting me excitedly with the words, 'You are my first white patient, welcome!' And that in her mother's shack in Harare, Vuyo was watching the Teletubbies.

I also knew that in Vovo Cash Store there were men, young and old, who had taught me the ways of the Xhosas, their respect, their humility and humanity. That all over Khayelitsha there were women who had given me compassion, conversation and love. They had seen the colour of my skin for what it was – nothing more than a covering for a body that was just the same as theirs, and blood, as so many of them had reminded me over and over again, 'red like mine'.

It had been a time for firsts – for me and for hundreds of my black countrymen and women in Khayelitsha. I'd learned a lot during my time there, and it wasn't just how to open a bottle with another bottle, a lighter, or my teeth. I'd gained a deeper understanding of a wide variety of often contradictory qualities, like patience, hunger, ubuntu, poverty, crime and eventually humility. I realised that if I had never lived in Khayelitsha, the culture shock of the Netherlands would not have been so great, with the Dutch priorities of individualism and self-sufficiency not that much more pronounced than in the suburbs at home.

The cliché that money does not always bring happiness was brought home to me. There, where almost everyone has enough of it, people don't need each other in the same way, with the result that the family unit is often confined only to parents, brothers, sisters and their spouses. And whereas compassion and charity is largely the domain of the social democratic government of the Netherlands, in South Africa they remain in the streets, boosted by a strong local culture and a liberal dash of poverty. In the townships the family unit is often hard to distinguish; friends, fellow clan members and even acquaintances are often included in it. Far more importantly, ubuntu goes beyond tribe, nation and race and cuts compassionately right through the whole of humanity.

After two years in Europe I took a one-month vacation to South Africa in January 2005. It was on this trip that I came to understand for the first time that there are different kinds of giving. It was a simple gesture of charity on the part of my old friend Fumanekile. His response, when a homeless woman in Cape Town's Long Street asked him for money, was so ingrained in his culture and personality that it came as naturally as breathing. On hearing the woman's request, Fumanekile dipped his hand into his pocket, separated his taxi fare to Khayelitsha from the rest of the coins, and handed the rest to her. He didn't even count what he gave her. I, on the other hand, looked closely at the coins in his palm, placing a value on my friend's kindness at around ten rand.

I may have been holidaying in my home country, but throughout my time in Cape Town, Uitenhage and on the Transkei Wild Coast I felt completely alienated. As I dolefully splashed out my euros, I longed for that feeling of being part of the solution to my country's problems, instead of being just another stereotypical European, throwing money where there should also be compassion.

I missed that spontaneous generosity when I returned to the Netherlands and my Dutch friends and I meticulously counted coins so as to pay our exact portion of a bill. I pined after the feeling of belonging, of being part of a powerful spirit of kinship. I yearned for that feeling of security where I knew that no matter what happened in my life, there would be hundreds willing to listen or offer their help. As if to confirm this, the Dutch people I met who had visited a South African township always cited the experience as the best in their tour of the country. Unlike me, however, and probably because they had spent a far shorter time there, they struggled to put their finger on the source of that conviction, managing only to say 'it had something to do with the people'.

'Blood is thicker than water', the old adage goes, but I knew that there was more to it than that. The people, the soil and the air of my homeland exerted a stronger pull than my family roots in Europe. My trip to the Netherlands, which I had hoped would be a journey towards the discovery of my true identity, had turned into an experience of exile. I had tried to ignore the teachings of the Xhosa whose spirit of ubuntu had shown me that even though love for homeland may mean different things to each of us, it is easily as powerful as the love for a woman.

I decided that I would leave Aletta and Europe behind and return to South Africa, to the place where people had said to me: 'You are white, my brother, and I am black, but if you cut our skin you will see that my blood is red, like yours.'

Walking home from Hlehle's Cool Spot. (Photograph: Lulama Zenzile)

The shack I shared with S'bu in 2005.

A stream running through TR Informal Settlement.

The train tracks are perilously close to the shacks.

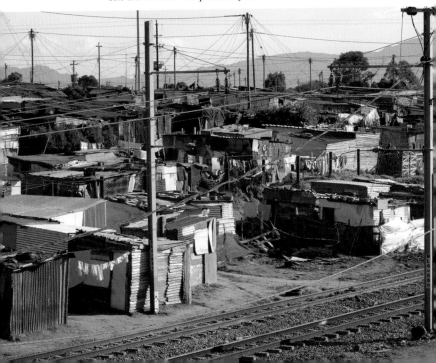

A typical street scene (above) and one of the local hair salons in TR.

One of the many furniture stores on Mew Way, between TR and W sections

A hangover from apartheid days, this old police watchtower overlooks TR residents.

Shacking Up

The Table Mountain sunset behind us was less than an hour away as we sped along the N2 highway past the turn-off to Cape Town International Airport. The rush hour traffic heading out of the city had thinned out slightly and we were racing down the busy highway towards Khayelitsha at a terrifying speed. But there was more to the adrenalin being pumped into my veins than that: after two and a half years away from the rambling black township I was coming back to live there. Europe could not have felt more distant as I watched the crooked shacks hurtling past on the right-hand side of the road. One of those shacks would be my home and the thought filled me with a combination of excitement and anxiety. This was the real Khayelitsha, the massive informal settlements known for their ugly poverty and rampant crime. This was the nemesis of the rich, where disorganised groups of tsotsis daily made the decision, consciously or otherwise, to take on the beneficiaries of the system.

It had been a mistake taking the middle front seat of the taxi, I realised as the taxi driver screeched to a halt on the grass verge of the highway. No matter your age, intelligence, religion or race, in the middle seat up front you are required to count the taxi fares sent forward from the back, not an easy task if someone forgets to pay, makes a mistake, or takes a chance. To be fair, the driver had handled my news that the money was 'short' quite well. Repeatedly turning his head towards the passengers seated behind us, he'd asked over and over again for the culprit to pay up. His ire having peaked, with a lightning quick glance in the left-hand side mirror, he'd swerved from the fast to the slow lane and applied the brakes.

'We are not going any further until that fare is in,' he said in Xhosa, as we ground to a stop.

After an angry conversation involving most of the passengers, the culprit, a shifty-eyed boy of around seventeen was eventually identified and paid up. He received a robust scolding from the mama sitting beside him, the driver started the engine and we were on our way again. The debate among the passengers had required a person by person explanation of their virtuousness.

'I gave you that ten rand note,' the woman sitting behind me had said, looking pleased with herself. 'Do you remember giving me change?'

And so it went on, until it became obvious that the devious youth had no evidence of his innocence. Once the mama's scolding was over, all was forgiven and we drove on in a comfortable silence.

It wasn't long before we were on Mew Way moving

over the bridge above the highway and heading towards TR Informal Settlement. As we neared the first four-way stop, a little hill sprinkled with shacks, some large, some small, some wide, some high, but all of them ragtag and decrepit, came into sight.

In the air above this beautiful scene, the evening fire was being taken on by darkness, with the dust from the shack lands and the smog from the city hanging wearily beneath the sky. The sun was already eroding the usually sharp contours of Table Mountain, its target the Atlantic Ocean flowing out before Camps Bay. Different worlds perhaps, but with the African sun they are linked forever.

Although there was not a tree in sight, I could feel by the ease with which the taxi crossed over the four-way stop that even the wind had paused for this sunset, its breath held in anticipation of reunion.

'Four-way please, my brother,' I said to the driver, who nodded that he'd heard.

Its momentum lost, the taxi moved over the little bridge leading to the four-way stop between TR and W Sections. The driver sluggishly dodged a few cars and brought us to a lazy halt.

'Sharp,' he answered my thanks.

And there he was, my old friend, on the other side of Mew Way. He was wearing beige baggy tsotsi-style pants with white braces. On his head, Fumanekile, aka Ta-fumsa, wore his lopsided revolutionary beret. Although this felt like a first meeting, this time, the gaps between his teeth, his rough skin, rugged looks and soft voice represented all that I liked most about this place in Khayelitsha's heart.

'Welcome back, my brother,' Fumanekile said just loudly enough for me to hear, as he crossed the road towards me.

I threw my heavy rucksack over my shoulder.

'Luvuyo,' he said, dragging the word out slowly, as he came out from behind the taxi, 'welcome home!'

We shook hands, going through the multifaceted hand-shake over and over again.

'This is Banana,' Fumanekile said, his left hand on the shoulder of the tall, thin man in his early twenties who was standing to one side, 'and this is your homeboy Gigs.'

I could see where Banana got his nickname. Exactly my height, he wore a pair of brown Bermudas which, with his sloping back, gave him the appearance of the longest KwaZulu-Natal banana ever. Gigs was a short man with a floppy white hat on his head. His lively eyes were set in a youthful face, untouched by cynicism or distrust.

'Are you from iLitha Park?' I asked.

'*Haai, mlungu*, from Uitenhage,' he said, shaking my hand vigorously.

'That's amazing,' I told him. 'I don't meet people from Uitenhage very often. I also don't like to admit that I come from there, you know?'

'Why? Uitenhage's a lekker place,' he replied. 'You know KwaNobuhle?'

I told him I did as we walked off, waiting on the island to cross the street, taxis hauling over the white lines in front of us. Fumanekile took my bag.

'Don't worry about it, Luvuyo,' he answered my protest.

'Yes, yes, hi, my brother,' Gigs said in a deep voice, the open smile on his face placing a lasting emphasis on his assertion that we were related. 'What clan are you from?'

'The Madiba clan,' I said, to laughter from all three of them.

As we headed down a side street in the direction of

Fumanekile's shack and into the centre of TR, the kwaito singer Zola's 'Bhambatha' blared out from a pair of speakers outside a roadside shebeen. Instead of making me feel homesick, as it had when I'd played it while braai-ing on my own in Europe, his tough township gangster rap inspired me to take the cue from my three companions – without thinking about it too much, I added an extra drag and a spring to my step.

In the distance I could see the other end of the road, up which I had walked from the Site C train station to visit Fumanekile more than three years before. The tar on the road where a group of children were playing a game of cricket, with a beer crate as the wickets, was as thin as everywhere else, looking like leftovers from an upgrading of the nearby highway. Whacked hard by a boy the height of my waist, the tennis ball the children were playing with shot between Fumanekile and me, with three boys in hot pursuit.

The smiles of passers-by, acknowledging us with a grin or a wave, ran contrary to the hardship written like graffiti all over my new surroundings, where the cheapest metals and the throwaway things of the wealthy had been used with great care to create the best living conditions possible. This was a great camping ground away from the rural areas, set up in acknowledgement of the contradictory magnetism of the city. Gone were the valley forests and green rolling hilltops of the Xhosa ancestral lands in the Transkei; in their place was a mix of sea sand, soil and never-ending flatness. The round, cow dung huts, which are cool in summer and warm in winter, had been sacrificed for tin shacks that would, if not for the cardboard insulators on the inside, have made the rough Cape Town seasons still worse, while the ancient radios – their aerials struggling periscope-like to catch a signal above the giant Transkei hills – had been exchanged for taxi rank hi-fis. The old-fashioned dark suit pants and collared shirts and traditional ladies' dresses, meanwhile, had been laid on the altar of tsotsi culture, where youthful rebellion lasted into the thirties. There was poverty all sides here, yet the smiles of the people told a different story – a story of cultural survival against all odds. As Zola rapped on in the distance, the angry tone in his voice intensified for a moment, then faded into his chorus, filled with courage and strength. Then a new track killed Zola's voice in that squatter camp that holds tens of thousands of residents, most of whom, like me, had initially travelled from the impoverished Eastern Cape in search of work.

We walked down the stairs and into Fumanekile's sunken lounge.

'What's on your mind?' he asked me.

'I've been away for too long,' I replied, and we both smiled.

I slept in Fumanekile's bed on my first four nights in TR Settlement. Fumanekile spent most of the daylight hours asking around TR for a vacant room for me in a shack with someone he knew, which meant I was saved the trouble of putting my name on the waiting list. Although he did take me to the community hall, the only brick building in the area, to introduce me to the neighbourhood leaders, Ta-fumsa said finding an empty shack would take weeks. The cost of a shack – around two thousand rand for the smallest and six thousand rand for the biggest – was within my range, but because of my sociable nature I preferred the idea of sharing.

I soon noticed that Ta-fumsa was extremely well connected. A source of wisdom to those in his area, with many coming to him in the evenings and at the weekends for advice on anything from their living arrangements to personal relationships, Ta-fumsa was as stable as I was moody. In the process of wrapping up his postgrad degree in journalism at Peninsula Technikon, I noticed that my friend still scraped together most of his family's living from the proceeds of a weekly story or two for the township's newspapers, *Vukani* and *City Vision*.

Because his natural generosity and the demands of his culture saw him vacate his bed for me, he spent the first three nights after my arrival at the homes of his girlfriends. I use the plural here because each evening he would walk off in a different direction. I had no reason to be concerned, though, for I knew my friend was the proud user of condoms – not only is there always a whole box of them under his bed, but from the steady drop in its level one can see that Ta-fumsa uses them.

'How many girlfriends do you have?' I asked him as he left on the third evening of my stay.

'This is not the suburbs,' he answered, obviously remembering his one and only meeting with Nigger in iLitha Park. 'The gardens here are bloody dry. Have you seen any trees around?'

'No,' I played along.

'But there are too many gardens,' replied Ta-fumsa, 'and somebody's got to water them. I am well-placed to do this, because my hosepipe is long!'

I came to like Ta-fumsa's three-bedroom shack. Wherever I walked I had only to take five steps at the most. Its smallness translated into cosiness, its haphazard yet neat

257

layout appealed to my chaotic but practical nature. Besides his, there were another two bedrooms, with the sunken lounge in the centre of the structure. Up one step from the lounge was a tiny kitchen containing two small cupboards with the strict necessities for cooking and eating. The shack smelt of paraffin at all times, a pleasant odour to emanate from a stove, although I could never quite get over my fear of fire.

Our fellow shack mates were good-natured and easy to live with. There were no quarrels or disagreements and Ta-fumsa's grandmother, Makhulu, Ruu, the youngster he had taken in some years before, and Ncebsi, his cousin, welcomed me into the family. Gigs and Banana, along with another of Ta-fumsa's friends named Skido, were regular visitors and were also an integral part of the household. Skido had the face and eyes of an old man and I was amazed to learn he was only in his late twenties. Sometimes they would bring food if it was close to a mealtime or, if we had already cooked some, they would get stuck into it as soon as it was warm.

Besides the money he got for his freelancing work and his grandmother's wages from her job as a domestic worker for a family in Fishhoek, Ta-fumsa's third source of income was from the loose cigarettes he peddled from his shack. At eighty cents a smoke, they were the cheapest in the area, so for most of the day and well into the evenings a steady stream of people would come down the stairs into Ta-fumsa's sitting room to purchase one or more cigarettes. Selling the cigarettes was a group effort and whoever was closest to the wide wooden tray with the small change would conduct the sale. I enjoyed this job and during the day, when Ta-fumsa and I sometimes took a little bench from the lounge and sat outside in the sun, I would always take the tray along with me. A substantial part of Ta-fumsa's income came from his cigarette business. It wasn't the first time I had been amazed at the simple, yet ingenious ways in which so many of Khayelitsha's residents made their money.

Sitting outside the shack was a good way for me to become known, since the sooner everyone knew me the sooner they would stop staring. The time I'd spent in iLitha Park had removed most of the groundless fears of my past, but in those first days in TR I never ventured more than a few hundred metres from Ta-fumsa's shack. In the place of those groundless fears a new realism had developed, and I knew I needed familiarity between me and my new neighbours before I travelled too far. Since my reasons for being careful had nothing to do with my prejudices of old, it took me some time to realise that they had been replaced by a new prejudice. How was I to know that the tsotsi-style clothes worn by almost every boy and man from the ages of thirteen to thirty was a simple expression of fashion? Ta-fumsa brought this error to my attention in reply to a comment I made as we sat outside one afternoon.

'Shit, man, most of the youngsters here are gangsters,' I'd said to him as he polished a pair of black shoes.

This was easily the hundredth group of youngsters clothed in tsotsi gear that had passed by his shack as we sat outside that day.

'Just because they're dressed like that doesn't mean they're skollies,' said Ta-fumsa. 'Take the way I dress, for example.'

I played the about-turn I had done on my initial perception of Ta-fumsa over in my head and instantly saw the truth in his words. After reaching the stage where I seriously thought I'd cleaned prejudice out of my mind, I had very easily walked into the trap again. And this time it was also based on appearance, skin colour having been replaced by dress style.

The Big Mouse

I moved into S'bu's shack on my fifth day in TR. The room had become available after S'bu's policeman father was posted to the Eastern Cape. There was no rent but Ta-fumsa advised me that S'bu and I would take turns to buy groceries. Only a hundred metres down the road from Ta-fumsa's home in the direction of the Site C train station, S'bu's was the only lean-to for miles with a front lawn. Inside were two bedrooms, a fair-sized lounge and a tiny kitchen. You could just make out the sex of the characters in movies, I noticed when Ta-fumsa took me there to discuss the move with S'bu, if you concentrated very carefully on the hazy shapes and elastic voices, but following the plot on his ancient television was impossible.

In his late teens, S'bu was very short and his spoken English consisted only of nouns. Considering that we had an equally rudimentary grasp of each other's languages, it was remarkable how well we got along. S'bu's already large eyes grew much bigger whenever he spoke English, a charming accompaniment to his comical sentences.

It wasn't a difficult move and we handled it in stages. Since the room had not a single item of furniture and my only possessions at this time were my clothes, professional camera, laptop and fair number of traveller's cheques in US dollars, I had no choice but to head into town to exchange a hundred dollar cheque into rands. On the taxi I spent a few minutes worrying about whether my camera and laptop would be safe while I was gone.

'The penalty for theft in TR Informal Settlement is death,' Ta-fumsa had told me on my first day there and from the look on his face I could see that he meant it. 'The people here have had enough of crime and we don't tolerate it any more.'

He went on to tell a story about an area of the shack lands where the residents had decided at a community meeting that they would no longer deal with the police. Their frustration at seeing tsotsis return home a day or two after their arrest had led to this extreme decision.

'The only call they make to the Khayelitsha police station is to tell them to come and pick up the body,' my friend told me, his eyes expressionless and his voice angry.

I had never seen Ta-fumsa's face so devoid of emotion and I told him I was uneasy about the naked anger in his voice.

'The only other people I don't have time for,' he said, smiling in spite of himself, 'are black diamonds, or *buppies* – I prefer to call them IMFs after the International Monetary Fund – those bourgeois young black yuppies who think they're special. They piss me off because they forget where they come from when it suits them.'

I understood my friend's dislike for those of the new black middle class who, he said, professed to be staunch traditionalists when they were around white people, but were ardent Westerners around poorer blacks. Their newfound confidence and self-assurance must have been especially disturbing for Ta-fumsa because of his humble surroundings and the humility of his fellow residents. I also worried that some of the residents of TR would harbour a disdain for me because, although my skin was white, I came from a similar class to the *buppies*.

I would often ask Ta-fumsa what other people were saying when it appeared they were discussing me in Xhosa. Although most of the time it seemed they were not talking about me, when they were, it was often complimentary – 'that white man is a real Xhosa', 'it's nice to see a white man who trusts us', or 'it's good to have a white man staying here with us'. Many people came up to me and said, 'Don't worry, my friend, as long as I am here you are safe.'

I caught a taxi back to TR from the foreign exchange agency in town and embarked on a mild shopping spree. My bed, purchased from a second-hand furniture store about fifteen minutes' walk from my new home, cost me three hundred and fifty rand, while the little desk and chair set cost two hundred rand. The prices included the delivery of the furniture, an affair that made me feel quite the exhibitionist. Being a Saturday, TR's residents were out in their thousands, some of them heading to the local shebeens, others returning from a morning of shopping in the city. And, from the way they were dressed, I could see that others were off to see their lovers in other parts of Khayelitsha, or in townships further afield, like Gugulethu and Langa.

My very public move began with Ta-fumsa, Banana, Gigs and me watching the two young furniture store employees argue over which one of them was going to help us. The dispute remained quite harmless as it moved from the inside of the store to a two-seater couch on Mew Way pavement, where the vast majority of worn items of the old owner's furniture were packed. What peeved Ta-fumsa even more, though, was that when we'd arrived the two had been sitting back on the very same couch doing nothing. It was Ta-fumsa who ended the lengthy debate.

'You, *kwedini*,' he said, using the Xhosa word for an uncircumcised boy, 'lift that side of the bed.'

With that, the five of us headed with my meagre furniture through the potholed streets in the early afternoon. On the way a number of residents shouted out polite questions to my friends, seeking an explanation for this rare sight. Each time Ta-fumsa slowed down, or he and Banana stopped to talk to our interrogator, explaining that I was now an official resident of TR. Now and then I would have to put down my side of the bed in order to shake hands with whichever of Ta-fumsa's friends wanted to meet me. I felt supremely carefree in this place where people were without airs, where I was already beginning to feel the importance of the individual contribution to the whole, where the biblical practice of 'Do unto others as you would have them do unto you' was a given, and not something that represented a threat to one's individualism. I'd always been averse to duty, but here one automatically adhered to it as a reaction to the unconditional kindness one experienced from others on a daily basis. These highly developed social skills were not so much a reaction to the density and poverty of the population in the shack area as an expression of a culture and attitude that was more powerful than individualism, duty or time.

S'bu was leaning on his garden fence when we arrived, with Laamy, a friend I had met the day before. Laamy's mock disapproval was hanging lightly in the air because I hadn't bought my new furniture from his store.

'Why didn't you buy those things from me?' he asked as we laboured slowly past him.

When Ta-fumsa had introduced me to Laamy I'd taken to him on the spot. Soft-spoken, yet confident, he'd impressed me with his knowledge of current affairs and the ease with which he discussed some of the books we'd both read. Nondescript in build and looks, Laamy told me he and his girlfriend, who had three children together, had been living in the same shack for fifteen years.

'The fact that for fifteen years I haven't paid lobola to her parents worries me the most,' he'd replied to my relentless search for something negative about what sounded like a perfect relationship.

Laamy's jocular complaints died away as we struggled to get the bed over the garden fence.

'Bed, gate,' S'bu was saying in his noun-based English. '*Eish*, difficult,' he added, the thick Xhosa accent adding emphasis to the difficulty involved.

After tripping over S'bu's hosepipe, from which water was sporadically spurting on to the lawn, I managed to rescue my bed from a particularly big puddle and hoist my side into the lounge.

'Where do you get the water for the hosepipe from?' I asked S'bu, who was helping on my side.

'Tap, everybody use,' he answered, which I took to mean that he attached it to the communal spout.

'Steve, I think we'd better get some pieces of wood to

insulate the walls,' Ta-fumsa suggested after we'd put the bed down in one corner of my room. 'It's going to be really hot in summer and very cold in winter if we don't insulate it.'

I nodded in agreement, looking around at the ragged corrugated iron walls, where shiny layers of rust and dust had made their home. At four by three and a half metres, the room wasn't much smaller than the one I'd occupied years before in iLitha Park, although the ceiling was a great deal lower. With the desk and chair in place opposite the bed, there was a fair amount of walking space between the two. The carpet was a dull orange and in good condition, considering there was nothing separating it from the sandy ground below. I took another proud look at my new home, taking in the electric wires weaving in and out of the beams propping up the ceiling and the little mouse droppings sprinkled here and there across the floor.

'Are there lots of mice?' I asked S'bu.

'Two,' he answered with such excitement in his big eyes that I felt quite elated by the news. 'Big mouse, Sbu room; small mouse, Steve room. Don't worry,' he added, 'small mouse too small, my big mouse sleep day, wake night.'

By the time the sun had descended down the other side of Table Mountain and into the Atlantic once more, I had unpacked my rucksack and made myself comfortable on the sofa in the lounge. S'bu had gone over the road to Laamy's hardware store to buy thin brown wooden boards and had expertly covered the walls of my room. They looked quite bland compared to the lounge walls, though, which were covered in light blue painted cardboard that was easier on the eye.

Three teenage girls had arrived a little while earlier, one of them my new shack mate's girlfriend, Viwe. She was a lovely girl and she spoke the most beautiful English. Plump and jovial, Viwe had obviously got together with S'bu fairly recently, it seemed. I watched him scribbling her phone number at the top of a list of girls' numbers on the short stretch of blue wall between the entrances to our two rooms. Surprisingly, for his age, S'bu had already gone to the bush and he reminded me often over the next few months that one's return from the bush harboured a new era of amazing popularity with girls.

It is never a good idea to go out on one's first night in a new home and I suppressed the urge that evening to visit friends. They streamed into our lounge over the next few hours anyway, Ta-fumsa, Banana, Gigs and Skido, all of them wanting to know if I was comfortable. I had made way for the girls on the couch and the five of us sat on the floor, our backs against the wall. The relaxed atmosphere was broken only by the confused sound of the television, whose screen changed colours and twitched excitedly whenever the slightest breeze came in through S'bu's frilled white curtains.

'That TV is going to give you a sore neck,' said Skido, to girlish giggling from Viwe, who was sitting on S'bu's lap.

The TV stood at an angle on an asymmetrical little table, one side of which was placed on bricks.

'No, the TV's fine,' I said, Skido's blatant honesty disconcerting me a little.

'You won't find a table like that in the suburbs,' said Banana, laughing into his hand.

'*Eish!*' exclaimed Gigs. 'We don't have tables like that in Uitenhage, hey, Steve?'

'Actually, I suppose it is quite skew,' I said above a howl of laughter from S'bu, who'd escaped from under Viwe and was standing shaking in front of his TV.

As earlier in the day, he was shirtless, his boyish stomach muscles heaving under the strain of his laughter.

Hours later, lying in my new bed, I wondered how many people had slept in it before me. Was its first owner a white person? How would I fall asleep with this racket, I wondered as my neighbour in the shack closest to my room played another kwaito track at full volume. My thin walls did nothing to keep the sound out. For a brief moment I considered going out for a while, but then abandoned the idea and decided not to allow the din to bother me.

I marvelled at how I had arrived at this shack in TR. It had been a long road that had wound its way from iLitha Park to the Eastern Cape, northern Europe and, after nearly three long years away from my country, back to Khayelitsha. With S'bu noisily washing dishes in the kitchen, I climbed out of bed in the darkness of my room and looked out of my little window. Gazing at the hardware and furniture store across the street, I could see that Laamy had long ago packed everything away. The dusty road was busy, with most pedestrians walking faster than in the daytime. From Ta-fumsa I'd learned that after 9pm it was better to go out only in a group of friends and I could see by the purpose with which the dark figures outside were walking that they knew it was getting late.

Suddenly I found myself thinking about Vuyo. I studied the faces of the passers-by, looking out for her walk and her smile. It was not the first time I'd thought of her since I'd left iLitha Park, but this time there was the possibility of seeing her. I hadn't had a photograph of her in my years away, but this had taken nothing away from her beauty and had left my memory of her unspoilt. The prospect of seeing Vuyo in the flesh excited me and I lay back in my bed and stared up at the vague lines of the corrugated iron ceiling, with long stabs of light from a giant lamp post somewhere nearby flickering through tiny holes here and there. I wondered whether Vuyo still lived in the same neat shack in Harare, close to where Nigger and I'd been held up. More than that, I wondered whether I would pluck up the courage to track her down, since I suspected that her life had probably changed much in two and a half years. Only rarely in my life had I tried to link my distant past to the present and I had always been unsuccessful. On more than one occasion I had tried to awaken love interrupted by circumstance, and I had always failed miserably.

'Goodnight, Bra Steve,' S'bu shouted from his bed next door.

'Goodnight S'bu,' I yelled back over the kwaito music. 'Sleep well, my brother.'

Just then, the wall that separated us trembled and shook under the weight of a loud roar from my shack mate's rear.

'*Sies*, you fucking pig!' I shouted at him.

'No, Steve, it's not me, it's the mouse,' he answered, between helpless snorts of laughter. 'I told you it was big mouse, very big mouse!'

Hardship is Everybody's Business

I quickly developed a comfortable routine in my new home. I still had enough money to keep me going for a few months, so I concentrated on the book I had decided to write on my time in Khayelitsha. While still in the Netherlands I'd begun writing about Khayelitsha to stem my nostalgia. Each morning I'd wake up at the crack of dawn to the sound of footsteps hurrying past in the street outside my window. In the distance I could hear the trains pulling into and leaving Site C station, their brakes screeching in the increasingly warm morning air. Usually by this time Ta-fumsa had already come jogging past my shack to follow the railway line from Site C to Mandalay station, the next stop on the way to town.

'Laaviistaa ...!' he would shout his specially extended version of my new nickname, as he marked time outside my window. 'Wake up, you lazy white man! Are you coming with us?'

Ta-fumsa had derived 'Lavista' from *lawaai*, a variation on the Afrikaans word for 'noise' as a nickname for me. It said a lot about me that, living among people who had been labelled noisy during my youth, I was considered to be the noisiest.

'Go away, Ta-fumsa!' I would yell back, to a chuckle from him and Nontombi, the pretty girl who ran with him most days.

With that, the two of them would run off towards the station, with the pitter-patter of footsteps following in their wake.

During the first few weeks waking up in my little room, with the thin wooden wall covers and the lopsided window with a torn-off piece of white sheet that barely covered it, came as a bit of a surprise to me. I woke up slowly, with the beat of the previous night's music from the shebeen next door still playing in my head. While at first I had put it down to a party animal neighbour living somewhere in the vicinity of our shack, I'd eventually tracked down the music to a jukebox in a large shebeen next door to my room. The most sparsely decorated tavern I had ever seen, it held only a pool table, which was in a terrible condition, and a single couch that leaned back dangerously whenever anyone took the courageous decision to plant their bum on it. My discovery of the jukebox also explained why a maximum of around five different songs were played over and over again from early evening until the small hours of the morning. The songs were obviously the going favourites. The repetition bothered me far more than the noise, but when I mentioned it to S'bu it became obvious it had never held even the remotest interest for him.

'African jazz better,' he said. 'You like kwaito?'

'Yes, I do,' I answered.

Since it would have seemed hypocritical to complain about music I liked, that was the end of that. Ta-fumsa, when I brought it up with him, was far more circumspect.

'Mmm ...' he said, adopting his thoughtful expression. 'This isn't the suburbs, my friend, where you can phone the police to complain. The shebeen owner makes money from that jukebox and he can't tell people what songs to play.'

After a series of stretches and yawns I'd head outside, crossing the road to the Somalian-owned café where, if I'd run out, I'd pick up some cereal and long life milk. Although these items were significantly more expensive than they were at the supermarket at the Site B shopping centre, it was useful to have a well-stocked café so close to home and I was one of hundreds who used it. This was before the time when Somalian shop owners in Cape Town's black townships became the targets of violent attacks by the community, but in TR relations between the Somalian refugees and the locals were good and have largely remained that way.

The practice of ubuntu was sidelined at all shops and drinking holes in the area, all of which had large signs that read 'No Credit!' either pasted to the outside walls of the establishment, or tied to the metal bars that shielded the counters.

Heading to and from the shop in the mornings I would invariably bump into someone I knew, although in their hurry to get to work they would often have time only for a friendly wave or smile. When I got home, S'bu would be ironing the various items of his school uniform on the coffee table in the lounge, still in his underpants. After making breakfast for both of us, I would sit down at my desk and begin to write.

Because of the vast numbers of unemployed people in

the area and the incredible denseness of its population, TR Informal Settlement is noisy all day. While I wrote, Laamy would set up his store outside, his three employees chatting and laughing among themselves as the sun warmed them. Toddlers stumbled and crawled about their feet.

Although movement to and from the station certainly slowed after the morning rush, it remained fairly constant all day. By the time I headed out midmorning for my first game of checkers, the sounds of talking and laughing adults formed a solid counterweight to the crying of babies and the footsteps of pedestrians. In the air above and around the crossroads were electricity cables hanging heavily under the weight of illegal connections, one of which headed into our shack through S'bu's kitchen window. To add to the constant noise, there were at least four shebeens within a hundred metre radius of my home, a different song emanating from each one's colourful jukebox, where the unemployed and those off sick placed their one rand coins.

It was in this environment and atmosphere that my routine developed. In those first weeks I moved casually from the laptop on my old wooden desk, to café, to checkers, and in so doing I gradually became well known. Playing checkers, in particular, was a good way to get to know people. I played thousands of games against Laamy and his workers and youngsters returning from school in the early afternoon. As the evening trains hauled in workers from across the city, some of those who still had a bit of energy would sit down on a low beer crate opposite me for a quick series of games before they embarked on the final part of their journey home on foot. The checkers board was set out between us on a table that hadn't been sold yet. I always had a good chuckle whenever Laamy sold a table from under the game and we had to relocate to another table, mattress or chair. It surprised me that Laamy never ever saw this as a nuisance, always helping us drag the next checkers table over from another part of the road.

It dawned on me very early on that TR was no iLitha Park. The latter, where the houses were far bigger than shacks and the streets were quiet in comparison, had far more in common with the suburbs than an informal settlement. I had found the people in iLitha Park friendlier than their counterparts in the suburbs of traditional white South Africa, but in TR friendliness took on another meaning entirely. Sharing was so pronounced that it was quite simply automatic. There was no hesitation about giving and there existed in everyone a natural socialist attitude towards neighbours, friends and acquaintances. It often took me an hour to walk the hundred metres from my shack to Ta-fumsa's – one friend wanted to play checkers, another wanted to chat and another would invite me to visit a shebeen or his or her home. These invitations were a long time coming, as the lengthy handshakes, initial greetings and questions about one's well-being and the health of one's family took a considerable time. For one who talks as much as I do, it was especially delightful to notice that almost everyone listened to every detail of my lengthy replies and I naturally began to put more effort into listening to others.

Over and over again I was amazed at how good manners, smiles and happiness can survive poverty of a level I had never been exposed to before. In TR, hardship is everybody's business: the hunger that pulses in the belly, the heat that pulsates under the corrugated iron roofs in summer, the acute cold that creeps easily through the walls of your home, then into your bones, and the physical exhaustion after another long day of toil. But just as these negatives are far more evident among the poor, so are the positives: a greater sense of belonging and community, ready laughter, and the caring and compassion that flows thickly through the streets.

Even though there always seemed to be enough food to go around, it wasn't very much. There also wasn't much variety, with the basics – like pap, eggs, sour milk, intestines, rice, beans, cabbage and pumpkin – making up the month's menus. Gone were the yoghurts, exotic cheeses, pastas, olives, juices and snacks I had been accustomed to while in Holland. S'bu did most of the cooking but despite the plentiful food, I seemed to be constantly hungry. At first I couldn't quite put my finger on why this should be, but I began to feel weak and sluggish and spent more and more time lying on the couch in our lounge reading. My skinny legs grew skinnier and my belly moaned and groaned under its lust for better nutrition. Sometimes I persuaded Ta-fumsa and one or two other friends to join me on a quick trip to the massive braai area across the road from the Site B taxi rank. There we would feast on enormous beef chops, helped down with a loaf of white bread and a litre and a half of Coke.

As the hunger for variety intensified, so I began to do more shopping, ensuring that I bought at the Site B Shoprite all the basics that good nutrition demanded. I found it fascinating to watch S'bu's reaction to the new cuisine I introduced some evenings. Most times when I asked him whether he liked my pastas or vegetable dishes, he told me quite honestly that he didn't. Not only did he seem suspicious of the ingredients in my meals, many of which fell outside his limited experience but, to be fair, I've never been a very good cook.

Another cause for my sudden interest in cooking unfolded one evening when I brought it to S'bu's attention that the chicken he was cooking was green. It was only when I lifted the lid on the pot that I realised where the terrible stench that had permeated our home was coming from. Having missed a bath that day I'd thought it was my feet and had apologised to my shack mate.

'Always eat this, very healthy,' S'bu replied to my index finger, which was pointed accusingly towards the rotten interior of the pot.

My other hand was cupped around my nose.

'You can't,' I said. 'You'll get sick.'

'Never sick,' answered S'bu, who had adopted a patient look. 'I show you.'

Sure enough, that night S'bu ate all three pieces of green chicken – his and mine, after I pushed mine away after only a few bites – and, in the days that followed, while I was gripped by the worst diarrhoea I had ever suffered, S'bu pumped mightily at the heavy iron bar and weights he kept in his room.

Fire!

Moving to Khayelitsha had been by far the most adventurous thing I had ever done, and I tried to analyse my motives for moving there more than three years earlier. I'd convinced my friends and family that moving to Khayelitsha had been a perfectly normal thing to do, but now I gradually came to terms with an entirely different set of reasons.

The thought of recording my experiences in Khayelitsha had only come to me during my last year in the Netherlands, so research was never a motive. Without that as a reason, though, it seemed almost as if I had moved into the township on a whim. This was certainly the easiest explanation, and the one initially believed by my family and friends, but it never really held water for me.

In an idealistic sense, I suppose I was trying to fix a problem and create a dream. Despite South Africa's segregated history, I had to ask myself whether, in the twenty-first century and in the new South Africa, there should still be 'officially' black areas, areas inhabited solely by a particular race group. Similarly, I fought against being controlled by rules that made no logical sense to me. While segregation by and large continues at this point in our history, my own make-up demanded that I make decisions based not on the expectations or norms of my society, but rather on the elements I believed should be part of an ideal South Africa. As a child I wondered what black South Africans did when they went home in the evenings and over weekends. To answer that question I went to see for myself.

I had always been wary of what I perceived as the simple-minded and hypocritical morals of English white South African society. We were not Afrikaners, so we felt we did not share responsibility for the evils of apartheid, even when we had gained so much from it. A small number of us wanted blacks to be enfranchised, and yet fled the country as soon as our wish was granted.

I had always had dual citizenship, so I was aptly described by the Afrikaners as a *soutpiel*, or saltdick. We had one foot in Europe and the other in Africa, leaving our dicks to hang in the ocean. At the first sign of trouble in South Africa, the Afrikaners implied, we would lift up our African foot and head for Europe.

Even though I attended English white boys' schools, I had never felt properly South African. Christmas was my only cultural experience of the year, when my mother would roast a rabbit (Austrian-style for my father), or a turkey (in vague acknowledgement of an even vaguer idea of England). These hazy memories of our distant roots left me confused, with the result that I thought of myself primarily as a white South

African. This identity imploded when I reached my late teens and for the first time learned about the many innocent black citizens and their leaders, such as Steve Biko, who had died in detention fighting for the rights of their people.

I eventually prevailed over this aspect of my identity crisis by living in northern Europe for a few years. It was there that I realised the extent to which I was African.

What my black compatriots had endured as a result of the actions of my people humbled me. The fact that none of them harboured any grudge towards me for the sins of my people humbled me still further. While reflections such as these have driven some white South Africans into a vicious circle where their racial arrogance increases in accordance with their guilt, for me it had the opposite effect. Instead of going along with the white Afro-pessimistic flow, I had constantly challenged it, not out of any feeling of moral superiority, but rather because I desperately wanted to be positive and optimistic about my new nation: more than anything I wanted to be a citizen of the new South Africa. I also came to believe that it was only through considerable cultural compromise on my part that I would be able to confront my prejudices, which I not only suspected were based on falsehoods and ignorance, but which were also suddenly rendered pointless by the dawn of our new democracy. The only sacrifice I ever wanted from my black friends was that they would accept me as an African, regardless of the colour of my skin. And that is exactly what they did.

Perhaps, I thought as I lay on my bed in my shack one evening a few weeks before Christmas 2005, I was being a little too dramatic. But I was certain of one thing – that in my effort to become a productive part of our new nation by confronting my prejudices, I had ended up doing far more.

Not only had I come to be accepted by my Xhosa brothers and sisters as one of them, but I had also learned so much more than I had ever expected to learn from black people. In precisely the same way as my prejudices about Khayelitsha and its people had been replaced by what we had in common so, too, had my first impression of Ta-fumsa changed until I realised a black man is my equal.

Of course, I knew I was flattering myself: Ta-fumsa is a better man than I am. His humility made me envious, which in turn made me resent his role as my teacher. But through his example and the example of other Xhosa people, I had learned to laugh at myself, to trust others of a different skin colour with my life, to love the good and bad in all people, to forgive, to share and, in one of the more telling ironies, to do unto others as I would have them do unto me – something that the white Christians who brought that doctrine to Africa had so often failed to do. At last I had taken on a fresh identity, an African identity. For the first time I knew that Africa would make it, whatever the odds.

Fire raged like the plague through Khayelitsha that summer. Almost every day I saw dark clouds of smoke rising out of the shack lands, signalling another overturned paraffin stove or carelessly discarded cigarette. As the fires rose on all sides, coming closer and closer to TR, I became increasingly fearful of being burnt alive. My fear climaxed into panic one morning when I noticed giant flames shooting up from X Section, just on the other side of Mew Way, a couple of hundred metres away. I joined scores of people at the scene, watching as scores more frantically helped to carry furniture,

TV sets, fridges, food, clothes, cupboards and the odd family photograph from their shacks while the fire raged like an angry, living monster above our heads. Young, bare-chested men, left at home by unemployment, stood on the roofs of shacks, emptying bucket after bucket of water into them in a vain effort to stop the inferno. A few seconds of burning; another shack lit; another massive explosion as a paraffin stove went up, flames arcing gracefully into the sky. And then the aeroplanes swooped through the smoke from beyond Harare to dump seawater on the blaze. Each dive of the little planes was greeted with a loud whooping from the crowd, which went on long after the planes had disappeared.

The fear of fire haunted my thoughts day and night. I slept lightly every night, listening carefully for the sound of flames.

And then one night they came for me. I was alone; S'bu was visiting his family in the Eastern Cape.

'Fire! Fire!' Shouted over and over again. I awoke slowly. 'Fire!' again, this time accompanied by a loud banging on the wall of my shack. Suddenly I was wide awake and panicking. The voice belonged to the old woman who lived in the next shack towards the station. Her voice was shrill and hoarse at the same time, a combination that shocked me into action.

I lurched out of bed and frantically pulled on a pair of green underpants, the roar of the flames beginning to reach me from the direction of the shacks bordering the railway lines. As the sound grew louder I grabbed my money belt and cellphone and dashed to the door. As I reached it the sound turned into train brakes screeching and my sense of urgency lessened. Looking at my phone, I noticed it was just after five, time for the first train of the morning. Thinking that I still had a minute to spare I raced back to my room and hurriedly grabbed my laptop, traveller's cheques and professional camera. My most valuable possessions safely tucked under both arms, I sprinted through the lounge to the front door. The five different locks and bolts, there to keep the tsotsis from breaking the door down in the early hours of the morning, made it impossible to open the door quickly, and my hands shook with the effort. Knowing I still had to open the gate to the street, I turned the last key as quickly as I could and fled out into the yard.

But there, instead of the flames I had expected, was a large group of my neighbours, each and every one of them, judging by the broad grins on their faces, delighted by my panic-stricken appearance. Standing in my underpants, my body trembling, I looked down the road to where the men of a single fire engine were lazily dousing the last, pathetic flames of a fire that had consumed just one little shack. The laughter from my neighbours enraged me and, with my skinny white legs and old-fashioned underpants as conspicuous as a black man in the snow, I focused every ounce of anger on the culprit.

'Voetsak!' I bellowed at my elderly neighbour, who deserved an Oscar for her performance. Faces fell; some of them looked hurt.

Later that day, my neighbour walked up to me where I was playing checkers at Laamy's store, her usual good humour replaced by a new sternness.

'Steven,' she said, 'I can't believe you swore at me this morning.' For a moment I thought I saw a tear in her eyes. 'Next time there's a fire,' she said, 'I definitely won't be waking you up.'

Harare Revisited

One Saturday afternoon at Hlehle's Cool Spot, owned by the delightful Ludwe and his wife, I was sitting on a chair with their pretty daughter Lenni, when in walked Punky and Bulelani, the two tsotsis I'd met on my one and only visit to TR a few years before. Punky patted Lenni's head gently as I shook Bulelani's hand. The lovely little five-year-old ran off to the family section of the shack, turning around once to wave at me. She always called me 'lungu', her attempt at '*mlungu*'; in a place where there was nobody else of my complexion she regarded me as a bit of a toy.

It delighted me that Lenni visited me regularly at home, where I would let her play with my laptop and camera. She was a clever little thing and I found it quite embarrassing that she adopted an attitude of almost patronising patience whenever she was with me. '*Kunjani?*' she would ask, before helping me pronounce the Xhosa reply properly. *'Ndiphilile,'* she would say slowly, extremely concerned that someone as big as me could say so few words in the only language she knew.

I sat down at a table with Punky and Bulelani and caught up on their news, all conveyed in slow, expressive tsotsitaal, peppered liberally with pidgin English.

I soon found out that their lives had undergone a mammoth change since I'd last seen them in the shack where they'd lustily puffed on a Mandrax pipe with Smiley.

'Smiley lives in Philippi,' explained Bulelani, as we recalled our last time together and I asked them if they still smoked.

'No,' replied Punky, 'we gave up that shit.' Looking at them more closely I could see that both had more flesh on their bodies and a healthier shade of pinkness in their cheeks than at our last meeting. Punky told me that a few weeks after I'd visited them, the community had thrown them out of TR and they'd relocated their drug business to Philippi.

'The people here were already upset with us for robbing that *winkel* down the road from Ta-fumsa's *hokkie*,' explained Bulelani. 'Then my mother put pressure on them to *skop* us out because of the buttons.'

'Is that why you went to Pollsmoor, because you robbed the shop?' I asked, taking a long slug from a one and a half litre Coke.

'Ja, *mfwetu*,' answered Punky, his eyes as soft as ever. 'We went there with guns.'

'So when the community caught us they beat us with sticks,' said Bulelani, 'and then they called the police. When we came out of Pollsmoor they forgave us, but the drugs made things go *swak* again.'

'So what do you do now?'

'I work for a construction company,' said Punky.

'Me too,' Bulelani replied.

'And your boss knows you were in jail?' I looked at Bulelani, who was cracking open a beer with his teeth.

'*Ja, my broer*,' Bulelani boasted. 'My boss doesn't mind that *ek was in die tronk*. I work hard for that *umlungu* and he *smaaks* me.'

After a few games of pool with my reformed friends I left Hlehle's for home, elated that their lives had undergone such positive change. Walking down the road from the tavern towards my shack, I reflected on how a paid job and the sense of responsibility that comes with it had altered Punky and Bulelani's attitudes towards life. Their sense of pride in their new lives had touched me and given me a renewed sense of hope. Their words had done much to improve my dark mood which had been brought on by a visit to Vuyo's mother's shack in Harare a couple of days before.

Using my monthly train ticket I'd travelled to Khayelitsha station, close to my first house in iLitha Park. From there I had walked the short distance to my old haunt, Vovo Cash Store. It was a weekday at the beginning of the school holidays and Steve's daughter Yoliswa was working behind the bar.

'Steven!' she shouted happily, running through the house to the front, where she jumped into my arms.

'Yoliswa, I missed you,' I said, holding her light body tightly.

She hadn't grown much taller in the time I'd been away, but as she leaned back to take a look at me I could see by her pimply face that she had become a teenager.

'How old are you now?' I asked her, feeing immensely happy to see her.

'I'm turning sixteen next month,' she said with pride. 'It's so nice to see you. Let me call my father, he's at home today.'

'Who?' I could hear Steve asking his daughter from his bedroom.

A minute later my friend came walking around the front of the house. Dressed in an old pair of tracksuit pants, he was shirtless, his healthy belly hanging proudly over his waist. We shook hands, smiling into each other's faces, with me touching the left-hand side of his upper body with the right side of my chest.

'Stevovo,' I said, looking him up and down.

Slapping his belly with the back of a hand, I grinned.

'You're fast becoming a chief,' I said.

'Yes, my friend,' he said proudly. 'My wife is still cooking well.'

'Is that the beer from last night?' I joked, pointing at his large belly.

'Some of it,' he answered, laughing. 'Where are you now?'

'I'm living in TR Informal Settlement,' I replied and the smile on Steve's face widened.

'You just can't get enough of the Xhosas, *eish*! Why don't you come back here?'

'I don't pay rent there,' I said.

'*Eish*,' Steve laughed. 'Yoli, give this poor white man a beer from me.'

It was refreshing to hear that not much had changed in Steve's life. His daughters had grown much in my absence and his wife had produced another one two years before. She was a scrawny little girl with a rather severe case of eczema.

'This one,' said Steve, as his latest daughter hid her face

behind his back, 'I don't know what to do about her skin. Look at this,' rubbing a palm softly against her cheeks.

Taking my leave of Steve and Yoliswa at Vovo Cash Store, I walked down Ntlazane Road towards Harare. As I entered John's hairdressing container, now surrounded by a number of new businesses, my spirits lifted somewhat. My old Ghanaian friend had forgiven me for Nigger's transgressions and he hugged me spontaneously.

'I left that bitch Nowie,' he said, putting his hair shaver on the lap of the customer he'd been busy with and beaming at me.

'I told you that you would be better off without her,' I said, feeling instantly guilty for this shifty display of 'I told you so'. 'Do you ever see Nigger?'

'Ja,' he said, having acquired a word of Afrikaans. 'I greet him too.'

'I'm glad,' I said, thankful that there were no hard feelings between any of us. 'John, I'm so sorry for what I ...'

'No way, my man, you did me a favour,' he said. 'What you did was wrong, but I also did not behave like a man that day. Everything turned out right, so forget about it. Hey, Steve man, your hair is growing like a girl's – you need John to cut it for free.'

'I'm going to grow it,' I declined the offer.

Years before Vuyo had said she liked my hair when it was long. Walking slowly onwards towards her Harare home, I'd passed the shack where I'd so often eaten smileys. I was surprised that the proprietor remembered me so well.

'*Uyapi*, my son?' she wanted to know my destination.

'An old friend,' I'd replied, Vuyo's beautiful features passing before my eyes.

Would I really see the pretty freckles on her nose again, would she smile and then giggle shyly when she saw me? All at once I was filled with a love for Vuyo that had remained untouched by distance or time.

And as I neared the house where I had seen a massive pig tied down in the back of a bakkie – the only sign of it on my return was the little boy chewing away at a last bone – I thought back to the time I had spent with Vuyo at the Technikon, where I had first fallen in love with her smile.

Even the few tsotsis sitting back against a shack wall or tree stump appeared respectful of the significance of this reunion. A wave, a 'hola 7', their index fingers and thumbs held up like a gun, not one of them even asked for a puff of my cigarette. Then, very suddenly, the shining silver of Vuyo's mother's shack, low against a backdrop of Harare's hilltop silhouette, rose up ahead of me. The shack was unworn and still looked as though it had been erected a week before.

'Hello,' I said loudly, heading around the side of the shack to the wooden kitchen door, 'Hello-ooo.'

I turned to the sound of a door opening behind me and there she was, a younger version of Vuyo, her sister Zodwa, coming out of the front garden loo.

'Where've you been?' she asked me, her English now easily as good as her sister's.

'First I was in the Eastern Cape, after that I went to Europe. But I missed Cape Town and came back. I live in TR Informal Settlement now, in a shack with a friend.'

'TR! There are too many skollies there,' Zodwa said.

For a moment my eyes glazed over, with memories of Vuyo flooding back, but I suppressed the urge to get straight to the purpose of my visit. Zodwa, standing there in old tracksuit pants and a yellow T-shirt with paint smears on it, waited politely for me to come back to her.

'How's school?' I asked her.

'I finished school in 2003,' she replied, 'I'm looking for a job now.'

'Why don't you study?'

'We don't have money,' she answered, making me see the insensitivity in my question.

'And your mother?'

'She's fine; she's working as a domestic.'

'Does she still not eat anything when Kaizer Chiefs lose a game?'

'Of course!' Zodwa laughed. 'That will never change.'

'And how's ...?' I began, but just then a young girl ran up to the fence and called out to Zodwa.

'My mother needs some sugar,' the bony girl said in Xhosa, rubbing her belly with a hand as she looked shyly at me out of the corner of one eye.

Zodwa walked past me towards the open kitchen door and the girl and I followed her into the shack.

Reaching into a cupboard, Zodwa took out a little packet of white sugar and placed it on the counter. The little girl continued to stare at me. Opening a drawer directly beneath the cupboard, Vuyo's sister took out a supermarket packet and poured about half of the sugar into it, tying a knot at its neck before handing it to the girl.

'Enkosi,' she thanked Zodwa, before flitting off, her eyes on me until she had moved out of sight.

'Vuyo is a mother now,' Zodwa said, as I turned back to look at her. 'She had to stop studying in her last year because my uncle ran out of money. She's at her boyfriend's house in Gugulethu now. I think she's coming back this evening.'

'That's nice,' I stammered, thinking that it wasn't nice at

all. 'I'm glad to hear that. How old is the baby?'

'Just over a year,' replied Zodwa. 'Her name is Zimkhita.'

Did she have to have a baby? I asked myself as I waved goodbye to Zodwa. A boyfriend I could have dealt with – or so my injured ego told me – but a child? In a way I was happy to have closure (I didn't have much of a choice) but I played Vuyo's sister's farewell over in my head for some months. I didn't have many lonely moments in TR, but when I did I often thought of her final words to me as I walked away.

'Why didn't you call her while you were in Europe?'

Epilogue

It is a beautiful winter morning in downtown Cape Town, the kind that makes you certain that everyone, everywhere else on the Peninsula is also celebrating the warmth. The wind blew itself out last night and the leaves lie in the sun. To those walking towards or away from us it must be obvious that we are in love. Hand in hand, we walk slowly along the road that leads through the wonderful greenery of the Gardens. Like so many young South African couples in so many South African cities, towns and villages, everything feels right to us.

You know the woman beside me, and her warmth, and her beauty and her smile. Like me, she is from Khayelitsha, and as she looks up at me and smiles, her nose wrinkles ever so slightly for a second and my heart is warm. Her pretty brown eyes soften as she looks at me and we walk on.

'That is wrong!' a *bergie* shouts after us, making us turn

our heads. 'A sheep and a pig can't be together!'

The bedraggled old hobo sits alone on the bench, his face twisted with the pain that we all know, the pain which comes from ignorance, distrust and contempt.

'Which of us is the pig?' I ask him.

He thinks for a moment, and when he replies, his voice is a despairing groan. 'I don't know!'

We walk away.

When I first see the dog, I am fascinated and amused, and we change course slightly so that we can get a better look. It has the jaw of a bulldog, and lips enough for three, but my laughter stops when I hear its voice and the earnestness of its words. I look more intently, as it speaks passionately and eloquently about this and that. And I see that its eyes are human.

Now the Gardens are gone, and the busy N2 highway roars nearby, with Khayelitsha sprawled beyond. I have a clear view over the shoulder of the reporter who is talking to the dog, and I can see that the lights of his television crew are illuminating a scene of destruction and fear, but I cannot see details. The dog continues to speak – it is Xhosa, I understand now – and as it drives home its message it steps from side to side, to show the camera the scene of devastation behind it.

I rubbed the sleep from my eyes. It was my last morning in Khaya, and I wandered over to Ta-fumsa and told him about my dream. He leaned back and smiled. It was the smile of a friend, a brother, and a man.

'It is our ancestors, my brother,' he said gently. 'They guide us in our dreams. And your dog, well, that is quite simple.'

He paused and looked away over the smoke, through the spider web of thousands of electric lines on wooden posts, up through the dust and into the sun that was rising over the southern tip of Africa. 'Our ancestors often appear in the form of a dog.' He smiled again. 'Perhaps your ancestors are wanting you to show something to your people, and to our people. Perhaps . . .' He laughed and shook his head, changing his mind.

'Eish,' he sighed. 'These things are too much difficult for a *mlungu*!'

Acknowledgements

Thanks go to the Penguin team for their excellent editing and production work. Penguin CEO Alison Lowry, editors Gemma Harries and Pam Thornley, along with Claire Heckrath and David Schröder, each of whom offered a crucial contribution to the editing and production processes – I am indebted to every one of you. Many thanks also go to Tom Eaton, whose structural editing was superb; to the brilliant photographer and my long-time friend Denzil Maregele, who not only spent a Saturday with me at Hlehle's Cool Spot, but has over the years given me encouragement; and to the talented Lulama Zenzile, who took the photo of me walking towards my TR shack from Hlehle's.

My gratitude must also go to Nonceba Mtwana, who shared her excellent knowledge of the Xhosa language and culture to ensure that the Xhosa people have received the respect and accuracy they deserve in this book. Many thanks also to Francine Townsley, my best friend in the Netherlands, who edited the first few chapters before I sent them off to Penguin. To Ian and Katrin, the wonderful owners of the Outsiders B&B and Restaurant in Nieu Bethesda, who asked me, 'how far is the book?' probably a thousand times over the months I spent writing in the delightful little Karoo town – thanks for your friendship, the game and those breakfasts.

To my boss, Independent Democrats President Patricia de Lille, who gave me a month off work to complete this book – I share your vision of bridging the racial and economic divides of the past.

To my lovely Andrea, who weathered my creative storms, fed me while I typed, listened while I read and still parties with me in Khayelitsha, thank you for your love and patience.

For their incredible emotional support and their undying faith in me, I am eternally grateful to my parents, who told me, 'you have a book in you – write it'. During my time writing in the desert they shelved the instinctive parental urge to say, 'get a job', instead giving me the encouragement I so desperately needed. My parents, Peter and Janet, my brothers Thomas and Albert, and my sister Bronwen showed so much courage in their willingness to discuss with me our family's past and the terrible economic and psychological effect of apartheid on the people of our South Africa.

There are so many people from Harare, iLitha Park, TR Informal Settlement, Gugulethu and beyond who gave themselves to me as friends (and sometimes a little more): Vuyo, Zane, Stevovo, Banana, Tarzan, Vuks, Xola, Lisa, Ayanda, Sivuyile, Lance, Thabo, X-man, Bulelani (aka Mpondo) and Punky, Laamy, Lucy, Moses, Ghost, Nana, Princess, Chris, Foamy, Frederick, Ludwe, Hlehle, Ruu, Ncebsi, Nontombi and Gigs. They are beautiful people, the people of Khayelitsha, and they accepted me, fed me, looked after me and taught me so much about their wonderful culture of ubuntu – I shall be forever indebted to you for your companionship.

To my good friend Nigger, who walked with me at all hours of the day and night deep into our 'new home', and who provided me with much laughter and wisdom – you will always be my friend.

Lastly, special thanks must go to my brother, Fumanekile Wisani – aka Ta-fumsa – whose mama remains a mother to me, whose *makhulu* remains a grandmother to me, whose family is my family and the other way around, and whose advice and guidance I shall always prize.